高等学校英语 拓展 系列教程

英语国家概况（修订版）
A GUIDE TO ENGLISH-SPEAKING COUNTRIES

语言文化类

◎ 主编：谢福之
◎ 编者：白晓煌　王瑞瑶　耿晓华
　　　　孙晓霞　郭立民　张淑娥

外语教学与研究出版社
FOREIGN LANGUAGE TEACHING AND RESEARCH PRESS
北京 BEIJING

高等学校英语拓展系列教程
编写委员会

顾问：刘润清　胡壮麟

主任：文秋芳　石　坚

委员：（以姓氏拼音为序）

曹　颖	常玉田	车丽娟	陈建辉	程冷杰	邓　杉	胡　超	胡英坤
冀成会	李　健	李小飞	李　毅	廖华英	刘爱军	卢志鸿	马龙海
秦荻辉	任书梅	沈素萍	宋　雷	孙　宁	田祥斌	王　斌	王　璐
王守仁	王维波	王秀银	谢福之	徐志英	余慕鸿	于晓言	张桂萍
张　健	章汝雯	张卫平	赵　蓉	赵　萱	郑仰成	祝凤英	

Andrew Lynn　　Donald M. Huffman　　Gary Rybold
Loren Steele　　Maxine F. Huffman

前　言

随着我国国际交往的日益频繁和涉外工作的需要，大学生不仅要学好英语，提高语言综合运用能力，还应加深对主要英语国家社会与文化的了解，提升文化素养，提高多元文化意识和跨文化交际能力。

《英语国家概况》是高等院校普遍开设、并深受学生欢迎的一门课程。本教材自2007年出版以来，被许多院校选用，并受到广大师生的一致好评。为了带给学生最新的文化体验，使学生及时了解主要英语国家的社会发展和变化，时隔六年之后，我们对教材进行了修订，更新了部分内容、信息，并补充了近几年这些国家社会文化发展的概况。同时，为了加深学生对文化信息的理解，带给学生更加直观的文化感受，修订版采用彩色装帧设计，并且甄选出教材中的重要文化信息辅以图片和文字说明。

本教材共分为18章，介绍了六个主要英语国家（英国、爱尔兰、美国、加拿大、澳大利亚和新西兰）的社会与文化，涵盖地理、历史、政治、经济、教育和文学等各个方面。对各国的介绍内容相对统一，但也根据各国的社会文化特点，选取其特色之处进行了重点介绍。

本教材具有以下主要特点：

一、**参考资料权威、丰富**。作者参考了众多国内外出版的权威报刊、杂志、教材、对外宣传材料及相关部门的官方网站，对大量的信息进行筛选，力求使编入教材的内容准确、客观、翔实。

二、**选材新，紧跟时代和社会的发展**。编写过程中，我们尽量选用最新的材料和统计数据，不仅涵盖了20世纪末到本世纪初所发生的重大事件，而且对于近期发生的事件，也介绍了其最新进展情况。

三、**内容编排合理，适合课堂教学**。教材每章围绕一个主题，各个章节既自成一体，又紧密联系。教师可根据学生水平和具体的课时安排选用部分章节进行课堂教学，其他章节可安排学生课外自学。

四、语言难易适中，有利于自主学习。教材尽量选用常用词汇，便于学生自主阅读和学习。对于较难的词汇和专有名词，教材给出了中文注释，便于学生理解章节内容，免去查证之苦；为一些重要文化信息提供了脚注，便于学生了解相关的背景知识，加深理解。

五、练习丰富、题型多样。每章提供了四种形式的练习，便于教师对学生进行测评和学生自测。此次修订，在每章前增设 Think and Talk 这一版块，以问题的形式提示章节中的重要文化信息，启发学生积极思考，并激发其学习兴趣。各章后增设 Learn and Check 这一版块，帮助学生回顾、总结章节的主要内容。

六、补充资源丰富，帮助学生拓展视野。教材配有四个附录，便于学生查找相关信息，也可作为学习内容。此外，教材还配有学习课件，提供补充文化信息、视频资源等，帮助学生更加全面地理解教材的文化内涵。

外语教学与研究出版社的领导和编辑在本教材的编写和修订过程中给予了很多支持和帮助；Matthew Korean（英）和 Oliver Ross（美）审阅了全稿，并提出了许多宝贵意见；胡永华和陈泳均两位老师帮助收集了很多资料，并参加了部分编写工作。在此一并表示感谢。

由于编者水平有限，本书难免有不足之处，敬请读者指正。

谢福之
2013 年 3 月

Contents

The United Kingdom of Great Britain and Northern Ireland

Chapter 1   Geography, People and Language   /2

Chapter 2   History   /13

Chapter 3   Government and the Commonwealth   /30

Chapter 4   Economy   /43

Chapter 5   Education, Media and Holidays   /53

Chapter 6   Literature   /66

The Republic of Ireland

Chapter 7   Society and Culture   /82

The United States of America

Chapter 8   Geography and People   /100

Chapter 9   History   /112

Chapter 10   Government   /125

Chapter 11   Economy   /139

Chapter 12   Education, Media and Holidays   /150

Chapter 13   Literature   /163

Canada

Chapter 14　Geography and History　/180

Chapter 15　Government and Society　/192

 ## Australia

Chapter 16　Geography and History　/206

Chapter 17　Government and Society　/222

 ## New Zealand

Chapter 18　Society and Culture　/242

Key to Exercises　/259

Appendices　/279

Appendix 1　Shires of the United Kingdom　/279

Appendix 2　States of the United States　/281

Appendix 3　Provinces and Territories of Canada　/283

Appendix 4　States and Territories of Australia　/283

References　/285

The United Kingdom of Great Britain and Northern Ireland

Chapter 1

Geography, People and Language

▼ Think and Talk

- Do you know the full name of Britain?
- Do you know the geographical features of this country?
- Do you know its major cities—London, Edinburgh, Cardiff, Belfast, etc.?
- Do you know how the English language develops into a universal lingua franca?

I. Geography

Geographical Features

The full name of Britain is the United Kingdom of Great Britain and Northern Ireland. When people refer to the country, they often use different names such as Britain, Great Britain, England, the British Islands, the United Kingdom or the U.K. Located to the northwest of mainland Europe, it is made up of many islands collectively known as the British Isles (不列颠群岛), covering an area of about 243,000 square kilometers. Great Britain and Ireland are two main islands of the British Isles. The island of Great Britain accounts for more than 90% of the country's landmass. That is why the country is also known as Great Britain. The island of Great Britain is geographically and historically divided into three parts: England, Scotland and Wales. The island of Ireland is divided into two parts: Northern Ireland and the Republic of Ireland. Northern Ireland is part of the United Kingdom, while the Republic of Ireland is an independent country.

Chapter 1 Geography, People and Language

England is the largest part of Great Britain, located in the south of the island, with Wales to the west and Scotland to the north. It has an area of 130,281 square kilometers and covers more than half of the whole island. The River Thames, the second longest and the most important river in Britain, originates in southwestern England and flows through the Midlands of England to London and empties into the North Sea. England is the most populous and wealthiest part of the country, so people sometimes refer to the whole country as England, a name that people of Scotland, Wales and Northern Ireland do not like very much. England is highly urbanized, with about 80% of the population living in cities. London, the capital of both England and the United Kingdom, is located in southeastern England.

Scotland, with an area of 78,772 square kilometers, occupies the northern part of Britain. It is the second largest of the four constituent parts of the United Kingdom, both in population and in area. The Clyde River (克莱德河) is the most important river in Scotland. For a substantial period in history Scotland remained a unified state independent of Britain. Edinburgh (爱丁堡) is its capital. Tourism is one of Scotland's most important industries. Tourists from all over the world come to enjoy the beauty of Scottish scenery, to drink Scotch whisky and to see Scotsmen wearing kilts (格子呢褶裥短裙) and playing bagpipes (风笛).

Wales is very close to the most densely populated parts of central England. Its entire area is 20,780 square kilometers and it covers less than 9% of the whole island. The capital of Wales is Cardiff (加的夫). The longest river of Britain, the Severn River (塞文河), originates in mid-Wales and flows through western England to the Bristol Channel (布里斯托尔海峡) and the Atlantic Ocean. Wales has been dominated by England longer than the other parts. However, it retains a powerful sense of its difference from England. Its own language, Welsh, is spoken by about 20% of the population, much more than those who speak Gaelic (盖尔语) in Scotland and Ireland.

Northern Ireland is the smallest of the four parts, both in population and in area. It has an area of 14,135 square kilometers and occupies the northern one-sixth of the island of Ireland. The capital of Northern Ireland is Belfast (贝尔法斯特). Lough Neagh (内伊湖), the largest lake in the British Isles, is located in northern Ireland. It covers an area of 396 square kilometers.

Climate

The climate of Britain is classified as temperate, with warm summers, cool winters and plentiful precipitation (降雨量) throughout the year. Its climate is generally mild and temperate due to its proximity (接近) to the Atlantic Ocean and the warming of the waters around the British Isles by the Gulf Stream (墨西哥湾流). The summer temperature is usually around 20℃, with the high rarely going above 32℃. The average temperature in January is around 0℃ and seldom falls below -10℃, even in northern Scotland.

The climate in Britain has three principal features. The first is the frequent fog that occurs in winter, for which London is famous. The second is the large number of rainy days. The third is its instability or changeability. Indeed, during a hot day in July the temperature can be the same as a mild day in January.

Major Cities

London, the capital of both England and the United Kingdom, is the political, industrial, cultural and financial center of the country. It is one of the world's leading banking and financial centers. Buckingham Palace (白金汉宫), Guildhall (市政厅), St. Paul's Cathedral (圣保罗大教堂) and Big Ben (大本钟) are some of the city's landmarks. The Port of London lies along the banks of the River Thames. The Tower Bridge of London (伦敦塔桥) over the River Thames has also become one of the symbols of the city. The West End of London includes many tourist attractions, as well as business and administrative headquarters. Some examples of London's cultural institutions are the University of London, the British Museum, the National Gallery, the Covent Garden (科芬园), the Royal Opera House and the Royal Festival Hall.

伦敦市政厅

Chapter 1　Geography, People and Language

爱丁堡大学老学院

Edinburgh is the capital of Scotland. Located on a river, the city is stunningly beautiful and its architecture is renowned the world over. Edinburgh is Scotland's administrative, financial, legal, medical and insurance center. It is also famous for the University of Edinburgh, one of the top-rated research universities in Britain.

威尔士国民议会大厦

Cardiff is Europe's youngest capital city and has been the capital city of Wales since 1955. The city has undergone an enormous amount of urban regeneration (重建) and restoration and has recently become one of the most fashionable cities in Britain. With modern shopping centers, historic Victorian shopping arcades (室内购物商场), an impressive selection of hotels, world-class restaurants and a trendy waterfront area, Cardiff has become a popular city attracting thousands of visitors each year from home and abroad.

Belfast is the largest city and the capital of northern Ireland. As an important historic city, it is crammed full of spectacular landmarks and monuments, most of which date back many hundreds of years. In recent years this city has undergone a remarkable transformation. Many areas have been redeveloped, new restaurants and hotels have been opened, and impressive new shopping areas have been built.

贝尔法斯特城堡

II. People

Britain has a population of about 63 million (2012). Its overall population density is among the highest in the world. About 53 million people live in England, with nearly 8 million in the capital. The rest are distributed in Scotland (around 5.2 million), Wales (around 3.1 million), Northern Ireland (around 1.8 million).

The majority of the population is descendants of the Anglo-Saxons*, a Germanic people from Europe who went to England between the 5th and 6th centuries. These people settled in England and drove the native Celtic people (凯尔特人) to the mountainous areas of Wales and Scotland. Their language became the official language of the country.

Most people in Wales and Scotland are descendants of the Celtic people who were the earliest known inhabitants of Britain. The Irish people are also of Celtic origin.

Besides the early groups from Europe, Britain has a considerable number of Italians, Greeks, Australians and New Zealanders who have settled in the country as permanent residents. In addition, there is a large number of immigrants from Africa and Asia. Most of them come from the former colonies of the British Empire, such as India, Pakistan, Bangladesh (孟加拉国), the Caribbean Islands and a number of African countries. All these immigrants have made Britain one of the most culturally diverse countries in Europe. In London, for instance, it is estimated that more than 300 languages and dialects are spoken.

---

* Anglo-Saxons: 盎格鲁－撒克逊人，属于日耳曼民族，包括盎格鲁人（the Angles）、撒克逊人（the Saxons）、朱特人（the Jutes）等。

Chapter 1　Geography, People and Language

大英博物馆

III. The English Language

English is a member of the Indo-European family of languages (印欧语系). This broad family includes most of the European languages spoken today. English is in the Germanic group of this family. This group began as a common language about 3,000 years ago and was later split into three distinct subgroups: East Germanic, North Germanic and West Germanic. English evolved from the West Germanic group. The development of the English language can be divided into three periods: Old English, Middle English and Modern English.

Old English

The Angles, the Saxons and the Jutes began populating the British Isles in the 5th and 6th centuries. They spoke a mutually intelligible language—now called Old English. They drove the original Celtic-speaking inhabitants out of what is now England into Scotland, Wales and Ireland, leaving a few Celtic words behind. The Celtic languages survive today in the Gaelic language of Scotland and Ireland, and in Welsh of Wales.

Old English was strongly influenced by Old Norse (古斯堪的纳维亚语) spoken by the Vikings (北欧海盗) and was closely related to the German and Dutch languages. The introduction of Christianity added the first wave of Latin and Greek words to the language. The Old English period ended with the Norman Conquest*, when the language was influenced by the French-speaking Normans.

---

* Norman Conquest: 诺曼征服，指诺曼底公爵 1066 年对英格兰的军事征服。

7

Middle English

征服者威廉

William the Conqueror (征服者威廉), the Duke of Normandy (诺曼底公爵), invaded and conquered England and the Anglo-Saxons in 1066.

In the early part of this period, French, spoken by the Normans, replaced English as the official language in England, while English was only used by the lower class. Numerous French words came into the English vocabulary. One interesting phenomenon was that the animals began to have different names from their meat because they were raised by servants who spoke English and so kept the English names. The meat gained a French name when it was served to the French-speaking masters. For example, "pig" became "pork", "sheep" became "mutton" and "cattle" became "beef".

In 1204, King John lost the province of Normandy to the King of France. Norman nobles of England began to estrange from their French cousins and to adopt a modified English as their native tongue. After the Black Death* (1347-1351), the laboring and merchant classes grew in economic and social importance, and English increased in importance compared to French. English evolved gradually into what is now referred to as Middle English.

Modern English

From the late 15th century onward, the English language changed further into what is now described as Modern English. The printing press was introduced to England in 1476 by William Caxton, who brought standardization to English. The dialect of London became the standard. Spelling and grammar became fixed. The first English dictionary was published in 1604. Samuel Johnson's dictionary—*A Dictionary of the English Language*, published in 1755, was influential in establishing a standard form of spelling.

English continued to assimilate foreign words, especially from Latin and Greek, throughout the Renaissance (文艺复兴). Despite some differences in vocabulary, the written material from the early 17th century, such as the works of William Shakespeare and the King James Bible (英王詹姆士钦定版《圣经》), is considered to be in Modern English.

---

* Black Death: 黑死病，14 世纪蔓延于欧亚两洲的鼠疫。

The Industrial Revolution and the rise of technology necessitated the introduction of new words in modern English for things and ideas that had not previously existed. Words like "oxygen", "protein", "nuclear" and "vaccine" were created using Latin and Greek roots. English roots were used for such terms as "horsepower", "airplane" and "typewriter". This proliferation (激增) of neologisms (新词) continues today, perhaps most visible in the field of electronics and computers. "Byte", "cyber-", "hard drive" and "microchip" (芯片) are good examples.

What is more, the rise of the British Empire and the growth of global trade led to the assimilation of words from many other languages. Hindi (印地语) and the other languages of the Indian subcontinent (印度次大陆) provided many words, such as "pundit" (专家), "shampoo", "pajamas" and "juggernaut" (不可抗拒的强大力量). Virtually every language on Earth has made a contribution to the development of English, whether slight, as in the case of the Finnish word "sauna" and the Japanese word "tycoon" (大亨), or vast, as with French and Latin.

Standard English

Standard English is based on the speech of the upper class of southeastern England, adopted as a broadcasting standard in the British media. It is used as much in printed materials as is normally taught at schools and to non-native speakers learning the language. It is also called "the Queen's English" or "BBC English", and has become the language preferred by the educated. It has developed and has been promoted as a model for the correct British English. Standard English also refers to the norm carried overseas for non-native speakers learning English.

Today, Standard English is codified to the extent that the grammar and vocabulary of English are much the same everywhere in the world where English is used. The variation among local standards is really quite minor, so that the Singaporean, South African and Irish varieties differ only slightly so far as grammar and vocabulary are concerned.

At present, it is estimated that a third of the world's population use English. It has become a universal lingua franca*.

---

* lingua franca: 母语不同的人之间使用的通用语。

Exercises

I. Read the following statements and decide whether they are true (T) or false (F).

_____ 1. People in different parts of Britain like to use the name England to refer to their country.

_____ 2. The Severn River is the longest river of Britain, which originates in Wales and flows through western England.

_____ 3. Today more than half of the people in Wales still speak the ancient Welsh language.

_____ 4. In terms of population and area, Northern Ireland is the second largest part of Britain.

_____ 5. Although the climate in Britain is generally mild, the temperature in northern Scotland often falls below -10℃ in January.

_____ 6. The majority of the people in Britain are descendants of the Anglo-Saxons.

_____ 7. The Celtic people were the earliest known inhabitants of Britain.

_____ 8. English evolved into what is now described as Modern English from the late 16th century.

II. Choose the best answer to complete each of the following statements.

1. The two main islands of the British Isles are _____.
   A. Great Britain and Ireland　　　　B. Great Britain and Scotland
   C. Great Britain and Wales　　　　 D. Great Britain and England

2. _____ is the capital city of Scotland.
   A. Belfast　　　　　　　　　　　　B. Edinburgh
   C. London　　　　　　　　　　　　D. Cardiff

3. Among the four parts of the United Kingdom, _____ is the smallest.
   A. England　　　　　　　　　　　 B. Scotland
   C. Wales　　　　　　　　　　　　 D. Northern Ireland

4. English belongs to the _____ group of the Indo-European family of languages.
   A. Celtic　　　　　　　　　　　　 B. Norman
   C. Germanic　　　　　　　　　　　D. Roman

Chapter 1 Geography, People and Language

5. The introduction of Christianity to Britain added the first element of _____ words to English.

   A. Danish and Finnish   B. Dutch and German
   C. French and Italian   D. Latin and Greek

6. The evolution of Middle English was reinforced by the _____ influence.

   A. Norman   B. Dutch
   C. German   D. Danish

7. Samuel Johnson's dictionary was influential in establishing a standard form of _____.

   A. grammar   B. handwriting
   C. spelling   D. pronunciation

8. At present, nearly _____ of the world's population communicate in English.

   A. half   B. a quarter
   C. one-third   D. one-fifth

III. Give brief answers to the following questions.

1. Why do tourists from all over the world like to go to Scotland?

   _____
   _____

2. How many periods can the development of the English language be divided into and what are they?

   _____
   _____

3. Why did English become more important after the Black Death?

   _____
   _____

IV. State your understanding of the following questions.

1. Who are the British people?
2. What is Standard English?

11

Learn and Check

Composing parts: England, Scotland, Wales, Northern Ireland

Climate: temperate, with warm summers, cool winters and plentiful precipitation throughout the year

Major cities: London, Edinburgh, Cardiff, Belfast

People: about 63 million (2012), the majority of the population being descendants of the Anglo-Saxons

Language: English. The development of the English language can be divided into three periods: Old English, Middle English and Modern English.

Chapter 2 History

▼ **Think and Talk**
- What is the Magna Carta?
- How did the Reformation take place in Britain?
- Why did the Industrial Revolution happen first in Britain?
- What is the British Empire?

I. The Founding of the Nation

Recorded history in Britain began in the year 55 BC, when Julius Caesar (恺撒大帝, 100BC-44BC) and his Roman troops invaded the island. British history before that time is largely undocumented. In 55 BC and 54 BC, Britain was twice invaded by Roman troops led by Julius Caesar and was invaded again by the Romans under Claudius I (克劳狄一世) in 43 AD. Britain subsequently became a Roman province and remained so until the beginning of the 5th century. Many of the native Celts were driven to the mountainous regions of Scotland and Wales, which remained unconquered by the Romans. The Romans constructed towns and cities which prospered far longer than any previous settlements on the island.

In 410, Germanic barbarians attacked Rome, forcing all Roman troops to leave Britain in order to defend their own nation, and thus ending the Roman occupation of the island.

Soon after the Romans left, the Angles, the Saxons and the Jutes landed in Britain. They drove the Britons to the mountains, and those that did not flee remained as slaves to the new invaders. The Angles settled in East Anglia, the Midlands and the North, the Saxons

恺撒大帝

in the South and Midlands, and the Jutes in the South and Southeast. From that time on, English replaced the old Celtic language as the dominant language of the land. The country became known as England, meaning "the land of the Angles".

The Anglo-Saxons were organized into tribes governed by a chief or king. They had a mixed economy of farming, hunting and animal husbandry (畜牧业). Their social union was not determined by kinship (亲戚关系), but rather by the village. Private ownership had come into existence, but everyone was subject to control by the village as a whole.

The Anglo-Saxons were not Roman Christians when they went to Britain. By order of Pope Gregory I (格列高利一世), St. Augustine (圣奥古斯丁) was sent to Britain to convert the Anglo-Saxons. St. Augustine arrived in Kent in 597 with 40 missionaries (传教士). They completed their task smoothly and converted many Anglo-Saxons to Roman Christianity. By the late 7th century, Roman Christianity became the dominant religion in Britain.

In the 8th century, the Vikings from the Scandinavian countries of Northern Europe, Norway and Denmark in particular, began to attack the English coast. In the process of resisting the Vikings, the seven Anglo-Saxon kingdoms[1] in England gradually became united under Alfred the Great (阿尔弗雷德大帝, 849-899). In 878 an agreement was reached between King Alfred and the Danish King of East Anglia, wherein the northern and eastern part of the island was to be subject to Danish law. However, the fight for territory was far from over. Alfred recaptured London from the Vikings in 886. For approximately the next 130 years the power constantly shifted between the Anglo-Saxons and the Danes.

In 1066, Edward the Confessor[2] (c. 1003-1066) died without an heir. Harold of Wessex, his brother-in-law, was crowned King. However, Duke William of Normandy (1028-1087) challenged Harold's succession.

On September 27, 1066, William crossed the English Channel with a formidable (强大的) army. On October 14, 1066, William and his army defeated the English army, killing Harold at the battle of Hastings (黑斯廷斯). On Christmas

---

1 seven Anglo-Saxon kingdoms: 七王国，包括肯特 (Kent)、埃塞克斯 (Essex)、萨塞克斯 (Sussex)、西萨塞克斯 (Wessex)、东盎格里亚 (East Anglia)、麦西亚 (Mercia)、诺森布里亚 (Northumbria)。
2 Edward the Confessor: 忏悔者爱德华，英格兰国王，因笃信宗教，获"忏悔者"称号。

Day, 1066, William was crowned King of England in Westminster Abbey (威斯敏斯特教堂). It is believed that the Norman Conquest of England marked the establishment of feudalism in England. Although officially known as William I of England, he is often referred to as William the Conqueror.

After William's death, many wars were fought for the crown among the nation's principal families. By 1154, Henry II, William's great grandson, ascended the throne and thus began the rule of the House of Anjou (安茹王朝, 1154-1485) in England, also known as the House of Plantagenet (金雀花王朝). Henry II built up a large empire which included England and more than half of France. He is best remembered for his reform of the courts and the laws. He improved the courts of justice, introduced the jury system and institutionalized common law throughout the country.

After Richard I, son of Henry II, was killed in France, his brother John ascended the throne in 1199. He demanded more feudal taxes and army service in order to avenge himself on France. Dissatisfied with John's leadership, the lords forced him to sign the Magna Carta (《大宪章》), or the Great Charter as it is more commonly referred to, on June 15, 1215.

威斯敏斯特教堂

The Magna Carta contained 63 clauses, the most important being the following: The King could not exact (强求) payment from the vassals (封臣) without their consent; no freeman should be arrested, imprisoned or deprived of their freedom unless they are convicted according to the law of the land; merchants should be allowed to move about freely; there should be the same weights and measures throughout the country; traditional rights and privileges should be given to the towns. If the King attempted to free himself from the law, the vassals had the right to force him to obey the law by every means possible, even by means of a civil war.

Although the Magna Carta was made in the interest of the privileged class, it was of progressive significance in that it granted the townspeople freedom of trade and self-government. The merchants and craftsmen appeared for the first time as a political force. The Magna Carta is regarded as the foundation of the British constitutionalism.

When King John died, his son Henry III was crowned in 1216, but he did not take the reins of government until 1234. He waged a series of wars on France to regain Normandy. Being unable to manage these with normal revenue, he exacted money from the English people under all pretexts (借口) in violation of the spirit of the Magna Carta. The outraged nobles, led by Simon de Montfort*, Earl of Leicester (莱斯特伯爵), drafted the Provisions of Oxford (《牛津条例》) in 1258, which attempted to limit the King's power by calling regular meetings of a 15-member Privy Council (枢密院). It was replaced in 1259 by the Provisions of Westminster (《威斯敏斯特条例》), which reformed the common law. In 1264, apart from nobles and clergymen, some commoners were also called to the Privy Council in order to gain the support of the middle class. Thus, it was through the efforts of Simon de Montfort that the modern idea of a representative parliament emerged.

Several important historical events took place in the 14th and 15th centuries. Among them were the Hundred Years' War and the Wars of the Roses.

The Hundred Years' War (1337-1453) was a series of wars fought between England and France over trade, territory, security and the throne. The English were eager to fight to regain the lost territory in France and to control Flanders (佛兰德), an important market for English wool. When Charles IV, King of France, died in 1328, the King of England

---

* Simon de Montfort: 西蒙·德·蒙特福特，英格兰贵族，被视为现代议会制的创始人之一。

Edward III held claim to the throne because his mother was the sister of Charles IV and because Charles IV had no sons. Another claimant (要求权利的人) Philip VI, the head of the Valois House (瓦罗亚王室), gained the throne. In 1337 Edward III renewed his claim to the French throne and the war broke out.

At first, the war went in England's favor. As time went on, however, guns and gunpowder appeared in war, which greatly reduced the effectiveness of the English bows and arrows. By the time the war ended, the English had lost all the territories they had gained during the war except the French port of Calais (加来).

The Hundred Years' War had a significant impact on English society. It promoted the concept of English nationalism and the development of the textile industry. In addition, the war raised the social position of the bourgeois class (资产阶级). All these factors contributed to the decline of feudalism in England.

The Wars of the Roses (1455-1485) were a series of civil wars between two great noble families: the House of York (约克王朝) whose badge was a white rose, and the House of Lancaster (兰开斯特王朝) whose badge was a red rose. Both houses battled for power, wealth and ultimately the throne. The wars started when Richard, Duke of York tried to displace the Lancastrian King Henry VI. Almost all the noble families were involved in the wars and suffered great loss. The wars lasted for 30 years. In the end, the House of Lancaster won and their leader Henry Tudor became King Henry VII and started the rule of the House of Tudor (都铎王朝).

The Tudor family ruled England from 1485 to 1603. Under the Tudors, England became a national state with an efficient centralized government and started changing from a medieval to a modern country.

玫瑰战争

II. Transition to the Modern Age

The Reformation

There was an inevitable conflict between the Roman Catholic Church and the King of England who had established an absolute monarchy. The resentment among the people toward the power of the Pope and the church was also growing because the English suspected that a large part of their wealth was taken to Rome and there was serious corruption in the church. However, the immediate cause for the Reformation was King Henry VIII's attempt to divorce his first wife, Catherine of Aragon.

At that time, the only person who could grant a divorce was the Pope, yet the Pope would never allow Henry to divorce his wife. Thus, Henry VIII started the Reformation by declaring a break with Rome. He carried out a wholesale suppression of the monasteries and confiscated (没收) the property of the church. In 1534 he issued the Act of Supremacy (《至尊法案》) and declared himself to be the Supreme Head of the Church of England. The Reformation was in essence a political movement in a religious guise.

For half a century the whole island went through the Reformation under Henry VIII and the Counter-Reformation led by his daughter and heir, Mary I. The bloody religious persecution came to a stop after the church settlement executed by Queen Elizabeth I (1533-1603). She was inclined to support the Protestants, but she tried her best to make peace by appeasing (平息) the Catholics. Although working for a compromise between different religious factions, she defended the fruit of the Reformation in essence. Under her reign the Church of England (also called the Anglican Church) was consolidated.

伊丽莎白一世

The Civil Wars

The major parliamentary clashes of the early 17th century were over monopolies. The King granted monopolies on certain commodities to his favorites, and thereafter no citizen could trade in these commodities without first purchasing the permission of the monopoly holders. This caused grave hardships to merchants and a sharp rise in prices followed, so Parliament declared that monopolies without its consent were illegal. However, King Charles I was dissatisfied and dissolved Parliament in 1629. For the next 11 years, he ruled the country without a parliament. Charles I afflicted the capitalist class as a whole and the demands for a new government increased.

The first Civil War broke out in 1642 between the Royalists known as the Cavaliers (保王党人) and the Parliamentarians known as the Roundheads (圆颅党人). Oliver Cromwell led the New Model Army (新模范军) and fought bravely against the King's troops. In 1646, Charles I could struggle no longer and surrendered. This ended the first Civil War. However, Charles I escaped and the Civil War broke out again until Charles I was recaptured and executed in 1649. In 1651, Cromwell destroyed Charles II's army, which marked the end of the Civil Wars. The monarchy was abolished and England was declared a commonwealth and governed as a republic.

克伦威尔

Cromwell became the head of the Commonwealth. He was conservative in social reforms and was committed to protecting the interests of the property owners. Taxes were increased to keep the army supplied and Cromwell became unpopular. Cromwell died in 1658 and was succeeded by his son, Richard. In 1660 Parliament decided to restore Charles II to the throne of England. This put an end to the Commonwealth.

Restoration and the Glorious Revolution

Charles II was crowned on April 23, 1661 and tried to restore the old social order during his reign. Upon his death in 1685, he was succeeded by his brother, James II. James soon showed his readiness to reestablish Catholicism in England. This was something the English bourgeoisie could not agree to. A group of important leading figures joined forces and asked William, who was then Head of the United Provinces of the Netherlands and had married Mary, James II's daughter, to come and rule England. William accepted the invitation and prepared to replace his father-in-law.

光荣革命

After William landed in England with an army in November, 1688, James II fled to France. A new Parliament declared the throne vacant and appointed William and Mary joint sovereigns in 1689. This was called the Glorious Revolution (光荣革命). In 1689, Parliament passed the Bill of Rights (《人权法案》), which limited the power of the monarch and guaranteed the authority of Parliament. William and Mary signed the bill into law. The Glorious Revolution was complete, in which Parliament succeeded in removing a ruling monarch they did not like and establishing a system known as constitutional monarchy*. From that time, the King ruled with an authority circumscribed (限制) by Parliament.

The Industrial Revolution

The Industrial Revolution took root in Britain in the 18th century for a variety of reasons. First, Britain had a huge market. After the Glorious Revolution, the British Parliament was made up of prosperous merchants and entrepreneurs who supported commerce and industry. Thus Britain became the single largest domestic market in Europe. Internationally, Britain fought and won a series of wars against France. During the Seven Years' War (1756-1763), Britain seized most of the French colonial territories in North America, including Canada. Britain also captured the French trading colonies in India and became the world's leading colonial power. The colonies provided Britain with necessary raw materials and a large market for its industrial products.

---

* constitutional monarchy: 君主立宪制，是相对于君主独裁制的一种国家体制。它在保留君主制的前提下，通过立宪，树立人民主权，限制君主权力，实现事实上的共和政体。

Second, England acquired from its colonies enormous wealth with which to develop its industry. The most well-known trading company was the East India Company, which had a trading monopoly in India and parts of East Asia. The Royal African Company was involved in trade with Africa, the slave trade in particular. All these activities accumulated a lot of capital for Britain's future industrial development.

Third, the enclosure movement (圈地运动) deprived many small landowners of their property. This new class of landless laborers now had to seek paid employment from the large landowners or to find work in the rapidly growing industrial areas.

England experienced rapid economic development in the 18th century. The market demand for manufactured goods exceeded the supply. This motivated entrepreneurs to search for new ways to improve productivity.

The Industrial Revolution began in the textile industry and was marked by a series of important inventions: Spinning Jenny (詹妮纺纱机), the water frame (水力纺纱机), the spinning mule (走锭纺纱机), the power loom (动力织布机) and the steam engine. These inventions completed the mechanization of the textile industry and prepared the way for a new system of production: large-scale industry.

With these developments came a need for a cheap means of transportation. Entrepreneurs invested in digging canals to ship goods to market. In 1814, the steam locomotive (蒸汽机车) was invented. The first railway was completed in 1825. By 1870, Britain had about 21,700 kilometers of railroad. Meanwhile, it had also built a large merchant fleet, which carried British-manufactured goods to all parts of the world.

蒸汽机车

By the middle of the 19th century, the Industrial Revolution was accomplished in Britain. It changed Britain in many ways. Its industrial productivity increased dramatically. Britain became the most advanced industrial country in the world. The country also underwent a process of mass urbanization. Many new cities sprang up, such as Manchester, Leeds (利兹), Birmingham (伯明翰) and Sheffield (谢菲尔德). The Industrial Revolution also created changes in the social class structure. The capitalist class became the most important force in the country. Meanwhile, the proletariat (无产阶级) came into being.

III. The Rise and Fall of the British Empire

Formation of the Empire

The British Empire began with the colonization of Newfoundland in 1583. By the time Queen Victoria (1819-1901) ascended the throne in 1837, Britain had long been an empire known as the First British Empire. It included the colonies in Canada, India and many small states in the West Indies (西印度群岛). These early colonies were usually started by individual businesspeople for the purpose of trade.

The Victorian Age witnessed the establishment of the Second British Empire. Queen Victoria ruled from 1837 until her death in 1901. Victoria's time was featured by tremendous achievements in almost every aspect. She encouraged further industrialization, the building of railways and the growth of trade and commerce. During Victoria's reign, especially from the 1870s, the British government adopted a very aggressive foreign policy known as the New Imperialism. By the end of the 19th century, the British Empire included about a quarter of the global population and a quarter of the world's landmass.

During the mid-19th century, Britain consolidated its existing colonies by bringing them under the direct control of the government. Australia, New Zealand and Canada became dominions (英联邦自治领) of the English Crown successively. In 1876, Victoria took the title "Empress of India" and India became her "jewel in the Crown". It served as a springboard (跳板) for the British colonists to expand their sphere of influence in Asia. In East Asia, the British government waged the Opium War (鸦片战争) against China and occupied Hong Kong with three unequal treaties it imposed on the Qing government. Meanwhile, Britain also

维多利亚女王

occupied Burma (缅甸), Sri Lanka (斯里兰卡), Singapore, Malaya (马来亚) and some other small countries and regions in Asia.

On the African continent, the British took control of the Suez Canal (苏伊士运河) and conquered Egypt in 1882. By the beginning of the 20th century, it occupied the Gold Coast (now Ghana), Nigeria, Sudan, Kenya, Uganda, Northern Rhodesia (today's Zambia), among others. It also controlled South Africa, where gold and diamonds had been found after the Boer War*. The war resulted in the creation of the Union of South Africa (南非联盟) in 1910, the fourth self-governing dominion of the British Empire after Canada, Australia and New Zealand.

On the eve of World War I, Britain was the largest colonial empire the world had ever seen. It controlled about a quarter of the world's landmass. The British boasted that they had "an empire on which the sun never set".

Britain in the World Wars

By the beginning of the 20th century, the world had entered the period of imperialism. Britain's dominance was challenged by other European nations and the United States, for they had also been industrialized and each was eager to protect their own markets and expand their influence. A conflict of interests and colonial rivalry involved two camps: the Central Powers (同盟国)—mainly Germany, Austria-Hungary, Turkey; and the Allies (协约国)—mainly France, Great Britain, Russia, Italy and from 1917, the United States. The conflict plunged the whole world into two devastating (毁灭性的) wars in the first half of the 20th century.

The immediate cause of World War I lay in the conflict on the Balkan Peninsula (巴尔干半岛). On June 28, 1914, the Austrian Archduke (大公) Francis Ferdinand was assassinated in Sarajevo (萨拉热窝). Austria-Hungary blamed Serbia (塞尔维亚) for the assassination and was determined to seek revenge. Both sides looked for support from their respective allies, Germany and Russia. This led to a showdown (决战) between the two camps and World War I broke out. The war ended with the victory for the Allies.

The cost of the war was great. Britain was drained of its manpower. Seventy percent of the merchant ships were sunk or damaged. As a result, Britain lost the sea

---

* Boer War: 布尔战争 (1899-1902)，是英国与南非布尔人为争夺南非殖民地而展开的战争。

supremacy (霸权). Though victorious, Britain came out of the war with a huge national debt. Business was slack (萧条的), many factories were closed down and taxes soared. The Great Depression from 1929 to 1933 brought additional problems to the British economy and society. Britain's position in the capitalist world was further weakened. With the rise of the Nazi Party in Germany, a new world war was imminent.

World War II was a continuation of World War I. According to the Treaty of Versailles (《凡尔赛条约》) which was signed at the end of World War I in 1919, Germany was required to relinquish (放弃) all its colonies and to permanently disarm. In addition, Germany was compelled to pay a vast sum in reparations (赔款). The Great Depression made things worse and led to the rise of fascism. Adolph Hitler aroused strong nationalism and racism in Germany, embarking (开始) on an ambitious plan to conquer Europe.

Reluctant to fight another war, the British government, led by Neville Chamberlain, followed a policy of appeasement (绥靖政策). However, Hitler invaded Poland on September 1, 1939. Britain and France were forced to declare war on Germany two days later. The next year Chamberlain resigned and Winston Churchill (1874-1965) became Prime Minister.

Germany invaded France and forced it to surrender in June 1940. Italy also entered the war on the side of Germany. Britain was in a very dangerous position.

In 1941 the pressure was somewhat alleviated (缓和) for Britain when Germany attacked the Soviet Union, and Japan attacked the United States at Pearl Harbor. These acts of aggression propelled the Soviet Union and the United States into an alliance with Britain. With the unified efforts of anti-Nazi forces, Germany surrendered unconditionally on May 7, 1945, one week after Hitler committed suicide.

Britain won the war, but at great costs. Around 357,000 people were killed or missing and 475,000 were wounded. The navy was 30% smaller than before the war and Britain lost its naval supremacy forever to the United States. In addition, the country had exhausted its reserves of gold, dollars and overseas investment, and was deeply in debt to the United States.

丘吉尔

The Fall of the Empire

As a result of World War II, most of Britain's colonies demanded and fought for independence. India and Pakistan became independent in 1947, followed by Burma in 1948. Egypt drove the British army out of the country and the Suez Canal Zone in 1956. In the 1960s, an independence movement swept the entire British Empire. More than 20 countries won their independence. The British Empire was replaced by the British Commonwealth of Nations, a loosely organized community of former British colonies.

IV. Britain Since World War II

Britain emerged from World War II as one of the Big Three. Perhaps she was not a superpower like the United States and the Soviet Union, but certainly the third wealthiest power. As a leading power, Britain adopted the foreign policy of "Three Majestic Circles" (三环外交). The first was the Commonwealth circle, which embraced much of Africa and Asia as well as the dominions of Canada, New Zealand and Australia. The second was Britain's special relationship with the United States, and the third was Britain's close relationship with Western Europe.

The process of decolonization transformed the British Empire into the British Commonwealth of Nations. The former colonies gained independence and then joined the Commonwealth. However, conflicts between members with different interests within the Commonwealth created a situation which no longer served the benefit of Britain. Therefore, Britain gradually reduced its involvement in the Commonwealth circle.

Britain cooperated closely with the United States after World War II, since they were allied during the war and shared the same concerns regarding the Soviet Union. Britain joined the North Atlantic Treaty Organization (NATO)* in 1949 and

---

* North Atlantic Treaty Organization (NATO): 北大西洋公约组织，1949 年由美国和西欧国家组建，旨在遏制苏联，控制西欧，争夺世界霸权。

followed the United States into the Korean War in 1950. Nevertheless, the special relationship was strained during the Suez Crisis. In 1956, Egypt tried to nationalize the Suez Canal, which harmed the British and French interests, so the two nations attempted to retake the canal by force. To the surprise of the British, America forced the Anglo-French forces to withdraw instead of supporting the action. The withdrawal marked the end of the British influence in the Middle East, and the United States took its place.

As for Europe, Britain adopted an isolationist policy immediately after World War II. It refused to join the European Economic Community (EEC)* when it was founded in 1957, and concentrated instead on its trade with the British Commonwealth nations. However, with few advantages gained from the Commonwealth, Britain gradually placed emphasis on trade with the European nations since the 1960s.

British Prime Minister Mrs. Margaret Thatcher (1925-2013) reestablished the special relationship with the United States. Thatcher promised that "Britain and America will stand side by side". However, the relationship was not always so friendly. Most notably, in 1983 President Reagan ordered the invasion of the Caribbean island of Grenada (格林纳达), ignoring the fact that it was a member of the British Commonwealth. Yet the disagreement did not last long, as was shown in 1986, when Britain allowed the United States to use its airbase to launch attacks on Libya (利比亚). By the end of the decade, relations had been successfully restored, so much so that when the former Iraqi President Saddām Hussein (萨达姆·侯赛因) ordered the invasion of Kuwait, Britain contributed 35,000 troops to a U.S.-led force which drove the Iraqis out in the "Operation Desert Storm" (沙漠风暴联合行动) in 1991. At the same time, Thatcher resisted European integration. She was deeply doubtful of the bureaucracy (官僚制度) of the EEC and determined to minimize Britain's contribution to the Community when the British economy was in recession. Due to this closeness with the United States and the constant arrogant attitude toward the European nations, she was not trusted by the Europeans.

Tony Blair (1953-), who became British Prime Minister in 1997, pursued a more positive policy toward Europe and participated actively in European affairs.

---

* European Economic Community: 欧洲经济共同体，推行欧洲经济、政治一体化。后逐渐演变、发展成为现在的欧洲联盟。

沙漠风暴联合行动

However, he refused to adopt the single European currency, the euro, when it was launched in January 1999, preferring instead to wait until the economic conditions were right for Britain. Blair was afraid that adopting the euro might damage the British economy, which had been stronger than that of other European countries since the mid-1990s.

The close relationship with the United States was further strengthened. Under the Blair government, Britain joined the United States in many military actions. In December 1998 the two countries launched a joint air strike "Operation Desert Fox" (沙漠之狐行动) against Iraq. A full-scale war against Iraq was launched in 2003 to overthrow Saddām Hussein's government. The war was sanctioned (认可) by the United States, but was opposed by most European countries. There was also strong opposition within Britain. Due to the British participation in the war, Blair faced a serious problem of credibility. The war was fought on the assumption that Iraq was making weapons of mass destruction, but no evidence could be found to support this claim. The Iraq crisis damaged Britain's relationship with Europe. It raised questions about the wisdom of Britain's special relationship with the United States, and it has even affected the image of the British government.

Exercises

I. Read the following statements and decide whether they are true (T) or false (F).

_____ 1. British history before 55 BC is basically undocumented.

_____ 2. The Anglo-Saxons came to Britain in the 5th century.

_____ 3. The chief or king of the Anglo-Saxon tribes exercised power at their own will.

_____ 4. The Vikings began to attack the English coast in the 8th century.

_____ 5. Henry II built up a large empire which included England and most of France.

_____ 6. The Magna Carta was designed to protect the rights of both the privileged class and the townspeople.

_____ 7. The Hundred Years' War was a series of wars fought between the British and the Vikings for trade and territory.

_____ 8. In an effort to make a compromise between different religious factions, Queen Elizabeth I actually defended the fruit of the Reformation.

II. Choose the best answer to complete each of the following statements.

1. The _____ attack on Rome ended the Roman occupation in Britain in 410.
   A. Norman   B. Danish   C. Celtic   D. Germanic

2. By the late 7th century, _____ became the dominant religion in England.
   A. Celtic Christianity   B. Anglo-Saxon Christianity
   C. Germanic Christianity   D. Roman Christianity

3. The _____ marked the establishment of feudalism in England.
   A. Viking invasions   B. signing of the Magna Carta
   C. Norman Conquest   D. adoption of common law

4. The end of the Wars of the Roses led to the rule of _____.
   A. the House of Valois   B. the House of York
   C. the House of Tudor   D. the House of Lancaster

5. The direct cause for the Reformation was King Henry VIII's effort to _____.
   A. divorce his wife   B. break with Rome
   C. support the Protestants   D. declare his supreme power over the church

6. The English Civil War broke out in 1642 between _____.
   A. the Protestants and the Puritans   B. the Royalists and the Parliamentarians
   C. the nobles and the peasants   D. the aristocrats and the Christians
7. _____ was passed after the Glorious Revolution.
   A. The Bill of Rights   B. The Act of Supremacy
   C. The Provisions of Oxford   D. The Magna Carta
8. The Industrial Revolution was accomplished in Britain by the middle of the _____ century.
   A. 17th   B. 18th   C. 19th   D. 20th

III. Give brief answers to the following questions.

1. What were Queen Victoria's major achievements?

2. What were the two camps in World War I?

3. Why did Britain cooperate closely with the United States after World War II?

IV. State your understanding of the following questions.

1. What were the results of the Industrial Revolution in Britain?
2. Explain the rise and fall of the British Empire.

Learn and Check

Famous people: Julius Caesar, Claudius I, Pope Gregory I, St. Augustine, Edward the Confessor, Alfred the Great, William I of England, Henry II, Henry III, Henry VII, Henry VIII, Queen Elizabeth I, Charles I, Oliver Cromwell, Charles II, Queen Victoria, Margaret Thatcher, Tony Blair

Important events: the Norman Conquest, the signature of the Magna Carta, the Hundred Years' War, the Wars of the Roses, the Reformation, the Civil Wars, the Glorious Revolution, the Industrial Revolution, the rise and fall of the British Empire

Chapter 3: Government and the Commonwealth

▼ Think and Talk

- Who is the head of state in Britain?
- Who is the most powerful leader in Britain?
- What are the three branches of the government and their respective functions?

I. Constitution

Britain is a parliamentary democracy with a constitutional monarchy. Although the King or Queen is the head of state, their power is largely symbolic. The government is elected by people and governs according to British constitutional principles.

The British Constitution is usually described as "unwritten", but this is misleading. Parts of the British Constitution are written and some are not. What is meant by "unwritten" is that it is not summarized into one single document as "the British Constitution". Therefore, it is more accurate to say that while much of the British Constitution is written down, it is not systematically codified into a single document. Of all the countries in the world, only Israel and New Zealand are comparable to Britain in having no single constitutional document.

The British Constitution is made up of three main parts: statutory law (成文法), common law (判例法) and conventions (习惯法). Statutory law is the most important and takes precedence (优先) over the others if there is a clash. Statutes are laws that have actually been passed by Parliament, for example, the Magna Carta (1215) which protects the rights of the community against the Crown, the Bill of Rights (1689) which extends the powers of Parliament, the Reform Act (1832) which reforms the parliamentary electoral system, the European Communities Act (1972) and the European Communities (Amendment) Act (1986) which define the relationship

Chapter 3 Government and the Commonwealth

between Britain and the European Community. Common law has never been precisely defined. It is deduced from customs or legal precedents and is interpreted in court cases by judges. Conventions are rules and practices which are not legally enforceable, but are regarded as vital to the working of the government.

The Constitution can be altered or amended by normal parliamentary processes. The flexibility of the British Constitution helps explain why it has developed so fully over the years. There is no single body which has the sole responsibility for interpreting the provisions of the Constitution. In other words, the Constitution is subject to interpretation by different bodies, the most important being politicians, judges and scholars.

As a parliamentary democracy, the British government is characterized by a division of powers among the legislature (立法机关), the executive (行政部门) and the judiciary (司法部门). However, the division among these three branches is not so absolute as that in the United States, because the Prime Minister, the head of the government, is also the leader of the majority party in Parliament. Furthermore, he advises the monarch on the candidates of the Supreme Court judges.

II. Government

The Legislature

Parliament is the law-making body of Britain. Strictly speaking, it consists of the Crown, the House of Lords (上议院) and the House of Commons (下议院). However, the monarchy is usually regarded as a separate institution because even though the King or Queen must consent to pass a law, that consent is given as a matter of course.

国会大厦

The United Kingdom of Great Britain and Northern Ireland

上议院

The stability of the British government owes much to the monarchy. Its continuity has been interrupted only once (the Republic of 1649-1660) in over a thousand years. Theoretically, the King or Queen is the source of all government powers. They are the head of the legislative, executive and judicial branches, the commander-in-chief of all armed forces and the "supreme governor" of the Church of England. In reality, they do everything on the advice of the Prime Minister, and their role is symbolic, ceremonial and unpolitical. This includes giving their Royal Assent* to any new law that has been passed by Parliament, meeting with the Prime Minister on a weekly basis at Buckingham Palace, and paying state visits to Commonwealth countries as head of state and non-Commonwealth countries on behalf of the British government. The importance of the monarchy is found in its effect on public attitude. It represents the continuity and adaptability of the whole political system and is a symbol of British unity, an indissoluble (牢不可破的) bond among people who retain many regional and cultural differences.

* Royal Assent: 御准，国王或女王对议会通过的议案的批准。

Chapter 3 Government and the Commonwealth

The House of Lords, sometimes referred to as the Upper House, consists of life peers* who are granted noble titles by the King or Queen on the advice of the Prime Minister, a limited number of 26 Church of England archbishops and bishops, and elected hereditary peers (世袭贵族). The main legislative function of the House of Lords is to examine and revise bills from the House of Commons. It also acts in a legal capacity as the highest court of appeal (上诉法院).

In recent years, the House of Lords has undergone a process of reform to make it more democratic and representative. Currently only 92 hereditary peers are allowed to remain in the House of Lords. The next phase of reform would be to remove the remaining hereditary peers and establish a fully elected chamber (议院).

The House of Commons, though often referred to as the Lower House, is the center of parliamentary power. It is usually composed of 650 Members of Parliament, known as "MPs" who represent the 650 constituencies (选区). The party which holds the majority of "seats" in the House of Commons forms the government, with its leader acting as the Prime Minister. After a government has been in power for five years, it must resign and hold a general election, in which all British adults (aged 18 or over) are given the chance to vote again for the MP who represents their constituency. However, whenever the government does not have the support of Parliament for its major policy, a new election is held and a new government is formed.

The House of Commons performs three major functions. The most important is drafting new laws. Although both houses are involved in the law-making process, the House of Commons has primacy over the House of Lords, especially in the ratification (批准) of "money bills" which dictate taxation and public expenditure. For any decisions made by the House of Commons on such matters, the House of Lords must give prompt approval without amendment. This is based on the principle that the House of Lords, as a revising chamber, should complement the House of Commons and not rival it. The second function of the House of Commons is to scrutinize (仔细检查) the actions of the government. It can force a government to resign by passing a motion of no confidence (不信任动议). In addition, it has the power to supervise finance. The government cannot legally spend any money without permission from the House of Commons. The third function is to influence future government policy.

---

* life peers: 爵位不能世袭的终身贵族，多为一些为英国社会做出杰出贡献的人。

The Executive

The government is made up of the Prime Minister, the Cabinet (内阁) ministers and assistants to the ministers. The government decides which policies should be taken to Parliament to become law. After a law has been passed by Parliament, the executive branch is responsible for making sure that it is carried out. Civil servants work in departments led by ministers to accomplish these tasks.

The Prime Minister is the leader of the majority party in Parliament. After each general election, the monarch will appoint the leader of the winning party as the Prime Minister and form a new Cabinet. Cabinet members are chosen by the Prime Minister from members of his own party in Parliament. Most of them are appointed as ministers in charge of government departments. The role of the Prime Minister is traditionally described as "first among equals". The Cabinet has always been led by the Prime Minister.

The Cabinet is at the center of the British political system. It is the supreme decision-making body in the British government. The Cabinet meets on a regular basis, usually weekly on Thursday mornings at 10 Downing Street, to discuss the most important issues of government policy. As the Prime Minister is also the head of the majority party in Parliament, the Prime Minister and the Cabinet can usually influence the legislation.

白金汉宫

Chapter 3 Government and the Commonwealth

The Cabinet works on the principle of collective responsibility and individual ministerial responsibility. Individual ministerial responsibility means that a Cabinet minister bears the ultimate responsibility for the actions of the ministry, while the collective responsibility means that members of the Cabinet must approve publicly of its collective decisions. Cabinet ministers that disagree with major decisions are expected to resign. When a vote of no confidence is passed in Parliament, every minister resigns and the entire executive branch is dismissed.

In addition to the Cabinet, the executive branch includes the Privy Council, serving as a body of advisors, which has about 500 members. They consist of Cabinet members, the leaders of all major political parties, the Speaker, Archbishops, senior judges and some other important public figures. Formerly, the Privy Council was a powerful institution, but it is now largely ceremonial. Most of its power is held by the Cabinet.

The Prime Minister, as the head of government, controls not only the Cabinet but also Parliament. Since the King or Queen's power is limited, the Prime Minister is in effect the most powerful leader in Britain.

The Judiciary

The judicial branch of the British government is rather complicated in that England and Wales, Scotland and Northern Ireland all have their own legal systems, with minor differences in law, organization and practice.

Different types of cases are dealt with in specific courts. For example, all criminal cases will start in the magistrates' court (地方法院), but the more serious criminal matters are committed to the Crown Court. Appeals from the Crown Court will go to the High Court, and potentially to the Court of Appeal or even the Supreme Court.

Civil cases will sometimes be dealt with by magistrates, but may well go to a county court (郡法院). Again, appeals will go to the High Court and then to the Court of Appeal.

In British criminal trials, the accused is presumed innocent until proven guilty. Trials are in open court and the accused is represented by a lawyer. Most cases are tried without a jury. More serious cases are tried in higher courts before a jury of 12 (15 in Scotland), which decides whether the accused is innocent or guilty.

III. Political Parties

The power to run the country lies in the elected Parliament. The British Parliament operates on a two-party system, which means that two political parties play the roles of the Government and the Opposition. The party whose political ideas are welcomed by the majority will be elected and consequently empowered (授权) to form the government. The leader of the party will become the Prime Minister.

The U.K. has many political parties, the three main being the Conservative Party, the Labor Party and the Liberal Democrats.

The Conservative Party

Before World War II, the leadership of Britain was almost continually in the hands of the Conservative Party. During the post-1945 period, however, the ruling party changed fairly frequently.

By and large, the Conservative Party is supported by those who have something to "conserve", such as landowners and businessmen, often from the middle and upper-middle class. For this reason, it is sometimes called the "Right". Many wealthy members of the working class also favor this party. One might infer that the higher one climbs in socioeconomic terms, the more likely they are to be a Conservative.

Economically, the Conservative Party supports free enterprise and privatization of state-owned enterprises. It is against too much government intervention, especially nationalization, which not only takes control away from the owners and builders of industry, but also leads to inefficiency. The Conservative Party favors reducing the influence of trade unions and minimizing expenditures on social welfare. Its policies are characterized by pragmatism (实用主义) and a belief in individualism.

Chapter 3 Government and the Commonwealth

The Labor Party

The Labor Party was created in 1900. It was one of the two major political parties of the U.K. during the 19th and early 20th centuries. It believes in an egalitarian (平等主义的) economy, wherein the function of the government is to act as a "redistributive" agent, transferring wealth from the rich to the poor by means of taxing the most affluent members of society and providing support for the poor. They also deem the government responsible for the provision of a range of public services, such as social welfare, education and public transport. The Labor government that came to power in 1945 had a major effect on British society. It set up the National Health Service to provide high-quality, free health care for all, "from cradle to grave", providing a range of welfare payments, and most controversially, it "nationalized" a wide range of industries, making a mixed economy of both private- and state-owned enterprises. All these government activities required money, so the Labor Party became known as a party of high taxation. The party activities are largely funded by the trade unions.

The Liberal Democrats

The Liberal Democrats was formed in 1988, by a merger of the Liberal Party and the Social Democratic Party. To some extent, the Liberal Democrats may be seen as a "middle" party, occupying the ideological ground between the two major parties. As such, at election times it may receive votes from those who usually vote for Labor as well as those who usually vote for Conservative. Many people see it as comparatively flexible and pragmatic in its balance of the individual and the social. It emphasizes the need for a change in Britain's constitutional arrangements in order to make the government more democratic and accountable (应负责任的).

IV. Election

A general election is held every five years. The candidate who wins the most votes in each constituency becomes a Member of Parliament. Each party has a local organization in the constituency, whose main task is to choose the candidate and help them win.

In elections, anyone who is eligible to vote can stand as an MP. It is only necessary to make a deposit of 500 pounds, which is lost if the candidate does not receive at least 5% of the vote. This is designed to prevent those unserious candidates from running in the election. Independent candidates are unlikely to win the election, for voters usually won't vote for them because even if they were to win the seat, they would be powerless in Parliament against the larger parties.

When political parties launch electoral campaigns, they use advertisements in newspapers, door-to-door campaigning and leaflets. The main parties are given several 10-minute slots (时段) on national television to present their policies to the public. Apart from the parties' own publicity, newspapers and TV programs spend a lot of time discussing the campaigns, interviewing politicians and predicting the results.

On election day, people go to their local polling station to vote. When the voting closes at the end of the day, the counting begins. By early morning of the next day, it is often clear who has won the election. The party which wins over half of the constituencies is the majority in the House of Commons, subsequently forming the new government. The head of the party becomes the Prime Minister.

V. The Commonwealth

Origin of the Commonwealth

The British Commonwealth of Nations is the successor of the British Empire. During the 19th and early 20th centuries, Britain possessed colonies as well as self-governing dominions such as Canada, Australia, New Zealand and the Union of South Africa. However, after World War II, the subject territories embarked upon an independence movement in order to gain a greater degree of autonomy. Gradually, the

Chapter 3 Government and the Commonwealth

British capitulated (屈服) to the pressures of such nationalist sentiment and had to reshape the relationship with its member states, thereby transforming itself into the British Commonwealth.

In 1949, the word "British" was dropped from the title of the British Commonwealth of Nations to reflect the new political status quo (现状). Numerous independence movements began within its member states. India gained independence in 1947, but still desired to remain as a part of the Commonwealth. In 1949 the London Declaration (《伦敦宣言》), often considered a milestone in the history of the modern Commonwealth, accepted and recognized India's continued membership as a republic. This paved the way for other newly independent countries to join the Commonwealth. From 1960 on, new members from Africa, the Caribbean region, the Mediterranean region and the Pacific region joined the Commonwealth, contributing to its immense diversity.

Characteristics and Functions

The Commonwealth of Nations is a voluntary association of independent sovereign states, all of which acknowledge the British monarch as the symbolic head of the association. Most of these states are former colonies of the British Empire and were once collectively known as the British Commonwealth of Nations.

The Commonwealth is not a political union of any sort, and its member states have full autonomy to manage their own internal and external affairs. It is primarily an organization in which countries with diverse economic backgrounds have an opportunity to interact closely as equals after gaining independence. The primary purpose of the Commonwealth is to advocate democracy, human rights and to promote economic cooperation and growth within its members. Membership in the Commonwealth is expressed in cooperation, consultation, mutual assistance and the periodic meeting of national leaders. The Queen of Britain is considered the head of the Commonwealth.

Members of the Commonwealth

The countries of the Commonwealth have a population of two billion people, some 30% of the world's total population. India is the most populous member, while Nauru (瑙鲁) and Tuvalu (图瓦卢) are the smallest.

The Commonwealth contains three groups of territories: white territories, non-white territories and mixed territories. Inhabitants of white territories are mainly of British descent and speak English as their mother tongue, for example, Canada, Australia and New Zealand. The non-white territories refer to places where the British have never settled, except temporarily as traders and administrators, such as Pakistan, Sri Lanka, some West African countries and Malaysia. The inhabitants of the mixed territories are of British and non-British origins, such is the case in Central and East African countries.

After many years of development, the Commonwealth has become an organization composed of 54 countries. With member countries spreading far and wide throughout the world, the nations of the Commonwealth occupy every time zone.

Organizations of the Commonwealth

The headquarters and the standing bodies of the Commonwealth of Nations are all located in London. Its major events include: a) the Commonwealth Heads of Government Meetings (CHOGM) wherein the heads of states from all Commonwealth nations meet. Every two years the meeting is held in a different member state to discuss matters of mutual interest; b) the Commonwealth ministerial meetings held annually. The Commonwealth has three intergovernmental organizations: a) the Commonwealth Secretariat, which is the central body of the Commonwealth of Nations. It implements the decisions taken by the association's 54 member governments and organizes the meetings of Commonwealth ministers; b) The Commonwealth Foundation, which helps civil society organizations promote democracy, development and cultural understanding; c) Commonwealth Learning, which encourages the development and sharing of open learning and distance education.

Commonwealth Day

Commonwealth Day is an annual event during which all the member countries of the Commonwealth celebrate their links with one another. It is celebrated on the second Monday in March each year. Today, Commonwealth Day has become an opportunity to promote understanding of global issues, international cooperation and the efforts of the Commonwealth to improve the lives of its citizens.

Chapter 3 Government and the Commonwealth

Exercises

I. **Read the following statements and decide whether they are true (T) or false (F).**

_____ 1. Conventions are regarded less important than the statutory law in the working of the British government.

_____ 2. The British monarchy has never been interrupted throughout the history.

_____ 3. In reality, the British King or Queen is the source of all government powers.

_____ 4. The British Parliament is the law-making body of the Commonwealth of Nations.

_____ 5. The members of the House of Commons are appointed rather than elected.

_____ 6. The British Prime Minister is the leader of the majority party in Parliament.

_____ 7. Cabinet members are chosen by the Prime Minister from various political parties in Parliament.

_____ 8. The legal systems in England, Wales, Scotland and Northern Ireland are much similar in terms of law, organization and practice.

II. **Choose the best answer to complete each of the following statements.**

1. The British government is characterized by a division of powers between three of the following branches EXCEPT the _____.
   A. judiciary   B. legislature   C. monarchy   D. executive
2. The importance of the British monarchy can be seen in its effect on _____.
   A. passing bills   B. advising the government
   C. political parties   D. public attitude
3. As a revising chamber, the House of Lords is expected to _____ the House of Commons.
   A. rival   B. complement   C. criticize   D. inspect
4. _____ is at the center of the British political system.
   A. The Cabinet   B. The House of Lords
   C. The House of Commons   D. The Privy Council
5. The main duty of the British Privy Council is to _____.
   A. make decisions   B. give advice
   C. pass bills   D. supervise the Cabinet
6. Generally speaking, the British Parliament operates on a _____ system.
   A. single-party   B. two-party   C. three-party   D. multi-party

41

7. The policies of the Conservative Party are characterized by pragmatism and _____.

    A. government intervention   B. nationalization of enterprises
    C. social reform   D. a belief in individualism

8. In Britain, the parliamentary general election is held every _____ years.

    A. three   B. four   C. five   D. six

III. Give brief answers to the following questions.

1. What are the three functions of the House of Commons?

2. What kind of public image does the Liberal Democrats have in Britain?

3. Why are independent candidates unlikely to win in the general election?

IV. State your understanding of the following questions.

1. What do British electoral campaigns usually involve during the process of a general election?
2. What is the Commonwealth of Nations?

Learn and Check

Constitution: statutory law, common law, conventions

Government: the legislature, the executive, the judiciary

Major political parties: the Conservative Party, the Labor Party, the Liberal Democrats

General election: every five years

The Commonwealth: 54 member countries

Chapter 4 Economy

▼ **Think and Talk**

▶ What are Thatcher's economic policies in the 1980s?
▶ What are the major products of British agriculture?
▶ Why is the service industry important in the British economy?

I. Recent History of British Economy

Britain was the first industrialized nation in the world and has remained an economic giant for the past two centuries. By the 19th century, the British economy had achieved global dominance, producing one-third of the world's manufactured goods, half of its coal and iron. The quantity of goods transported in Britain's shipping industry was greater than that of the rest of the world put together.

Although Britain remained a member of the Group of Seven* after World War II, its economy experienced a period of great difficulty and relative economic decline for the following reasons. First, Britain suffered great losses in the two World Wars. It went heavily into debt to finance both wars, which resulted in economic problems during the post-war period. Second, by the mid-20th century, the era of the British Empire was over. Shortly after the end of World War II, India, which provided raw materials and a large market for British goods, gained independence, quickly followed by the rest of the Empire, leaving Britain a medium-sized European country. Third, Britain was forced to maintain an expensive military presence in many overseas locations until the end of the 1960s, when the process of decolonization was

---

* Group of Seven: 七国集团，是主要工业国家会晤和讨论政策的论坛。其成员包括：美国、英国、法国、德国、日本、意大利和加拿大。后因俄罗斯的加入，七国集团演变为八国集团。

completed. Moreover, as one of NATO's major partners and a member of the U.N. Security Council (联合国安全理事会), Britain had to make substantial financial contributions. The result was that Britain spent a higher proportion of its national wealth on military expenditure than most of its competitors. Fourth, Britain failed to invest in industry after World War II. During the war, British industry survived and was comparatively unaffected. However, some of its competitors, especially the defeated Germany and Japan, had to start from nothing. This ostensible (表面的) disadvantage may have worked in their favor because they were compelled to invest in industry. It was no surprising that they were able to catch up with and even overtook Britain.

In 1945, the Labor Party carried out drastic reforms and laid the foundation for the post-war British social and economic development. Economically, it implemented the nationalization of industries and exercised a considerable amount of control over private enterprises in order to revive the primary industries and help balance trade. However, inflation and trade deficit (贸易赤字) were persistent problems that prevented rapid economic development. British industry appeared to be performing poorly, with imports increasing compared to exports. The economic difficulties caused unemployment to rise. The oil crisis of 1973 impaired an already declining economy with the fall of the pound and very high inflation rates. Although the government changed from one party to another, the economy remained stagnant (停滞的). Britain's economic growth fell behind that of other European countries. The negative economic situation led to a change in government at the general election. In 1979, the British people voted in the Conservative Party under Mrs. Margaret Thatcher, who promised radical economic reform.

撒切尔夫人

Thatcher was the first woman to become Prime Minister of Britain. Her government introduced the biggest changes in the British economic policy since World War II. She privatized state-owned industries and promoted a more competitive spirit in the British economy. In terms of social welfare, Thatcher's government reduced old age pensions, shortened the period of unemployment benefits and cut child benefits. Believing that a free labor market was essential for a successful economy, she curbed (控制) the power of the trade unions.

Thatcher's revolution seemed in some ways to be a success as inflation came under control and business profits increased. The 1980s saw the recovery of the British economy although it continued to grow at lower rates than its competitors. However, the negative aspect of Thatcher's reform was a rapid increase in unemployment. In 1982, the unemployment rate was comparable to that of the years during the Great Depression, with three million people out of work.

Thatcher and her policies were, and remain, highly controversial. Her supporters contended that she was responsible for reviving the British economy, while her opponents argued that she was responsible for mass unemployment and a vast increase in inequality between the rich and the poor. However, if judged merely by the economic records, by any standard, Mrs. Thatcher's economic record from 1983 onward was impressive.

She served as Prime Minister until 1990, when she lost the support of the voters because of the stagnant economy, the unpopular poll tax (人头税) her government had levied (征收) and her reluctance to integrate the British economy with the European Union. She was succeeded by John Major, who worked hard to revive the economy. However, the public lost confidence in the Conservative Party due to its internal division regarding policies toward the European Union.

In 1997, the Conservative Party was voted out of office after 18 years in power. The Labor Party won a major victory in the election and its leader, Tony Blair, became Prime Minister. Blair called for the "Third Way" which was different from the old Labor Party's commitment to nationalization of economy and the Conservative Party's emphasis on extreme individualism. In order to separate politics and economic policy, Blair made the Bank of England independent. In social policy, the Blair government changed the old Labor Party's practice of using tax system, public expenditure and price controls to reduce inequality and put an emphasis on the minimum wage and supplementing low incomes. It also emphasized individual responsibility.

The Blair government was successful in limiting government spending, keeping inflation under control and reducing unemployment. By the end of the 20th century, British economic growth surpassed that of other major European countries.

布莱尔

II. Current British Economy

Agriculture

Britain's agriculture is characterized by a small proportion of the population (about 1.5% of the workforce) engaged in agricultural activities with a high degree of mechanization. But the country is so heavily populated that it produces only about 60% of the food it consumes.

Britain's mild climate provides the country with a favorable environment for agriculture and stock raising (畜牧业). Upland areas generally lend themselves to sheep farming, flat areas to crop production, wet and warm areas to milk and beef production. Although the country's land area is small compared with that of other European nations, some 70% is devoted to agriculture, with two-thirds of it reserved for stock raising.

Important crops in Britain are wheat, barley, sugar beet (甜菜) and potatoes. Dairy farming is distributed throughout the country, but is predominant in western England. Britain is the world's leading exporter of cattle, sheep, pigs and horses. Britain's beef, especially that of Scotland, is well known for its excellence, and Welsh mutton is the country's favorite meat. However, the beef industry was crippled by BSE (疯牛病) in 1996, leading to a ban on beef exports until 2006.

Britain has a large ocean fishing fleet and fish is a basic element of the national diet. The fishing industry fulfills two-thirds of Britain's demand for fish. The major fishing areas are the North Sea, the English Channel, the waters off the Irish coast and the sea area between Britain and Iceland.

Energy Production

Coal mining industry is a traditional energy industry in Britain. It not only provides tens of thousands of jobs, but also a quarter of the energy consumed nationally. Most of the coalfields are located in Central Scotland, Central England and South Wales, particularly around such big cities as Glasgow (格拉斯哥), Manchester, Sheffield and Newcastle (纽卡斯尔). Rio Tinto Group (力拓集团), one of the world's largest mining companies, operates mines all over the world.

Britain's oil industry is relatively new. In 1975, oil first came ashore from the North Sea. Britain produced nearly 2.5 million barrels per day during 2009. However, production is certainly past its peak. Since 1999, when Britain was the world's six-largest oil and gas producer, yields have fallen by an average of 6.2% a year. Some of the giant energy companies include: Shell (壳牌集团), British Petroleum (BP) and British Gas (BG).

Another major source of energy in Britain is nuclear power, with the first nuclear power plant constructed in 1956. Its subsequent development has been sufficient to make Britain a world leader in nuclear energy. Today, it has a total of 16 nuclear power plants.

Manufacturing Industry

Britain's manufacturing sector remains important, being the third largest sector in the U.K. economy after the business services and the retail sector in terms of share of GDP. British companies are active in all major fields of the manufacturing industry, but are particularly strong in pharmaceuticals (药品), chemicals, aerospace, and food and drink. Britain also has a substantial electronics industry. Its automobile industry is, in many cases, foreign-owned.

Service Industry

The major trends in the British economy since the end of World War II have been a further decline in the already small agricultural sector (by European standards), a reduction in the industrial sector and a sizable expansion of the service sector (retailing, banking, tourism and public services). Like most developed economies, Britain has seen a relative shrinkage in the importance of secondary industries and a spectacular growth in the service industry.

Britain boasts one of the world's oldest, most extensive and most highly developed financial systems. London is one of the three principal financial centers of the world, with the other two being New York and Tokyo. It has the greatest concentration of foreign banks in the world and is the world's largest foreign exchange market. At the heart of the British financial system is the Bank of England, which was founded in 1694 and nationalized in 1946. It functions as Britain's central bank, working in close contact with the government to control monetary policy and give directives to commercial banks.

The London Stock Exchange*, located in the heart of London, is one of the world's largest centers for trading stocks and bonds. It is also the most international of all the world's stock exchanges, with around 3,000 companies from over 70 countries admitted to trading on its markets.

---

* the London Stock Exchange: 伦敦证券交易所, 世界四大证券交易所之一。

英国银行

Chapter 4 Economy

温莎城堡

Other financial institutions based in London include many insurance companies, such as the prestigious (有威望的) Lloyd's[1], shipping companies, merchant banks and discount houses (贴现公司), as well as foreign banks and many of the world's major commodity markets like the London Metal Exchange and the Baltic Exchange[2].

Tourism is one of the largest industries in Britain. It employs 2.1 million people in hotels, restaurants, pubs, travel agencies and museums. More than 25 million people visit England every year from all over the world. England has much to offer, with magnificent countryside views which vary from region to region and a wide variety of cultures. There are wonderful Dorset and East Devon Coast[3], the Lake District, Stonehenge[4], Windsor Castle[5], and the beautiful university towns such as Oxford and Cambridge.

Exhibition and conference services provide Britain with another source of revenue. Britain is one of the world's largest centers for international conferences.

---

1 Lloyd's: 劳埃德社，又称劳合社，英国最大的保险交易市场。
2 the Baltic Exchange: 波罗的海交易所，是由全球航运市场核心成员组成的会员组织。
3 Dorset and East Devon Coast: 多塞特和东德文海岸，位于英格兰南部海岸，2001 年被评为世界自然遗产。
4 Stonehenge: 巨石阵，英国南部索尔兹伯里平原上的古代巨石建筑遗迹。
5 Windsor Castle: 温莎城堡，英国王室的行宫之一，位于伦敦附近的温莎镇。

巨石阵

Foreign Trade

Britain has been a trading country for hundreds of years. Trade still plays a very important role today. The principal exported goods are manufactured goods, mineral fuels, chemicals, foodstuffs, beverages and tobacco. Britain is also a major supplier of machinery, vehicles, aerospace products, electrical and electronic equipment, etc. Britain's major export partners are Germany, the United States, the Netherlands and France.

British imports mainly consist of manufactured goods, machinery, fuels and foodstuffs. Britain's most important trade partners for imports are Germany, China, the Netherlands and the United States.

Exercises

I. **Read the following statements and decide whether they are true (T) or false (F).**

_____ 1. Britain was the first industrialized nation in the world.

_____ 2. The British economy experienced a relative decline during the post-war period.

_____ 3. Limited resources and high unemployment rate were persistent problems that prevented rapid economic development in Britain after World War II.

_____ 4. Thatcher's revolution turned out to be a great success in dealing with all the British economic and social problems.

_____ 5. The economic approach adopted by Tony Blair was different from that of the old Labor Party and the Conservative Party.

_____ 6. Blair made the Bank of England independent in order to separate politics from economic policy.

_____ 7. Britain is an important oil exporter since its oil industry has a long history.

_____ 8. Nuclear power is one of the major energy sources in Britain.

II. Choose the best answer to complete each of the following statements.
1. The _____ in the early 1970s worsened an already stagnant economy in Britain.
   A. oil crisis
   B. high inflation rates
   C. large imports
   D. unemployment problem
2. Of the following practices, _____ did not belong to Thatcher's social welfare reform.
   A. reducing child benefits
   B. shortening the period of unemployment benefits
   C. reducing unemployment
   D. lowering old age pensions
3. The Blair government was successful in all the following aspects EXCEPT _____.
   A. limiting government spending
   B. keeping inflation under control
   C. reducing unemployment
   D. reducing inequality
4. Britain has devoted about _____ of its land area to agriculture.
   A. 50%   B. 60%   C. 70%   D. 80%
5. Britain's important fishing areas include all the following EXCEPT _____.
   A. the North Sea
   B. the English Channel
   C. the sea area around the Irish coast
   D. the sea area between Britain and Ireland
6. Coal mining industry in Britain provides _____ of the energy consumed in the country.
   A. one-third   B. one-fourth   C. one-fifth   D. two-thirds
7. The car industry in Britain is mostly _____.
   A. foreign-owned
   B. state-owned
   C. joint-venture
   D. privately-owned
8. Of the following sectors in Britain, _____ has experienced spectacular growth since the end of World War II.
   A. agriculture
   B. the energy industry
   C. the service sector
   D. the manufacturing industry

III. Give brief answers to the following questions.

1. What was the negative aspect of Thatcher's reform in the early 1980s?
   _____
   _____

2. What are the characteristics of Britain's agriculture?
   _____
   _____

3. What happened to Britain's beef industry in the mid-1990s?
   _____
   _____

IV. State your understanding of the following questions.

1. What were the major causes of Britain's relative economic decline in the post-war period?
2. Why do developed nations like Britain encourage the development of the service industry?

Learn and Check

Prime Ministers: Margaret Thatcher, John Major, Tony Blair

Economic sectors: agriculture, energy production, manufacturing industry, service industry, foreign trade

Important trade partners: Germany, the United States, the Netherlands, France, China

Chapter 5 Education, Media and Holidays

▼ **Think and Talk**
▶ What do you know about Oxford University and Cambridge University?
▶ What do you know about Christmas and Easter?
▶ What is "Trooping the Color" in London?

I. Education

Educational Policy

Historically, education was voluntary and many British schools were set up by the church. Before 1870, only 40% of children under 10 went to school regularly. From then on, in response to changes brought about by the Industrial Revolution and social and political movements, the government started to take responsibility for education.

Education in Britain is compulsory for all children between the ages of 5 and 16 (17 from 2013). In the 1960s, comprehensive schools[1] were introduced, which ended the division between grammar schools[2], where the most academically capable pupils were sent to prepare for university, and vocational schools, where the less successful pupils were sent to learn a trade. The National Curriculum was introduced in 1988. Today all children must study the following subjects: mathematics, English, science, geography, history, technology, music, arts, physical education and a foreign language. They must also pass national tests and schools are ranked according to their students' performance on these tests.

Now, education in Britain is divided into four stages: primary education, secondary education, further education and higher education. Children start primary

---

1 comprehensive school: 综合学校，无论学生能力如何均可入学，学生可以在校学习多种科目。
2 grammar school: 文法学校，一种采取优选制的中学，侧重人文学科，帮助学生通过考试进入高等学府。

school at the age of 5 and go on to secondary school at the age of 11 and stay there until 16. After that, they can choose to study for two more years in preparation for higher education. Students start their university education around the age of 18.

Educational System

1) Primary and Secondary Education

There are two parallel school systems in Britain for primary and secondary education. One is the state system, where education is provided free of charge. The other is the independent system where fees are required. At present, there are over 2,500 independent schools across the country, including some prestigious and time-honored seats of learning such as Eton and Winchester*. Over 7% of all British children receive primary and secondary education through the independent system. The National Curriculum is compulsory in the state system, but optional in the independent system. However, in practice, most independent schools teach what the National Curriculum demands.

Between the ages of 5 to 11, students mainly attend state primary schools. These schools are called co-educational or mixed schools because they admit both boys and girls. State secondary schools take in students aged 11. Then compulsory education continues for five years until they reach the age of 16.

Secondary schools are mostly comprehensive, which provide a general education. Students study both academic subjects, like literature and science, and more practical ones, like cooking and carpentry.

---

* Eton and Winchester: 伊顿公学和温彻斯特公学，英国著名的私立贵族学校。

伊顿公学

Chapter 5 Education, Media and Holidays

When children finish their schooling at 16, they are required to take a national examination, the General Certificate of Secondary Education (GCSE)[1], which certifies that they have achieved the standard expected after 11 years of compulsory education. Having completed their GCSE, students may choose to leave school and begin working, or to continue full-time education in what is called the "sixth form"[2], which lasts for two years, and then take a further set of standardized exams, known as the A-levels (General Certificate of Education—Advanced Level[3]), in three or four subjects. Since admittance to universities depends largely on A-level results, the two years spent in the sixth form are crucially important and stressful for students. Other students who decide not to go to university may choose to take vocational training.

In the private sector, a number of independent schools are commonly and somewhat confusingly called public schools. Independent schools receive their funding through the private sector and tuition fees, with minimal government assistance. They are generally much better funded than most state schools and are likely to recruit the best teachers and provide superior facilities. As a result, graduates of independent schools are more likely than those of state schools to be accepted by famous universities. Yet the high fees of independent schools have made education at independent schools a privilege of the wealthy.

2) Higher Education

Higher education has a long history in Britain. Oxford and Cambridge dated from the 12th and 13th centuries, while the Scottish universities of St. Andrews, Glasgow, Edinburgh and Aberdeen were founded in the 15th and 16th centuries. Other universities were mainly established in the 19th and 20th centuries. In the 1960s there was a large expansion in the number of universities and many new institutions were founded. In 1992 the number grew again when polytechnics (工艺专科学校) were given the right to become universities. Now there are more than 100 universities in Britain. Along with universities, colleges also play an important part in the British higher education system. They vary greatly in size and range of disciplines. Some of them specialize in certain fields of study like art or design; others are multi-disciplinary and can award degrees up to the doctoral level. There are also professional colleges which specialize in teacher training.

All British universities are partially funded by central government grants, except Buckingham University and BPP University College. The rest funds come from tuition fees, donations or corporate contributions. Before 1998, university students did not pay tuition for their education. In addition, students from poor families could receive the maintenance

---

[1] General Certificate of Secondary Education (GCSE): 普通中等教育证书。
[2] the sixth form: 第六级学院，为升大学做准备的预科教育机构。
[3] General Certificate of Education—Advanced Level: 普通教育高级证书。

grant (助学金), a form of financial aid based on need, from the central government. In 1998, the Labor government abolished the maintenance grant and implemented a tuition plan for university education, which varied according to the university.

Britain's universities are legally independent and enjoy complete academic freedom. They appoint their own staff, decide which students to admit, provide their own courses and award their own degrees. Admission is by selection based on A-level results, school references and an interview. Degrees are awarded according to students' performance throughout their studies, yet are often dependent upon final examinations. Students spend three years studying full-time for the first degree—Bachelor of Arts (B.A.) or Bachelor of Science (B.S.). Then, if they want to obtain a Master's Degree in Arts (M.A.) or a Master's Degree in Science (M.S.), they usually need another one-year of full-time study. To obtain a doctoral degree requires three to four years of additional study and research.

The Open University* offers a non-traditional route for people to take university-level courses and receive a university degree. People can register without having any formal educational qualifications. They follow university courses through textbooks, TV and radio broadcasts, correspondence, video and a network of study centers. Tens of thousands of British people, from housewives to coal miners, from teachers to ballet dancers, "attend" the Open University each year.

3) Famous Universities

Oxford University and Cambridge University are sometimes referred to collectively as Oxbridge. The two universities have a long history of competition with each other as they rival each other in prestige.

Oxford, located in the city of Oxford, England, is the oldest university in the English-speaking world. The exact date of the university's foundation is unclear, but there is evidence of teaching there as early as in 1096. In the following century, the first

牛津大学博德利图书馆

---

* the Open University: 开放大学，成立于1969年的远程教育大学。

Chapter 5 Education, Media and Holidays

residence halls were founded, which later became colleges. Each college has its own distinct characteristics.

Cambridge is one of the oldest universities in the world and one of the largest in Britain. It was founded in the 13th century, by some scholars who left Oxford. Its reputation for outstanding academic achievement is known worldwide and reflects the intellectual achievement of its students, as well as the world-class original research carried out by the university staff.

Cambridge has 31 colleges and consists of over 100 departments, research centers, plus a central administration. Each college is an independent institution with its own property and income. The colleges appoint their own staff and are responsible for selecting students in accordance with the university regulations. Teaching responsibilities are shared by the college and university departments.

Cambridge has more Nobel Prize winners than any other institution in Britain. It is the result of both the learning opportunities offered at Cambridge and its extensive resources, including libraries, museums, etc. Teaching consists not only of lectures, seminars and practical classes conducted by experts in their fields, but also more personalized teaching arranged through the colleges. Many opportunities are provided for students to interact with scholars at all levels, both formally and informally.

剑桥大学

Founded in 1836, the University of London was first comprised of just two colleges, University College London (UCL) and King's College London (KCL), but now it has 18 colleges and 10 other smaller specialist research institutes. The university is a federation of colleges, which together constitute one of the world's largest universities. Its colleges are treated as individual universities and have the same status as Oxford and Cambridge. About 10% to 20% of British students attend one of its colleges.

King's College London, one of the two founding colleges of the University of London, has a multicultural student body and an academic reputation that goes from strength to strength. It has more than 24,000 students from 150 countries. Four of King's campuses are within a single square mile along the Thames, making it the most central university institution in London.

The London School of Economics and Political Science (usually referred to as the London School of Economics) is the only university in Britain specializing in the study of social sciences and has a worldwide reputation in the field. The British Library of Political and Economic Science, one of the largest libraries in the world devoted to the economic and social sciences, is housed there. The school is also a public lecture venue. Nelson Mandela, Kofi Annan and Bill Clinton have given lectures at the school, and ministers, EU commissioners (委员) and others regularly speak to students at public events.

伦敦大学

Chapter 5 Education, Media and Holidays

II. Media

For most British people, a day begins with the morning newspaper and ends with television. It is obvious that the media is central to British leisure culture. It is no exaggeration to say that the media shapes the public opinion, determines people's moral and political orientation (倾向) and consolidates or undermines (削弱) the rule of a government.

Newspapers

Britain has one of the world's oldest established newspaper industries. In the late 18th and 19th centuries, as the British economy began to industrialize and as literacy levels rose due to mass education, more and more newspapers began to appear. *The Observer* (《观察家报》), first appeared in 1791, making it the world's oldest Sunday newspaper, while *The Times* (《泰晤士报》), first published in 1785, is one of Britain's oldest and influential newspapers.

There are 10 different daily national papers, which are available throughout the country and cover issues of national importance. About half of these are usually referred to as the "quality press". The "quality press" carries in-depth articles of political and social importance, reviews and feature articles about "high culture" and is generally read by a well-educated, middle-class audience. *The Times*, *The Guardian* (《卫报》) and *The Daily Telegraph* (《每日电讯报》) are referred to as Britain's "Big Three". *The Times* has a reputation for its cautious attitude. It often reflects the view of the government. *The Guardian* is recognized as a platform for liberal and left-wing opinions. *The Daily Telegraph* appeals to readers who favor free enterprise over social programs.

There are also "tabloids" (通俗小报), smaller-format newspapers with color photos and catchy headlines. They deal with scandals and gossip, usually about famous people. The stories are short, easy to read and often rely more on opinions than facts. In 2012 *The Sun on Sunday* was launched to replace the defunct *The News of the World*. It carries mainly crime, sport and sex stories and becomes one of Britain's popular newspapers.

Television and Broadcast

The British Broadcasting Corporation (BBC) (英国广播公司), affectionately referred to as the "Beeb", is Britain's main public service broadcaster. The BBC started daily radio broadcasts in 1922 and made its first TV broadcast in 1936. The BBC has always been funded by levying television license fees. The BBC does certain things particularly well: documentaries, especially wildlife programs, including the best-selling *Life on Earth*, which has been sold to over 100 countries and watched by an estimated 500 million viewers; "costume dramas" (古装剧), which are loved at home and abroad and have served to bring the "classics" to a wider audience; and the "BBC Shakespeare" series, now a standard visual aid in many secondary schools.

The international branch of the BBC is the BBC World Service, which broadcasts in 32 languages throughout the world. Its global weekly audience is estimated to be about 180 million people.

The BBC remained the sole television news provider in Britain until 1955, when Independent Television (英国独立电视台), a commercial company, was founded. In 1990, the BBC had a much bigger competitor, when SkyTV merged with British Satellite Broadcasting (BSB) to form the British Sky Broadcasting Group PLC (BSkyB) (英国天空广播集团), Britain's top pay-television provider.

英国广播公司

Chapter 5 Education, Media and Holidays

III. Holidays and Festivals

Throughout the year the British celebrate many holidays which reflect the religious, historical, social and cultural diversity of their country. Some holidays are celebrated throughout the nation and mark important events in the Christian calendar. Other holidays are based on local customs and traditions. What almost all of the holidays have in common is that they provide an opportunity for families and friends to get together to exchange good wishes and enjoy each other's company.

Christmas commemorates the birth of Jesus Christ and is celebrated on December 25. Schools close for the holiday period, as do shops and offices. Most British people celebrate it by exchanging gifts and Christmas cards, preparing holiday foods and decorating homes and workplaces with colored lights, Christmas trees and ornaments.

There are three Christmas traditions which are particularly British. One is the Christmas pantomime (童话剧), a comical, musical play. The pantomime is usually based on traditional children's stories like *Cinderella* (《灰姑娘》) and includes songs and jokes which can be enjoyed by adults and children alike. Another tradition is the Queen's Christmas message, broadcast on both television and radio. She usually talks about the year that is ending and expresses her hopes for the future. A third British tradition is Boxing Day (节礼日), which falls on the day after Christmas. This day is entirely unrelated to the sports from which its name comes. Traditionally, it was on Boxing Day that people gave Christmas gifts or money to their staff or servants. Nowadays, Boxing Day is usually the day when members of the extended family come together if they spent Christmas Day in their own home. It is also customary to give small gifts or tips to regular service workers (the milkman, dustman, paperboy and mail carrier) and to give a Christmas bonus to employees. These gifts are called "Christmas boxes".

For church-goers it is Easter (复活节), not Christmas, which is the most important Christian festival. Easter commemorates the Resurrection of Jesus Christ (耶稣复活) three days after his Crucifixion (耶稣被钉死在十字架上). It falls on a Sunday between March 22 and April 25, depending on the date of the first full moon after the spring equinox (春分). While Christians attend many church services over the Easter period, for most people the main symbol of Easter is the Easter egg. From earliest times the egg had been a symbol of rebirth. The Easter egg later

复活节彩蛋

The United Kingdom of Great Britain and Northern Ireland

皇家军队阅兵式

became a religious symbol, representing the tomb from which Jesus broke forth and the new life within. Nowadays people give each other Easter eggs made of chocolate or candy which are often very large, elaborate and expensive.

One of Britain's most impressive and colorful festivals takes place on the second Saturday in June, when the Queen's birthday is officially celebrated with "Trooping the Color" around Buckingham Palace in London. It is also known as the Queen's Birthday Parade. Britain, unlike most countries, does not have a national day, so the ceremony of the Queen inspecting her troops draws a great deal of people.

Bonfire Night—sometimes called Guy Fawkes Night (盖伊·福克斯之夜) or Fireworks Night—is a national festival on November 5 which commemorates a historical event. On November 5, 1605, the conspirator (密谋者) Guy Fawkes (one of the Royalists) put gunpowder in the House of Parliament in order to blow up the English Parliament. However, the plot was discovered and Guy Fawkes was arrested. Therefore, when the day arrives, children make "guys"—life-sized men made of straw and other available materials—and beg for money to buy fireworks. On Bonfire Night, they let off fireworks and burn the guys in a big bonfire (篝火).

There are also many other smaller festivals, such as Mother's Day, April Fools' Day, Remembrance Sunday* and various saints' days. Among them, Remembrance Sunday is a singularly important demonstration of patriotism. It commemorates those who died in the two World Wars. This remembrance is coupled with a widespread plea that such horrors will never happen again.

* Remembrance Sunday: 阵亡将士纪念日，通常在最接近11月11日的那个星期日。

Chapter 5 Education, Media and Holidays

Exercises

I. **Read the following statements and decide whether they are true (T) or false (F).**

　　_____　1. The British government has been responsible for education since the early 1800s.

　　_____　2. Education in Britain is compulsory for all children between the ages of 6 and 15.

　　_____　3. The National Curriculum is compulsory in both the state system and the independent system.

　　_____　4. When children finish their schooling at 16, they are required to take a national GCSE examination.

　　_____　5. Graduates from state schools in Britain have a less favorable chance to enter famous universities than those from independent schools.

　　_____　6. *The Times* is the world's oldest Sunday newspapers.

　　_____　7. The BBC World Service broadcasts only in English throughout the world.

　　_____　8. Some British holidays are celebrated to mark important events in the Christian calendar, and some others are related to local customs and traditions.

II. **Choose the best answer to complete each of the following statements.**

1. In Britain, the division between grammar schools and vocational schools was ended by the introduction of comprehensive schools in the _____.
   A. 1930s　　　　B. 1940s　　　　C. 1950s　　　　D. 1960s

2. Over _____ of British children receive primary and secondary education through the independent system.
   A. 5%　　　　B. 6%　　　　C. 7%　　　　D. 8%

3. Partially funded by central government grants, most of the British universities receive their remaining funds from all the following sources EXCEPT _____.
   A. tuition fees　　　　　　　　B. loans
   C. donations　　　　　　　　　D. corporate contributions

63

4. To be admitted to the Open University, one needs _____.
   A. some educational qualifications
   B. no educational qualifications
   C. the General Certificate of Education—Advanced Level
   D. the General Certificate of Secondary Education
5. Among Britain's quality press, the following newspapers are regarded as the "Big Three" EXCEPT _____.
   A. *The Times*   B. *The Guardian*
   C. *The Observer*   D. *The Daily Telegraph*
6. *Life on Earth* is a kind of _____ program produced by the BBC and is popular worldwide.
   A. radio   B. drama   C. documentary   D. soap opera
7. _____ is Britain's top pay-television provider.
   A. BSB   B. SkyTV   C. BBC   D. BSkyB
8. The following Christmas traditions are particularly British EXCEPT _____.
   A. Trooping the Color   B. the Queen's Christmas message
   C. Boxing Day   D. the Christmas pantomime

III. Give brief answers to the following questions.

1. What used to be the major functions of grammar schools and vocational schools in Britain?

2. What kind of subjects do British comprehensive schools provide?

3. In what ways do British universities enjoy complete academic freedom?

4. What role does the media play in British leisure culture?

Chapter 5 Education, Media and Holidays

IV. **State your understanding of the following questions.**

1. What are the general features of Britain's independent schools?
2. What are the "quality press" and the "tabloids" in Britain?

Learn and Check

Educational system: primary education, secondary education, higher education

Famous independent schools: Eton, Winchester

Famous universities: Oxford, Cambridge, the University of London, King's College London, the London School of Economics and Political Science

Major newspapers: *The Observer, The Times, The Guardian, The Daily Telegraph, The Sun on Sunday*

Television and broadcast: BBC, Independent Television, BSkyB

Holidays and festivals: Christmas, Easter, Trooping the Color, Bonfire Night, Mother's Day, April Fools' Day, Remembrance Sunday, various saints' days

Chapter 6 Literature

▼ **Think and Talk**
- How many famous English writers can you think of?
- What is Chaucer's *The Canterbury Tales* about?
- What do you know about the Renaissance?
- What do you know about Shakespeare and his plays?

I. The Old English Period and Middle English Period

《坎特伯雷故事集》

The most famous work in the Old English period is the epic *Beowulf*. Beowulf is a 6th-century Swedish warrior. On hearing the news that the great hall of Hrothgar, King of Danes, is raided by a dreadful sea monster named Grendel, Beowulf comes to help him, killing Grandel and Grandel's equally dangerous mother. Later, Beowulf, King of his own land, dies killing a dragon that is threatening his people. *Beowulf* is a folk legend brought to England by the Anglo-Saxons from their continental homes. It had been passed down by word of mouth for hundreds of years before it was written down in c. 1000.

With the Norman Conquest in 1066, Britain entered the Middle Ages. The most significant Middle English author is the poet Geoffrey Chaucer (c. 1342-1400). He was the first court poet to write in English. *The Canterbury Tales* (1387-1400) is his masterpiece and one of the monumental works in English literature. It is a collection of stories told by pilgrims to entertain each other on their way to the Christian church in Canterbury. The stories cover practically all the major types of medieval literature, such as romance, folk tale, fable and sermon (布道).

II. The Renaissance

During the 14th and 16th centuries an intellectual movement known as the Renaissance swept Europe. It was characterized by admiration of the Greek and Latin classic works. The sonnet (十四行诗) and other Italian literary influences began to appear in English literature.

The highest glory of the English Renaissance is unquestionably drama. The first professional theater opened in London in 1576, and others followed, producing the works of many famous playwrights, including Christopher Marlowe and William Shakespeare.

Christopher Marlowe (1564-1593) is the greatest pioneer of English drama, whose efforts in reforming it paves the way for Shakespeare. His most important play is *The Tragical History of Dr. Faustus* (1604), in which Faustus, a young and brilliant scholar, sells his soul to the devil in return for power. In spite of Marlowe's literary success, his involvement in political activities brought him many troubles. It was rumored that his short life was ended in a deliberately planned political murder.

William Shakespeare (1564-1616) is recognized in much of the world as the greatest of all dramatists. A complete, authoritative account of Shakespeare's life does not exist, but it is generally accepted that he came from a middle-class family in Stratford-upon-Avon and became a successful playwright and director in London.

Shakespeare's plays fall into three categories: comedy, tragedy and historical play. His comedies include *A Midsummer Night's Dream* (1600), *The Merchant of Venice* (1600), *As You Like It* (1623) and *Twelfth Night* (1623). His great tragedies include *Hamlet* (1603), *Othello* (1622), *King Lear* (1608), *Macbeth* (1623) and *Romeo and Juliet* (1597). His major historical plays are *Richard III* (1597), *Henry V* (1600) and *Antony and Cleopatra* (1623).

Among the best-known is *Hamlet*, which is regarded as a milestone in Shakespeare's dramatic development. Shakespeare achieves artistic maturity in this work through his brilliant depiction of the hero's struggle with two opposing forces: moral integrity and the need to avenge his father's murder.

There are many reasons why Shakespeare is so famous. The basic one lies in his great understanding of human nature and his ability to find universal human qualities and put them in dramatic situations.

莎士比亚

III. The Neoclassical Period

The 17th century witnessed the Bourgeois Revolution and the Restoration. The Glorious Revolution marked the end of a century of disputes and battles. The state structure of England was settled, within which capitalism developed freely. English literature of this period was often concerned with the tremendous social upheavals (剧变) of the time.

约翰·弥尔顿

John Milton (1608-1674), English poet, pamphleteer and historian, is considered the most significant English author after William Shakespeare. The twin poems *L'Allegro* (1645) and *Il Penseroso* (1645) describe respectively the cheerful social mood and the meditative (沉思的) solitary mood of the poet. Apart from poems, he wrote pamphlets on religious and political subjects. The most famous of them is *Areopagitica* (1644). It is in the form of a speech addressed to the Parliament of England, in which he appeals for freedom of speech. After the establishment of the Commonwealth, Milton served as Latin secretary to Cromwell, composing many state documents in Latin. With the restoration of Charles II, Milton was imprisoned. After his release, he retired into obscurity (隐匿) and produced his masterpiece, the epic *Paradise Lost* (1667), its sequel *Paradise Regained* (1671) and the poetic tragedy *Samson Agonistes* (1671).

After the social changes of the Reformation and the Restoration, Britain entered a period of comparatively peaceful development in the 18th century. The Industrial Revolution brought about rapid growth of industry and commerce. English literature during this period correspondingly catered to the rising bourgeoisie. Neoclassicism prevailed for the most part of the century with Alexander Pope as its representative. Conversationalists and letter writers flourished in literary circles and gathered in London clubs. The theater was lively with satirical comedies. Satire, making fun of people, was prominent not only on the stage, but also in novels.

Alexander Pope (1688-1744) is considered the greatest English poet of the classical school in the first half of the 18th century. His first major contribution to the literary world is considered to be *An Essay on Criticism* (1711). This is followed by *The Rape of the Lock* (1712, 1714), his most popular poem, which reveals the idle vanity of the court life. Pope also translated Homer's *Iliad* and *Odyssey*. The commercial success of his translations made Pope the first English poet who could live off the sales of his works alone. Pope's works were once considered part of the mental furniture of the well-educated people.

Jonathan Swift (1667-1745) is probably the foremost prose satirist in the English language. *Gulliver's Travels* (1726) is his greatest work. It is a fanciful account of Gulliver's four voyages to Lilliput, the land of tiny people; Brobdingnag, the land of giants; the Island of Sorcerers, where he speaks with great men of the past and learns from them the lies of history; and the land governed by horses. In the fourth part, *Gulliver's Travels* reaches a powerful climax. The human race, represented by filthy creatures called Yahoo, is inferior to and governed by a noble breed of reasoning and high-minded (高尚的) horses known as Houyhnhnms. Swift's *Gulliver's Travels* gives an unparalleled satirical depiction of vice, folly (愚蠢) and mere weaknesses of mankind.

《格列佛游记》中的场景

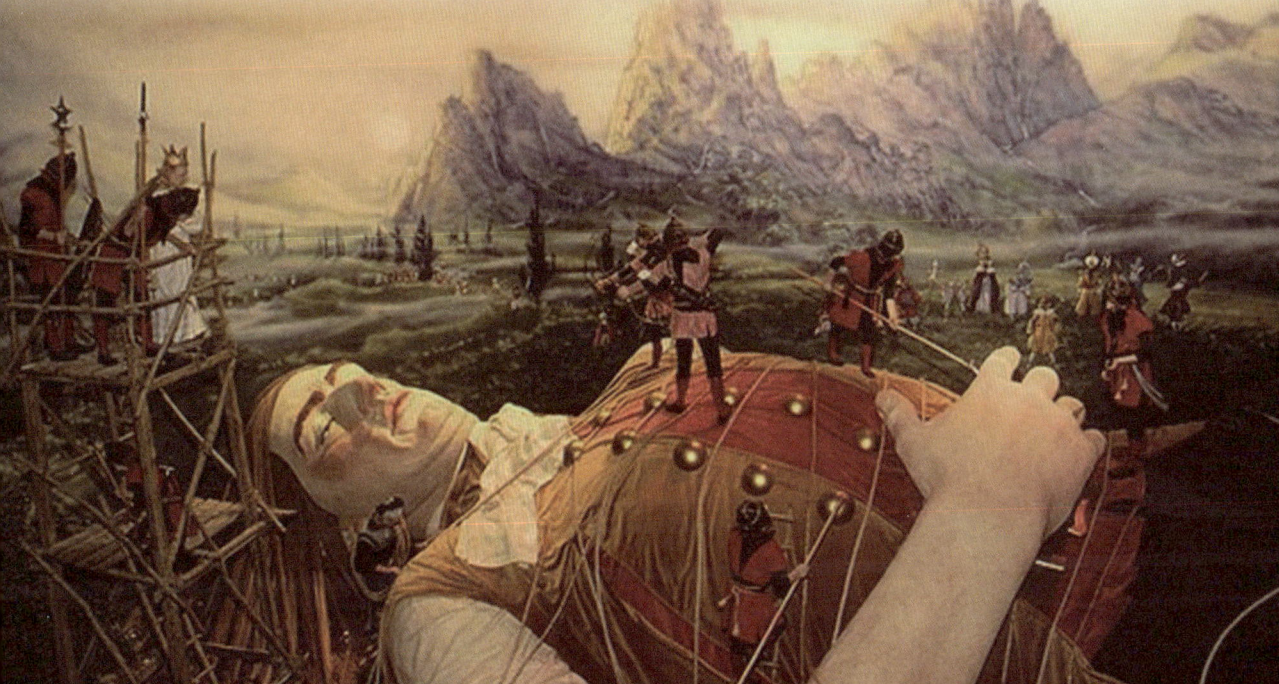

Daniel Defoe (1660-1731) is a famous English pamphleteer, journalist and novelist. More than once his opinions carried him to prison. He wrote many books and was viewed as one of the progenitors (创始人) of the English novel. The novel *Robinson Crusoe* (1719) won him great acclaim. It is the most famous tale of a shipwreck and solitary survival in literature. The best part of the novel is the realistic account of the successful struggle of Robinson alone against the pitiless forces of nature on the uninhabited island. Robinson is representative of the English bourgeoisie in its earlier stage of development.

IV. The Romantic Period

At the turn of the 19th century, Romanticism appeared as a new trend in English literature. It is a revolt against the prescribed rules of Classicism. Writers of Romantic literature are more concerned with imagination and feeling than with reason and intellect. William Wordsworth (1770-1850) and Samuel Taylor Coleridge (1772-1834) began the trend, bringing emotionalism and introspection (自省) to English literature with a new concentration on the individual and the common man. They are also representatives of the Lake Poets* who lived in the Lake District to explore nature. Discontent with the development of capitalism, they sought literary refuge.

Lyrical Ballads (1798) is a volume of poems written by Wordsworth and Coleridge. In its preface, Wordsworth states his belief that poetry results from the spontaneous overflow of powerful feeling. It is viewed as Romantic poetry's "Declaration of Independence". Wordsworth's other great works include his long, autobiographical poem *The Prelude* (1850) and such short poems as "My Heart Leaps Up" and "I Wandered Lonely as a Cloud". Coleridge's most famous poem is "The Rime of the Ancient Mariner" (1798).

The major second generation of Romantic poets includes Lord Byron, Percy Bysshe Shelley and John Keats. They brought the Romantic Movement to its height. They scorned social convention and often used poetry as a political voice.

---

* the Lake Poets: 湖畔派诗人，19 世纪英国浪漫主义运动中的一个流派。主要代表有华兹华斯和柯尔律治等。由于他们曾一同隐居于英国西北部的昆布兰湖区，以诗赞美湖光山色，所以有"湖畔派诗人"之称。

George Gordon Byron (1788-1824), known as Lord Byron, traveled extensively in Europe. He derived poetic material from his travels and produced the partly autobiographical *Child Harold's Pilgrimage* (1812-1818). His masterpiece is *Don Juan* (1819-1824), which owes its title and parts of its story to the old legend of the great lover Don Juan.

Percy Bysshe Shelley (1792-1822) is justifiably regarded as a great poet of revolutionary Romanticism in England. His writings encompass a broad range. The long poem "The Revolt of Islam" (1818) preaches revolution; the political lyric "The Masque of Anarchy" (1832) sings for the working class; and the essay "A Defense of Poetry" (1840) upholds the place of imagination and love in arts. His masterpiece *Prometheus Unbound* (1820), a lyrical drama, symbolizes the victory of man's struggle against tyranny and oppression. The lovely musical quality appears in his short poems on nature, such as "Ode to the West Wind" (1819) and "To a Skylark" (1820).

拜伦

The English Romantic poets' emphasis can also be found in such prose works as the essays of Charles Lamb (1775-1834) and William Hazlitt (1778-1830) and in Thomas De Quincey's (1785-1859) autobiographical *Confessions of an English Opium-Eater* (1821).

V. The Victorian Period

It was in the Victorian Era that the novel became the leading form of literature in the English language. Critical Realism of the 19th century flourished in the 1840s and the early 1850s. The critical realists described the chief traits of society and criticized the capitalist system from a democratic viewpoint. The greatest English realist is Charles Dickens.

电影《简·爱》的海报

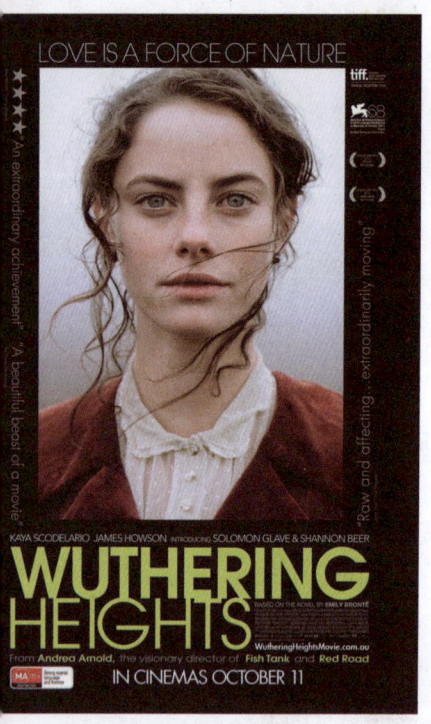

电影《呼啸山庄》的海报

Charles Dickens (1812-1870), having suffered as a child worker, brought to light the suffering of the poor. He was a fierce critic of the poverty and social stratification (分化) of Victorian England. Throughout his works, Dickens retained an empathy (同情) for the common man and a skepticism for the fine folk. Dickens' novels are works of social commentary. His first novel, *The Pickwick Papers* (1836-1837), which showed a rare comic gift, brought him immediate fame and this continued right through his career. Among his best-known works are *Great Expectations* (1860-1861) which traces the growth of Philip Pip from a boy to a man of depth and character; *Oliver Twist* (1837-1839), the story of an orphan child drawn into crime in the London underworld only later to discover the error of his ways through the love and understanding of an older mentor (指导者); *A Tale of Two Cities* (1859), which takes the French Revolution as the subject; and *David Copperfield* (1849-1850), which is argued by some to be his best and most autobiographical novel.

Among the distinguished English novelists of the 19th century are several women. They are Jane Austen, the Brontë sisters and George Eliot.

Jane Austen (1775-1817) is noted particularly for her vivid description and lively interplay of her characters, superb sense of comic irony and moral firmness. Her works focus on practical social issues, especially marriage and money, ridiculing the silly, the affected (做作的) and the stupid. She is regarded as one of the great masters of the English novel, and her most notable works include *Sense and Sensibility* (1811), *Pride and Prejudice* (1813), *Mansfield Park* (1814) and *Emma* (1815).

The story of the three Brontë sisters, Charlotte (1816-1855), Emily (1818-1848) and Anne (1820-1849), all talented and all dying young, is one of the saddest pages in the history of English literature. Given their short lives, they did not produce a great many works, but among their masterpieces are some of the best-loved novels in English: Charlotte's *Jane Eyre* (1847) and Emily's *Wuthering Heights* (1847), both being filmed several times.

George Eliot is the pen name adopted by Mary Ann Evans (1819-1880), a gifted woman writer who adopted a masculine name in order to survive in a male-dominated world which refused to take what a woman wrote seriously. Her works excellently refute this sexual discrimination. Few male writers could surmount (超越) her in both profundity (深刻) of thinking and the exquisiteness (细腻) of expression. Her representative works include *Adam Bede* (1859), *The Mill on the Floss* (1860) and *Silas Marner* (1861). *Middlemarch* (1871-1872) is not only her masterpiece but also one of the greatest novels in the world literature. Taking the novel not merely as a vehicle for entertainment but a means of revealing the human condition, Eliot explored the interior life of human beings and studied the impact of the environment on the individual. Her profound thinking and complex representation of life won her the name "philosophical writer".

Thomas Hardy (1840-1928), English novelist and poet, is one of the representatives of English Critical Realism at the turn of the 19th century. His major works are *The Return of the Native* (1878), *The Mayor of Casterbridge* (1886), *Tess of the d'Urbervilles* (1891) and *Jude the Obscure* (1895), the latter two being considered his masterpieces. The characters in Hardy's novels are for the most part from the poor rural class and are often sympathetically portrayed. At the end of the 19th century Hardy turned entirely to poetry and mastered the field of philosophical lyrics.

New literary trends prevailed at the end of the 19th century, such as Neo-Romanticism[1] and Aestheticism[2]. Dissatisfied with the ugly social reality, some writers led the novel back toward storytelling and romance. Those who advocated the new trend of Neo-Romanticism put emphasis on the invention of exciting adventures and fascinating stories. Robert Louis Stevenson (1850-1894) is one of its representatives, with his *Treasure Island* (1881) and *Kidnapped* (1886) thrilling readers young and old. His most famous work is *Strange Case of Dr. Jekyll and Mr. Hyde* (1886), a story of the double personality in human nature and the struggle between good and evil within a single person.

Aestheticism is the belief that artists have no obligation other than to strive for beauty—"art for art's sake". The most important representative of Aestheticism is Oscar Wilde (1854-1900). *The Picture of Dorian Gray* (1891), a novel full of descriptions

---

1 Neo-Romanticism: 新浪漫主义，19 世纪末兴起的文艺思潮，其主旨是反对现实主义，恢复曾经风行于 19 世纪初的浪漫主义。
2 Aestheticism: 唯美主义，19 世纪末流行于西欧的资产阶级文艺思潮，以艺术的形式美作为绝对美的一种艺术主张。

of the depraved (堕落的) life and divided personality of a young hedonist (享乐主义者) and *Salome* (1893), a play about the horrible sadism (虐待狂) of an ancient Jewish woman, are typical products of this trend.

VI. The Modern Period

The 20th-century English literature can be roughly divided into two periods: Modernism[1] and Postmodernism[2]. Modernism prevailed before World War II. It can be viewed as a deliberate departure from tradition and is characterized by the use of innovative forms of expressions. Modernist writers express in their works the difficulty they see in understanding and communicating in real life. Therefore, modernist writing seems disorganized and hard to understand. It often portrays the action from the viewpoint of a single confused individual, rather than from the viewpoint of an all-knowing impersonal narrator.

Fiction

Joseph Conrad (1857-1924) is a Polish-born British novelist. His literary works bridge the gap between classical literary tradition and the emerging Modernist Schools of writing. With the moral ambiguity of modern life, he is classified as a forerunner of Modernism. Conrad's most famous story is "Heart of Darkness" (1902), an interesting story as well as a social commentary on imperialism.

Virginia Woolf (1882-1941) is one of the leading writers of Modernism. Her best-known novels include *Mrs. Dalloway* (1925), *To the Lighthouse* (1927) and *Orlando: A Biography* (1928). In her works she experiments with the stream of consciousness: the apparently unorganized flow of thought onto page. Writers who adopt this technique give precedence to the depiction of the characters' mental and emotional reactions to external events, rather than the events themselves. Woolf is an influential feminist. Her best-known non-fiction work, *A Room of One's Own* (1929), discusses the failed role of women in literature and the future of women in education and society.

弗吉尼亚·伍尔芙

1 Modernism: 现代主义，20世纪上半叶各种文学新流派的总称，包括象征主义、超现实主义、未来主义、意识流小说等文学流派。
2 Postmodernism: 后现代主义，产生于20世纪50年代末、60年代初的文化思潮，其基本特征可以概括为：不确定性的创作原则、创作方法的多元性、语言实验和话语游戏。

James Joyce (1882-1941), Irish novelist, is another well-known novelist of the stream of consciousness school. Joyce's technical innovations in the novel include an extensive use of interior monolog (独白), a complex network of symbolic parallels drawn from mythology, history and literature, and the creative use of invented words, puns (双关语) and allusions (典故). His greatest works are *Ulysses* (1922), a story of the wandering Leopold Bloom, a modern Ulysses, during 24 hours, and *Finnegans Wake* (1939), which depicts a dream of Mr. Earwicker, a Dublin innkeeper, in a dream language.

D. H. Lawrence (1885-1930), who was less experimental, wrote novels which were critical of the modern world. Lawrence felt that society forced too many rules onto people and kept them from living a full, natural life. He advocated the principle of saving the decaying civilization through a rearrangement of personal relationships, especially those between men and women. His best-known books include *Sons and Lovers* (1913), partly based on his own life, *The Rainbow* (1915), which is about the relations between men and women in marriage, and *Lady Chatterley's Lover* (1928), the most controversial of his works.

Poetry

During the first half of the 20th century, William Butler Yeats and T. S. Eliot were the leading figures of the Modernist Movement in English poetry.

William Butler Yeats (1865-1939) is an Irish poet, dramatist and prose writer. He wrote poetry, drama and prose, but his fame rested chiefly on his poetry. He used an elaborate system of symbols in his poems, which provided the reader many memorable lines. His representative poems include "The Wild Swans at Coole", "Michael Robartes and the Dancer" and "The Tower". Yeats won the Nobel Prize for Literature in 1923.

T. S. Eliot (1888-1965) is an American-English poet, dramatist and literary critic. His long poem *The Waste Land* (1922) is one of the principal examples of the new trend in English poetry and represents the disillusionment of a generation of intellectuals after the end of World War I. *Four Quartets* (1943), his masterpiece, consists of four long poems, "Burnt Norton", "East Coker", "The Dry Salvages" and "Little Gidding". The main ideas are time and eternity, history and the present, the intervention of the divine in human life and the possibilities of reconciliation. T. S. Eliot was awarded the Nobel Prize for Literature in 1948.

Drama

George Bernard Shaw (1856-1950) is an Irish dramatist, literary critic, socialist spokesman and winner of the Nobel Prize for Literature in 1925. He established himself as a leading music and theater critic in the 1880s and the 1890s and became a prominent member of the Fabian Society*, for which he composed many pamphlets. He decided to write plays in order to illustrate his criticism of English society. His earliest dramas are called *Plays Pleasant and Unpleasant* (1898), of which the most famous are *Widowers' Houses* (1892), *Mrs. Warren's Profession* (1902) and *Arms and the Man* (1898). His comedy, *Pygmalion* (1913), is a popular success and has been adapted into films and musicals. However, his popularity declined after his publication of a controversial pamphlet "Common Sense About the War", which was considered unpatriotic. With *Saint Joan* (1924), he regained his acceptance by the post-war public.

电影《窈窕淑女》的海报
该电影改编自萧伯纳的喜剧《皮格马利翁》

VII. The Postmodern Period

Fiction

One of the most famous novels in the post-war period is George Orwell's (1903-1950) *Nineteen Eighty-Four* (1949). It is a prophetic (预言的) novel describing the dehumanization of a mechanistic and totalitarian (极权主义的) world. This depressing story is characteristic of the post-war years. Postmodernism differs in some ways from Modernism. Modernism, for example, tends to present a fragmented view of human

---

* the Fabian Society: 费边社，英国改良主义组织，成立于 1884 年，主张以渐进方式而不是革命方式传播社会主义原则。

subjectivity, but presents that fragmentation as something tragic, something to be lamented as a loss. Postmodernism, in contrast, doesn't lament the idea of fragmentation but rather celebrates it. Modernists look for the buried meaning below the confusing surface, while postmodernists abandon that search.

William Golding (1911-1993) is the winner of the Nobel Prize for Literature in 1983. Golding deals principally with evil and his works are characterized by a kind of dark optimism. His novel *Lord of the Flies* (1954) introduces one of the recurrent themes of his fiction, the conflict between humanity's innate barbarism (野蛮) and the civilizing influence of reason.

V. S. Naipaul (1932-2018) is a Trinidadian (特立尼达人的)-British writer, known for his pessimistic novels set in developing countries. Writing with increasing irony and pessimism, he details the dual problems of the Third World: the oppression of colonialism and the chaos of postcolonialism. Among Naipaul's works of international analysis are *The Middle Passage* (1962) and an Indian trilogy—*An Area of Darkness* (1964), *India: A Wounded Civilization* (1977) and *India: A Million Mutinies Now* (1990). His novels include *The Mystic Masseur* (1957), *In a Free State* (1971), *A Bend in the River* (1979) and *Half a Life* (2001). Naipaul was awarded the Nobel Prize for Literature in 2001.

Drama

Samuel Beckett (1906-1989) is an Irish novelist and playwright, and one of the great names in the "Theater of the Absurd"*. His plays are concerned with human suffering and survival, and his characters are struggling with meaninglessness and the world of the Nothing. Beckett won the Nobel Prize for Literature in 1969. His most famous work is *Waiting for Godot* (1952). In this tragicomedy (悲喜剧) of two acts, Beckett discusses the tedium and meaninglessness of human life.

Harold Pinter (1930-2008), English playwright, theater director, actor, poet and political activist, was awarded the Nobel Prize for Literature in 2005. His plays are noted for the use of silence to increase tension, understatement and small talk. Equally recognizable are themes of nameless menace, erotic (色情的) fantasy, obsession, jealousy, family hatred and mental disturbance. His most famous plays include *The Birthday Party* (1959), *The Caretaker* (1960), *The Homecoming* (1965), *Betrayal* (1978) and *Moonlight* (1993). Since the 1970s, Pinter had been active in human rights and politics.

* Theater of the Absurd: 荒诞派戏剧，兴起于第二次世界大战之后，主要表现人生与世界的无意义与荒诞。

Exercises

I. Read the following statements and decide whether they are true (T) or false (F).

_____ 1. *The Canterbury Tales* is a representative work of the Old English period.

_____ 2. The Renaissance is characterized by admiration of the Greek and Latin classic works.

_____ 3. As a great English poet, Alexander Pope also translated Homer's *Iliad*.

_____ 4. Jonathan Swift is probably the foremost prose satirist in the English language, and *Robinson Crusoe* is his masterpiece.

_____ 5. William Wordsworth and Samuel Taylor Coleridge brought the Romantic Movement to its height.

_____ 6. Lord Byron distinguished himself by the musical quality of his short poems, such as "Ode to the West Wind".

_____ 7. Jane Austen is a well-known novelist of the stream of consciousness school.

_____ 8. Joseph Conrad is classified as a forerunner of Modernism, which prevailed before World War II.

II. Choose the best answer to complete each of the following statements.

1. The most significant achievement of the English Renaissance is _____.
   A. poetry B. drama C. novel D. pamphlet

2. _____ is viewed as Romantic poetry's "Declaration of Independence".
   A. "I Wondered Lonely as a Cloud" B. *Don Juan*
   C. The preface to *Lyrical Ballads* D. *Prometheus Unbound*

3. Of Dickens' novels, _____ is considered most autobiographical.
   A. *A Tale of Two Cities* B. *David Copperfield*
   C. *Oliver Twist* D. *Great Expectations*

4. _____ is a representative of English Critical Realism at the turn of the 19th century.
   A. Robert Louis Stevenson B. John Milton
   C. Joseph Conrad D. Thomas Hardy

5. Of the following books, _____ is NOT written by Thomas Hardy.
   A. *Jude the Obscure*   B. *Tess of the d'Urbervilles*
   C. *Adam Bede*   D. *The Return of the Native*
6. _____ is NOT included in the modernist group.
   A. Oscar Wilde   B. Virginia Woolf
   C. William Butler Yeats   D. T. S. Eliot
7. Of the following writers, _____ is NOT a Nobel Prize winner.
   A. Samuel Beckett   B. James Joyce
   C. William Golding   D. V. S. Naipaul
8. *Waiting for Godot* is written by _____.
   A. Samuel Beckett   B. George Orwell
   C. William Golding   D. D. H. Lawrence

III. Give brief answers to the following questions.
   1. What are the three categories of Shakespeare's plays and their representatives?

   2. What is Critical Realism?

   3. What are the two new literary trends prevailing at the end of the 19th century?

   4. What is the stream of consciousness?

IV. State your understanding of the following questions.
   1. What is Romanticism?
   2. What are the characteristics of English literature in the 20th century?

Learn and Check

Major literature periods and their representative authors/works:

The Old English Period
Beowulf

↓

The Middle English Period
Geoffrey Chaucer, *The Canterbury Tales*

↓

The Renaissance
Christopher Marlowe, William Shakespeare

↓

The Neoclassical Period
John Milton, Alexander Pope, Jonathan Swift, Daniel Defoe

↓

The Romantic Period
William Wordsworth, Samuel Taylor Coleridge, Lord Byron, Percy Bysshe Shelley, Charles Lamb, William Hazlitt, Thomas De Quincey

↓

The Victorian Period
Charles Dickens, Jane Austen, the Brontë sisters, George Eliot, Thomas Hardy, Robert Louis Stevenson, Oscar Wilde

↓

The Modern Period
Joseph Conrad, Virginia Woolf, James Joyce, D. H. Lawrence, William Butler Yeats, T. S. Eliot, George Bernard Shaw

↓

The Postmodern Period
George Orwell, William Golding, V. S. Naipaul, Samuel Beckett, Harold Pinter

The Republic of Ireland

Chapter 7 Society and Culture

▼ Think and Talk
- Where is the Republic of Ireland situated?
- How did the Irish people gain independence?
- How is the Irish government organized?
- Why do we regard emigration as an Irish characteristic?

I. Geography

The island of Ireland is the third largest island in Europe. It lies in the North Atlantic Ocean, separated from the island of Great Britain by the Irish Sea and from mainland Europe by the Celtic Sea.

The island of Ireland is currently divided into two parts: the Republic of Ireland, which is an independent country, and Northern Ireland, which is part of the United Kingdom.

Geographical Features

The Republic of Ireland occupies approximately five-sixths of the island of Ireland, about 70,200 square kilometers. It is bordered on the west by the Atlantic Ocean and on the northeast by the North Channel (北海峡). To the northeast, Ireland's only land border is with Northern Ireland. To the east, it is separated from the United Kingdom by the Irish Sea and to the southeast by Saint George's Channel (圣乔治海峡) and the Celtic Sea.

The main geographical features of Ireland are low central plains surrounded by a ring of coastal mountains. Numerous rivers and lakes, as well as bogs (沼泽), are scattered throughout the country. The longest river in Ireland, the Shannon (香农河), runs about 360 kilometers from the northwest to the southwest before it reaches the

Chapter 7 Society and Culture

Atlantic Ocean. Corrib (科里布湖) in the west, with a total area of about 176 square kilometers, is the largest lake in the country. The west coast of Ireland consists mostly of cliffs, hills and low mountain ranges. Carrantuohill (卡朗图厄尔山) in the county of Kerry is the highest peak in Ireland, rising to some 1,041 meters above sea level.

Climate

The Republic of Ireland has a temperate maritime climate, with little seasonal or regional variations. Meanwhile, the temperature throughout the entire island is highly uniform. The coldest months are usually January and February, with an average temperature of 4℃-7℃, while the hottest months are July and August, with an average temperature of 14℃-16℃.

Average annual precipitation in Ireland varies from about 760 mm in the east to more than 2,533 mm in the western areas. The average number of rainy days per year is large, though regional variation is significant. Generally, the west coast receives more than twice as much rainfall as the east. The sunniest part of the country is the southeast.

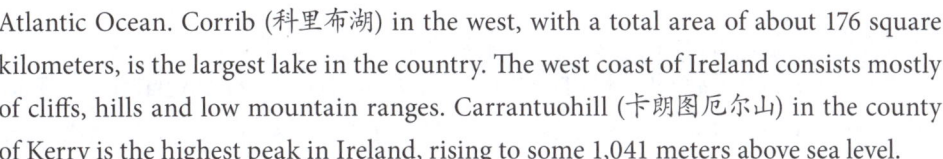

莫赫悬崖

83

Major Cities

The capital city of Ireland is Dublin, which is located in Dublin Bay. It straddles (横跨) the mouth of the River Liffey (利菲河), which flows through the city center. With one-fourth of the country's total population living there, Dublin is the largest city in Ireland. It is also the country's chief port, the commercial and financial center, and the seat of culture.

Cork (科克) is the second largest city in Ireland. The city has a reputation for independence dating back to 1491, when its people fought to overthrow the English rule. The people of Cork are proud of their participation in the Irish War of Independence (1919-1921) and the Irish Civil War (1922-1923). Hence, the city earned its nickname, "the Rebel County".

Other major cities include Galway (戈尔韦) and Limerick (利默里克) in the west, and Waterford (沃特福德) on the southeast coast.

II. History

Early History

Human habitation in Ireland dates back to almost 6,000 BC, when hunter-gatherers from Britain occupied the island. They settled down, farming and developing the culture of the island. In the 6th century BC, Ireland was invaded by a number of Celtic tribes. Though the Celts did not unite Ireland politically, they established a unified Irish culture and language. It is believed that the most significant invasion occurred in the 4th century BC, when the Gaels arrived on the island and established a flourishing Gaelic civilization. Subsequently, the arrival of St. Patrick in 432 transformed the island into a center of learning and Christian culture. The Vikings came and settled on the island in the 8th century. English involvement in Ireland began with the arrival of the Normans in the 12th century, but they did not have full control until the 17th century.

Chapter 7 Society and Culture

In 1801, the British and the Irish Parliament passed the Act of Union (《联合法案》), which merged Ireland and Great Britain to create the United Kingdom of Great Britain and Ireland. Thus, Ireland became an integral part of the United Kingdom. This integration did not bring prosperity to Ireland. On the contrary, Ireland suffered severe economic depression and Great Potato Famine* from 1845 to 1849. Consequently, in the late 19th and early 20th centuries, Ireland experienced a series of vigorous but unsuccessful campaigns for Irish home rule.

Process Toward Independence

Sinn Féin (新芬党) was founded at the beginning of the 20th century by Arthur Griffith. It strongly opposed British rule and fought for self-government. Sinn Féin won 73 of 105 seats allotted (分配) to Ireland in the British Parliament in 1918. In January 1919, the 73 Irish Members of Parliament refused to take their seats in the British House of Commons. Instead, they set up an Irish Parliament, issued a Unilateral Declaration of Independence (《单方独立宣言》), and proclaimed an independent Irish republic, which directly led to the Irish War of Independence.

都柏林饥荒纪念碑

In the early 1920s, representatives of Sinn Féin and the British government held a series of peace negotiations, resulting in the Anglo-Irish Treaty (《英爱条约》) of 1921. The treaty ruled that the 26 southern counties of Ireland became the Irish Free State (爱尔兰自由邦), as a dominion within the British Commonwealth of Nations, while the remaining six northern counties remained part of the United Kingdom. Under the treaty, the Irish Free State government would control its own police and armed forces. However, like other British Commonwealth dominions such as Canada, Australia, New Zealand and the Union of South Africa, the Irish Free State was required to pledge an oath of allegiance to the British monarch. According to the treaty, a Governor General would be appointed to represent the British monarch. In addition, Britain would continue to control a limited number of ports in the Irish Free State.

---

* Great Potato Famine: 爱尔兰马铃薯大饥荒。由于种植马铃薯失败，超过 800 万人遭受这次大饥荒的危害。

The Anglo-Irish Treaty brought about the pro-treaty and anti-treaty factions within Sinn Féin. The pro-treaty forces claimed that the treaty was an interim (暂时的) step toward full independence. They argued that the rejection of the treaty at this crucial stage would cause conflict and fighting and that the victory already achieved, like the ratification of the treaty, would be taken away by the British. The anti-treaty forces were dissatisfied that the treaty made Ireland a state with "dominion status" rather than a fully independent state. This divergence (分歧) resulted in the bloody Irish Civil War, in which more people lost their lives than in the Irish War of Independence.

In 1932, Fianna Fáil (共和党), organized by the anti-treaty forces under the leadership of Eamon de Valera, gained control of the government. On December 29, 1937, the Constitution of Ireland came into force. Under the new Constitution, the Free State was renamed Ireland; an elected President of Ireland replaced the Governor General to act as head of state; a new, more powerful prime minister came into being as head of government. In addition, the new Constitution declared that Ireland's jurisdiction encompassed the whole island of Ireland and the Irish government had the right to pass laws for both the North and the South, even though the Constitution could only be enforced in the 26 southern counties. Although it had a President, Ireland was not technically a republic. It still belonged to the Commonwealth. The British monarch continued to act as King or Queen of Ireland, but only to play a symbolic role in diplomatic relations with other nations. The President served only within the territory of Ireland.

When Britain declared war on Germany in 1939, Eamon de Valera announced that Ireland would remain neutral. Behind the scenes, Winston Churchill offered Eamon de Valera a united Ireland at some point in the future if Ireland would enter the war and allow the British navy to use its ports. Eamon de Valera refused this proposal despite German air raids on the city of Dublin in 1941. The state's neutrality is largely due to its anti-British sentiment and lack of military preparation for involvement in a war.

In the immediate post-war period, Ireland experienced severe economic strain, as World War II had caused economic devastation in Britain and mainland Europe. Eamon de Valera was defeated in the 1948 national election and replaced by John A. Costello as Prime Minister. Under Costello's leadership, a series of legislation was passed to reduce inflation and the cost of living, such as lower taxes, expanded industrial production and establishment of closer commercial relations with Britain.

Republic of Ireland

On April 18, 1949, Ireland declared itself a republic, completely independent of Britain and no longer a member of the Commonwealth of Nations. Britain recognized the independence of the Irish Republic, but refused to return the six northern counties.

Throughout the 1950s and the 1960s, Ireland made significant progress in stimulating its national economy. Under the First Program for Economic Expansion (1958-1963), economic protection was removed and foreign investment was encouraged; the economic growth rate reached 4%. This prosperity brought profound social and cultural changes to what had been one of the poorest and most backward countries in Europe. Emigration substantially declined and consumer spending increased.

Despite a brief economic boom, serious problems became evident in Irish society by 1980. These included declining agricultural prices, increasing premium (加付款) for imported oil, rising foreign debt, growing unemployment and inflation. By the mid-1980s, with a program of comprehensive cuts in public spending, the economy showed signs of improvement. Though the budget deficit and high level of unemployment continued to pose considerable problems, inflation was at its lowest level in nearly two decades.

In 1985, after successful negotiations with the British Prime Minister Margaret Thatcher Ireland signed the Anglo-Irish Agreement (《英爱协议》) with Britain. This agreement gave the Irish government a consultative role in the administration of Northern Ireland.

Ireland Since 1990

On December 3, 1990, Mary Robinson was inaugurated (使正式就任) as the first female President of Ireland. She considerably improved Anglo-Irish relations in the seven years of her presidency. Robinson was the first Irish President to visit Queen Elizabeth II at Buckingham Palace, and she also invited senior members of the British royal family to visit Ireland. Robinson resigned in 1997 and has been regarded as the most popular President in Ireland to date.

In 1993, Irish Prime Minister Albert Reynolds and British Prime Minister John Major signed the Downing Street Declaration (《唐宁街宣言》). This declaration was an agreement between Ireland and Britain to enforce a ceasefire (停火) in Northern Ireland. Consequently, the Irish Republican Army (IRA) (爱尔兰共和军) announced a ceasefire in 1994. However, the IRA resumed its terrorist activities in 1996 because it strongly opposed the British demand for complete disarmament (裁军). After Tony Blair became Prime Minister of Britain, the British government revoked (撤回) its demand for complete IRA disarmament, and the IRA announced its second ceasefire in 1997.

On April 10, 1998, the Belfast Agreement (《贝尔法斯特协议》) (also known as the Good Friday Agreement) was reached between the Irish and British governments. This agreement called for devolved government in Northern Ireland, and was approved in both the Republic of Ireland and Northern Ireland. Though much progress had been made in the relations between the Republic of Ireland and Britain, the issue of IRA disarmament still remained unresolved and continued to undermine the peace process.

In July 2005 the IRA formally declared an end to its armed campaign against the British rule in Northern Ireland. The IRA stated that it had ordered its members to renounce (宣布放弃) all violence and to disarm. The disarmament revived the peace process in Northern Ireland and at the same time further strengthened Anglo-Irish relations.

玛丽·罗宾逊

III. Government

Ireland is a republic with a parliamentary government. The Constitution (1937) is the basic law of the state. The Constitution states that all legislative, executive and judicial powers of the government derive from the people. It sets out the form of government and defines the power of the President, the two houses of Parliament and the government. It also defines the structure and power of the courts, sets out the fundamental rights of citizens and contains directive principles of social policy for the general guidance of Parliament. The Constitution includes a section that outlines the fundamental rights of the people.

The Legislature

Under the Constitution, Ireland has a bicameral (两院制的) Parliament, which consists of the House of Representatives and the Senate. The House of Representatives has 166 elected members and the Senate is composed of 60 members. The Senate has fewer powers than the House of Representatives. It cannot amend taxation or money bills, but can reject or amend other bills submitted by the House of Representatives. Parliament members from both houses are elected every five years.

The Executive

The Irish executive branch includes the head of state, the head of government and the Cabinet. The head of state is the President, elected by direct vote of the people for a term of seven years and may not serve more than two terms. The President has little executive power, but represents Ireland on official state occasions. In addition, the President signs and promulgates (颁布) all laws passed by the legislature. Under certain circumstances, the President can submit a legislative bill to the people in a referendum (全民投票) or ask the Supreme Court to rule on the constitutionality of a bill.

The head of government is the Prime Minister, appointed by the President on the nomination of the House of Representatives. The Prime Minister is normally the leader of the political party that wins the most seats in the national election. The

Cabinet ministers are appointed by the President with previous nomination by the Prime Minister and the approval of the House of Representatives.

The Judiciary

Judicial authority in Ireland is vested in the Supreme Court, the High Court / the Central Criminal Court, the Court of Criminal Appeal, circuit courts (巡回法院) and district courts. The Supreme Court is the court of final appeal and may also determine the constitutionality of bills submitted by the President. Judges of the Supreme Court are appointed by the President on the advice of the Prime Minister and the Cabinet.

四法院

Political Parties

Ireland has three main political parties, Fianna Fáil, Fine Gael (统一党) and the Labor Party. The Progressive Democrats, once a conservative political party founded in 1985, officially dissolved in 2009.

> Fianna Fáil, constituted in 1926, has remained the dominant political party in Ireland since the 1930s. It pursues a policy of complete political separation from Britain and supports peaceful reunification of the island.

> Fine Gael was founded in 1933, in support of the Anglo-Irish Treaty of 1921 that established the Irish Free State. The party accepts the British partition of Ireland and has generally been less anti-British. Fine Gael bases its outlook on the following key principles: equality of opportunity, pro-enterprise policies, security, integrity and hope.

> The Labor Party is the main party of the left in the Republic of Ireland. The party was organized in 1912 and was formally established as an independent party in 1930. It has participated in a number of coalition governments, mostly with Fine Gael. The party advocates liberalization of laws on divorce and contraception, an active role for the state in managing the economy, and a moderate position on the question of eventual unification with Northern Ireland.

IV. People

The population of Ireland is about 4.6 million (2012), with a relatively low population density in the EU. The population is predominantly of Celtic origin, with French, English, and more recently Chinese and Indian minorities. Ireland also has a small indigenous (本土的) minority known as Travellers, who move and camp across the Irish countryside.

Emigration, a characteristic of the Irish, has a long history and has traditionally taken place on a large scale. Emigration began in the early medieval period, when Irish missionaries settled throughout the continent of Europe. With the overthrow of the Gaelic political order by the English in the 17th century, the first major migration of the modern period began.

From the 16th century on, Irish Catholics migrated to the Catholic countries of continental Europe, where they sought safety and help from religious strife (冲突) in their own nation. The social and political disadvantages encountered by the Catholic nobility and gentry (贵族阶层) encouraged many of them to emigrate to Europe. Since entry to EEC in 1973, new opportunities to live and work in continental Europe have been created and increasing numbers of young Irish people have migrated into the main EU countries, and this tendency is likely to grow.

High rates of emigration to Britain occurred during the Great Potato Famine. Mass emigration was again recorded during the 1950s in Britain, which coincided with the depression in Ireland. It is estimated that there may be up to six million people of Irish birth (including those from Northern Ireland) in Britain today.

In the early 19th century increasing numbers went to the United States and Canada. The Great Potato Famine accelerated emigration and approximately five million people emigrated over the course of the century. Recent statistics indicate that over 40 million people in the United States claim some Irish ancestry, and that 25% of them claim solely Irish ancestry.

Up to 30% of the Australian population is estimated to be of Irish descent, making Australia probably the most "Irish" country in the world outside of Ireland itself. However, in the 1990s immigrants to Ireland outpaced emigration from the country.

V. Economy

Throughout its history, Ireland has been an agricultural country. Cattle, sheep and pigs are raised in large numbers. The main crops are wheat, barley (大麦) and potatoes. Agriculture yields the country's principal exports. Farm products, mainly related to livestock, have been the country's major exports for more than a century. The traditional market for these exports has been Britain.

In the 1920s, public policies were directed toward expanding employment opportunities. Agricultural production and marketing were reorganized on a more competitive basis. High tariffs were placed on imported goods, so small-scale industries could be developed to serve local needs. After World War II, energetic policies of industrialization were pursued not only to increase production in agriculture and industry, but also to foster the increasingly important tourist trade. Foreign-owned firms, especially those with export potential, were encouraged to be set up in the country. Since the 1960s, manufacturing has occupied an increasingly important position in the economy.

The high-tech industries of the 1990s, such as software and biological engineering, gave further impetus (促进) to the development of the national economy. As a result, Ireland's economy finished its transition from an agriculture-based economy to a knowledge-based one. During the 1990s, Ireland experienced a period of considerable economic growth. The Irish government continued to encourage foreign investment. Many large foreign corporations, especially those in the computer and electronics industries, opened facilities in Ireland. Computer giants such as Dell began assembling computers in Ireland, and Microsoft established its European Development Center in Dublin. By the early 2000s, Ireland's per capita income had exceeded the EU average and Ireland has now become one of the richest among the European countries. The main areas of growth in Irish exports are the computer/electrical machinery, chemical and pharmaceutical industries.

VI. Languages

There are two dominant official languages in Ireland, Irish and English. The Constitution states that Irish is the first official language; English is the second official language. Irish language was once spoken by nearly all the Irish. However, the use of Irish has been declining. Today it is taught in all government-sponsored schools. English is by far the dominant language and is universally spoken. Public signs are usually bilingual throughout Ireland.

VII. Education

Ireland has a free public school system, with compulsory attendance for all children of 6 to 15 years old. The public school system starts from primary schools. Secondary schools are private institutions and are mainly operated by religious communities. Most of the secondary schools receive financial assistance from the government. Other educational institutions include comprehensive and community schools, which are completely state-owned, and vocational schools, regional technical colleges and teacher-training colleges, which are partly state-subsidized. Ireland has two major universities, which are self-governing but receive state grants. The University of Dublin, or Trinity College, is a Protestant institution, which was founded in 1592. The National University of Ireland (NUI) was founded in 1908, fostering Irish culture and values. NUI is a federal university comprised of three constituent universities and five recognized colleges.

都柏林大学

Chapter 7 Society and Culture

VIII. Religion

The Irish Constitution guarantees religious freedom. In Ireland, about 90% of the population is Roman Catholic, and the Church exercises a strong influence on the nation's affairs. Catholicism is a matter of public identity more than merely a private faith. There are also small communities of believers such as Muslims, Jews and Presbyterians (长老会教徒). It is true that Ireland is exceptionally religious by the standards of the West. For example, more people attend church once a week than in any other country in the world. When asked how important God is in their lives, the Irish rank Him higher than any other people.

Exercises

I. Read the following statements and decide whether they are true (T) or false (F).

_____ 1. The Republic of Ireland occupies the entire area of the island of Ireland.

_____ 2. The earliest inhabitants in Ireland were Celtic tribes from Europe.

_____ 3. In the 1800s, Ireland gained in prosperity because it became a part of Britain.

_____ 4. In the 1930s, Ireland was not indeed a republic, but belonged to the British Commonwealth of Nations.

_____ 5. Ireland's economy wasn't affected by World War II because it remained neutral during the war.

_____ 6. In 1949, Britain recognized the independence of the Irish Republic and returned the six northern counties.

_____ 7. English is the only official language in Ireland because the majority of people speak it as their mother tongue.

_____ 8. Catholicism in Ireland is more than a mere matter of private faith, but of public identity.

II. Choose the best answer to complete each of the following statements.

1. _____ established a unified Irish culture and language in the 6th century BC.

    A. Hunter-gatherers from Britain   B. Celtic tribes

    C. British invaders   D. The Vikings

2. Divergent views about _____ resulted in the Irish Civil War.

    A. the Act of Union

    B. the Unilateral Declaration of Independence

    C. the Anglo-Irish Treaty

    D. the Anglo-Irish Agreement

3. _____ was the first Irish President to visit Queen Elizabeth II.

    A. Eamon de Valera   B. John A. Costello

    C. Mary Robinson   D. Albert Reynolds

4. _____ brought Anglo-Irish relations to a new height.

    A. The British recognition of the Irish Republic

    B. The signing of the Downing Street Declaration

    C. The signing of the Belfast Agreement

    D. The IRA's formal declaration of disarmament in 2005

5. In Ireland, the head of state is _____.

    A. the Prime Minister   B. the President

    C. the British monarch   D. the General Governor

6. _____ has been the dominant party in Ireland since 1930s and supports peaceful reunification of the island of Ireland.

    A. Fine Gael   B. The Labor Party

    C. Fianna Fáil   D. The Progressive Democrats

7. Emigration in Ireland started since the _____.

    A. medieval period   B. 17th century

    C. Great Potato Famine   D. early 18th century

8. Ireland now has a _____ economy.

   A. agriculture-based   B. knowledge-based

   C. industry-based   D. foreign investment-based

III. Give brief answers to the following questions.

   1. Why was Cork given the nickname "the Rebel County"?

   _____

   _____

   2. Who were the first groups of people that came to Ireland?

   _____

   _____

   3. Why did Ireland remain neutral in World War II?

   _____

   _____

IV. State your understanding of the following questions.

   1. What is the significance of the following documents: the Act of Union, the Anglo-Irish Treaty, the Anglo-Irish Agreement and the Belfast Agreement?
   2. What are the goals of the main political parties in Ireland?

Learn and Check

Geography: occupying about five-sixths of the island of Ireland

Climate: a temperate maritime climate

Major cities: Dublin, Cork, Galway, Limerick, Waterford

Important documents: the Act of Union (1801), the Unilateral Declaration of Independence (1919), the Anglo-Irish Treaty (1921), the Anglo-Irish Agreement (1985), the Downing Street Declaration (1993), the Belfast Agreement (1998)

Government: the legislature, the executive, the judiciary

Major political parties: Fianna Fáil, Fine Gael, the Labor Party

People: about 4.6 million (2012)

Official languages: Irish and English

Major universities: the University of Dublin (or Trinity College), the National University of Ireland (NUI)

Religion: mainly Roman Catholic

The United States of America

Chapter 8 Geography and People

▼ **Think and Talk**

▸ What do you know about such famous American cities as New York and Los Angeles?
▸ Why is America regarded as a "nation of immigrants"?
▸ What is the dominant American culture?
▸ How did Chinatown come into being?

I. Geography

Geographical Features

The United States is located in the central part of North America, except Alaska and Hawaii. The country is bordered by Canada to the north, Mexico and the Gulf of Mexico to the south, the Atlantic Ocean to the east and the Pacific Ocean to the west. The total area of the country is 9.6 million square kilometers. It is the fourth largest country in the world in size after Russia, Canada and China. The country includes 50 states and a federal district of Columbia, which is the seat of the federal government. For many years there were 48 states, then in 1959, Alaska and Hawaii became the 49th and 50th states. The two newest states are separated from the continental United States. Alaska borders northwestern Canada, and Hawaii lies in the central Pacific Ocean. Alaska is the largest in area and Rhode Island (罗得岛州) is the smallest of all the 50 states. On the mainland Texas is the largest state.

The United States can be divided into three distinct areas according to their geographical features: the eastern part, the western part and the Great Plains in between.

The eastern part consists of the highlands formed by the Appalachian Range (阿巴拉契亚山脉). It holds one-sixth of the continental American territory. These highlands are relatively low. The average altitude is only 800 meters above sea level. The Appalachian Range begins from the Canadian border and stretches to central Alabama (亚拉巴马州), covering a distance of 3,200 kilometers.

The western part consists of high plateaus (高原) and mountains, which extend from Canada through the western part of the United States to Mexico and further south. The whole area of this part holds one-third of the country's territory on the continent. The Rocky Mountains (落基山脉) are a spectacular scene on the western plateaus and stretch more than 4,830 kilometers from Montana (蒙大拿州) and Idaho (爱达荷州), through Wyoming (怀俄明州), Utah (犹他州) and Colorado (科罗拉多州), into New Mexico with an average altitude of over 4,000 meters above sea level.

The Great Plains lie between the Appalachians in the east and the Rocky Mountains in the west. The Great Plains occupy almost one-third of America's landmass on the continent. They stretch from the Great Lakes* in the north to the Gulf of Mexico in the south.

Connected by rivers and canals, the Great Lakes are open to navigation by large steamers and are linked to many inland industrial areas. The famous Niagara Falls (尼亚加拉瀑布) is located on the U.S.-Canadian border between Lake Erie and Lake Ontario.

The Mississippi River is the longest river in North America. It flows from the Lake Itasca (艾塔斯卡湖) in northern Minnesota (明尼苏达州) to the Gulf of Mexico, having a length of 3,780 kilometers and a drainage area of more than three million square kilometers. It is known to some native American Indians as the "Father of Waters".

The United States can be typically divided into six regions: New England, the Mid-Atlantic States, the South, the Midwest, the Southwest and the West. These regions are formed by history and geography and are shaped by the economy, literature and folkways that all the parts of the regions share.

New England consists of six states, Connecticut (康涅狄格州), Maine (缅因州), Massachusetts, New Hampshire (新罕布什尔州), Rhode Island and Vermont (佛蒙特州). They are all located in the northeastern corner of the country.

---

* Great Lakes: 五大湖, 美国和加拿大边境上的五个淡水湖, 包括苏必利尔湖 (Lake Superior)、休伦湖 (Lake Huron)、伊利湖 (Lake Erie)、安大略湖 (Lake Ontario) 和密歇根湖 (Lake Michigan)。

New England is famous for its long history. The Europeans made their first settlements here. Geographically it features mountains, valleys and rivers, with many historic cities and towns concentrated in this area. New England is also famous for having some of the top-ranking universities and colleges, including Harvard, Yale and Massachusetts Institute of Technology (MIT).

The South is composed of 16 states and the District of Columbia. The region is blessed with plentiful rainfall and a mild climate. Crops grow easily and can be grown frost-free for at least six months of the year.

In recent years, a great deal of industry has moved into the South from the North, therefore, the population is growing rapidly. Despite its great size, the South has few large cities. The notable ones are Miami, New Orleans, Memphis (孟菲斯), Atlanta and Birmingham.

The West includes 13 states, including Washington, Oregon (俄勒冈州), California, Alaska, Hawaii, among others. This area has various natural advantages, which have enabled it to grow rapidly. Oregonians are proud of their state's wealth of beautiful forests and streams, and place great importance on proper use of their environment.

California has striking natural features, including a huge fertile central valley, high mountains and hot dry deserts. Its notable cities are San Francisco, Los Angeles and San Diego (圣地亚哥). Its agricultural yield is predominant. It is one of America's high-tech industry centers.

Alaska lies in the northwestern part of America, stretching southward from the Arctic Ocean to the Pacific. Alaska is known as a world full of glaciers (冰川), waterfalls and lakes. The temperature is low throughout the year. About half of all native Alaskans are Eskimos (爱斯基摩人). Alaska's main agricultural output is seafood. Its industrial outputs are crude petroleum, natural gas, precious metals and timber.

Chapter 8 Geography and People

Hawaii is comprised of eight major islands, stretching about 2,400 kilometers long from east to west in the central Pacific like a chain of beads. The temperature is mild, and sugar cane (甘蔗), pineapple, flowers and dairy products are the chief products. Hawaii also grows coffee, bananas and macadamia nuts (夏威夷果). The tourist business is Hawaii's largest source of income.

Climate

Taking the country as a whole, the climate of the United States can be classified as temperate, with some mild subtropical zones. The southern Florida and Hawaii are tropical.

Almost through the middle of the country, north to south, runs a well-known 50-centimeter rainfall line, to the east of which there is comparatively more rain. To the west there is much less rain (less than 50 centimeters a year) with the exception of the coastal areas along the Pacific.

尼亚加拉瀑布

The United States of America

Major Cities

曼哈顿

New York is the commercial and financial center of the United States. It includes three islands, Manhattan Island, Long Island and Staten Island (斯塔滕岛) at the mouth of the Hudson River (哈得孙河). New York is composed of five boroughs (行政区) which include Manhattan, Brooklyn (布鲁克林区), the Bronx (布朗克斯区), Staten Island and Queens (昆斯区). Manhattan is not only a financial, but also an entertainment center, and you will find Broadway, Times Square, Wall Street, Fifth Avenue and Central Park here. The headquarters of the United Nations is also located in New York. The Statue of Liberty standing at the gate of New York Harbor is the symbol of America.

Washington is in Washington D.C. It is governed directly by the federal government. The city was named after George Washington (1732-1799), the first President of the United States. Washington hosts the headquarters of all the branches of the American federal system. Apart from the government buildings, for example, the White House, as a leading cultural center, Washington has numerous museums, theaters and centers of interest, such as the Washington Monument, the Lincoln Memorial, the Jefferson Memorial, the Kennedy Center and the Library of Congress. The city has little heavy industry, and its residents are mainly engaged in light and service industries to meet the needs of the federal government and the cultural institutions.

华盛顿纪念碑
和国家广场

Chapter 8　Geography and People

金门大桥

San Francisco is a center of oil-refining, chemicals, commerce, finance and the shipping industry. The transcontinental railroad connects San Francisco with the industrial and agricultural centers of the Midwest and the East. The Golden Gate Bridge is a spectacular scene for visitors. Chinatown in San Francisco is one of the largest Chinese settlements in the United States.

Los Angeles is the second largest city in America after New York, spreading far and wide. Los Angeles is an important electronic center. It is known for the manufacture of tires, automobiles and aircrafts, and is also the center of atomic research. Hollywood, located in Los Angeles, is regarded as the heart of world's motion picture industry and draws a lot of ambitious young people seeking their dream of stardom (明星地位).

好莱坞

Chicago, "the Windy City", is the nation's third largest city. Founded in the early 1800s, Chicago served as the main connection between the eastern coast cities and the West. The city is one of the country's leading industrial cities where both heavy and light industries are highly developed. It is now considered a center of industry, transportation, commerce and finance in the Midwest Region. It is also a cultural center, for it has one of the world's best collections of modern architecture, such as the 110-story Willis Tower (威利斯大厦) and the Art Institute of Chicago.

威利斯大厦

II. People

Population

The United States is the third most populous nation in the world, ranking behind China and India. According to the U.S. Census Bureau, America has a population of 314 million (2012), with white people constituting about 80%.

The distribution of the population in the U.S. is rather uneven. The most densely populated region is the northeastern part of the country. The region takes up about one quarter of the total land area, but about half of the population is living there. The Great Plains have a comparatively small population. The South has a population of over 100 million. The West is not densely populated, except for some metropolitan centers like Los Angeles and San Francisco.

Nation of Immigrants

The United States is a nation of immigrants. In no other country have as many varied ethnic groups congregated (聚集) and amalgamated (混合) as they have in America. America is not merely a nation, but a nation of nations. There have been waves of immigrants to the United States during different periods of American history.

The first people on the American continent came from Asia as early as 12,000 years ago. When Columbus arrived in the 15th century, there were perhaps 10 million people called Indians. The Westward Movement (西进运动) meant the destruction of the Native Americans. Today there are about 2.9 million Native Americans in the United States. Poverty and unemployment are the major problems for them, especially on the reservations (居留地).

The majority of American people are descendants of the European immigrants. It is not easy to ascertain the exact time when their ancestors first came to settle. However, modern Americans look back to their Pilgrim Fathers, a group of Puritans who came from England in 1620, as a symbol of their origins in this new country.

From the 16th century through the 19th century, about 12 million people were brought to America from African countries as slaves, working on plantations or large farms of the South. Today about 13% of America's population is black.

After the early periods of settlement, the first sharp increase in immigration took place in the 1830s and the 1840s, bringing Northern Europeans and particularly Irish craftsmen displaced by the dreadful poverty of the Great Potato Famine. In the 1890s, another tremendous tide of immigration appeared, this time largely from Southern and Eastern Europe.

During this period, the United States was changing from a mainly agricultural society to an industrialized country. Many immigrants settled in cities and worked in factories. Being poor and accustomed to poverty, they were willing to work for very low wages. This made other workers, especially those in labor unions, afraid that the immigrants would lower wage levels and take jobs away from them. This opposition finally led to the Immigration Act* of 1924 that restricted further immigration, particularly from Europe. Some other groups continued to come and concentrate in different areas—Mexicans in Texas and California and Cubans in Florida. Many recent immigrants are from Central American countries.

In the 19th century, laws limited Asian immigration. Asians in the United States such as Chinese and Japanese met with widespread discrimination. In 1965, the Immigration and Nationality Act Amendments (《移民与国籍法修正案》) gave an equal chance to all foreigners seeking entry into the United States regardless of where they came from. In the 1980s, almost half of all immigrants were Asians. Among them, the Chinese Americans have proved to be industrious, intelligent and doing fine today.

The United States is often called a "melting pot" where various racial and ethnic groups are assimilated into the American culture. However, It has been more recently called a "salad bowl", which means that immigrants of different backgrounds mix harmoniously, but at the same time keep their distinct culture and customs.

Racial Assimilation

The dominant American culture is English-speaking, Western European, Protestant and middle-class in character. The first immigrants formed the land's basic cultural values as freedom, equality and desire to work hard for a higher standard of living.

---

* Immigration Act: 美国 1924 年《移民法》。该法规定各国移民美国的人数不得超过 1890 年人口普查时该国侨居美国人数的 2%。

曼哈顿的唐人街

In its early years the United States was a successful "melting pot". The original settlers were of similar background, coming largely from Northern Europe, and were easily assimilated into society. Although the later immigrants were from different backgrounds, they tended to be drawn together.

As time went on, the characteristics of the dominant majority got solidified and determined to what extent other groups were accepted. A large number of immigrants with significantly different characteristics tended to be viewed as a threat to basic American values and the American way of life. During the late 19th and 20th centuries, most immigrants came from poverty-stricken nations. For them, assimilation was much harder because of the differences between their culture and language and those of the established Americans. These new immigrants, feeling lost in strange surroundings, clustered together in close-knit communities. Soon, many cities had ethnic neighborhoods such as "Chinatown".

Various American agencies, public and private, offered English instruction and citizenship classes to new immigrants to assist in their assimilation and becoming American citizens. It took quite some time for the adult immigrants to learn, while the children quickly learned the American ways by imitating their schoolmates.

Through new opportunities and new rewards, the immigrants came to accept most of the values of the dominant American culture and were, in turn, accepted by the great majority of Americans. The immigrants now have a much stronger feeling about being an American.

The immigrants' attitude toward their old-world background has changed markedly, especially since the mid-20th century. People of various origins have become interested in their foreign past and proud of their cultural heritage. Courses have been organized for them to study their native language and culture that they once tried to forget. Books are now published to acquaint young people with their foreign ancestors. Many of today's descendants of immigrants respect the culture that they had once rejected. Furthermore, they believe that the United States, a land of immigrants, could benefit from retaining its diverse cultural backgrounds. The contributions made by those people have helped America achieve its rapid social and economic development.

Exercises

I. Read the following statements and decide whether they are true (T) or false (F).

_____ 1. The eastern highlands formed by the Appalachian Range hold one-third of the country's continental territory.

_____ 2. The climate in the United States can be classified as temperate, with some mild subtropical and tropical zones.

_____ 3. A 50-centimeter rainfall line runs through the middle of the United States.

_____ 4. New York is composed of five boroughs, including Manhattan, Brooklyn, the Bronx, Staten Island and Queens.

_____ 5. San Francisco is the second largest city after New York and the world-famous Hollywood is located here.

_____ 6. During the 1830s and the 1840s, many Northern Europeans and Irish immigrants came to America.

_____ 7. Almost half of the immigrants coming to the United States in the 1980s were Asians.

_____ 8. Basic American cultural values are freedom, equality and desire to work hard for a higher standard of living.

II. Choose the best answer to complete each of the following statements.

1. The U.S. lies in _____ North America, with Canada to the north, Mexico to the south, the Atlantic to its _____ and the Pacific to its _____.
   A. northern, east, west
   B. central, east, west
   C. southern, west, east
   D. western, west, east

2. The continental United States has _____ states.
   A. 50   B. 49   C. 48   D. 35

3. The state of _____ is the largest in area of all the U.S. states.
   A. Alaska   B. Hawaii   C. Texas   D. Florida

4. The longest river in the U.S. is _____.
   A. the Missouri River
   B. the Mississippi River
   C. the Ohio River
   D. the Lake Itasca

5. Some of the world-famous universities like Harvard, Yale and MIT are located in _____.
   A. the South
   B. the West
   C. New England
   D. the Midwest

Chapter 8 Geography and People

6. San Francisco, Los Angeles and San Diego all belong to _____.
   A. Montana   B. Utah   C. Maine   D. California
7. The Immigration Act of 1924 restricted further immigration into the United States, particularly from _____.
   A. Europe   B. Asia   C. Africa   D. South America
8. The characteristics of the dominant American culture are _____.
   A. English-speaking, Northern European, Roman Catholic and middle-class
   B. English-speaking, Western European, Roman Catholic and upper-class
   C. English-speaking, Northern European, Protestant and upper-class
   D. English-speaking, Western European, Protestant and middle-class

III. Give brief answers to the following questions.

1. How is the American population distributed?

2. Why was the Immigration Act of 1924 instituted?

IV. State your understanding of the following questions.

1. Why is the United States regarded as a "melting pot" and a "salad bowl"?
2. What do you think is the best way to help assimilation in a multicultural society?

Learn and Check

Regions: New England, the Mid-Atlantic States, the South, the Midwest, the Southwest, the West

Climate: temperate, with mild subtropical and tropical zones

Major cities: New York, Washington, San Francisco, Los Angeles, Chicago

Population: 314 million (2012)

Immigrants: America being called a "melting pot" and recently a "salad bowl"

Chapter 9 History

▼ **Think and Talk**

▶ How did America get its name?
▶ What was the cause of the American War of Independence?
▶ What do you know about Abraham Lincoln?
▶ How did the Bush administration respond to the September 11 event?

I. America in the Colonial Era

It is traditionally believed that the first Americans were Indians, descendants of the Mongoloid (蒙古人的) people in Asia. About at least 12,000 years ago, they traveled to the North American continent. From that time on, they made their home and lived there.

Christopher Columbus is believed to have discovered America. In 1492, financed by the Spanish King and Queen, he sailed west in search of a new sea route to India. He failed to reach India, but found the islands of the Caribbean instead. He believed he had reached India and called the natives on the islands Indians. Following in his footsteps, Amerigo Vespucci, an Italian navigator, discovered the continent of South America. The newly-found continent was later named after him and became known as America.

The first successful English colony in North America was founded at Jamestown, Virginia, in 1607. In 1620, the Pilgrim Fathers sailed for Virginia on a ship called the *Mayflower*. They had been persecuted in England because they refused to abide by the rules of the Church of England. They finally landed in what is now Plymouth (普利茅斯), Massachusetts.

By 1733, English settlers had occupied 13 colonies along the Atlantic coast. Elsewhere in North America, the French controlled Canada and Louisiana. After the Seven Years' War, England gained control of Canada and all of North America east of the Mississippi in 1763.

Soon afterward, England and its colonies were in conflict. England imposed new taxes partly to defray (支付) the cost of fighting the Seven Years' War and expected Americans to lodge British soldiers in their homes. The colonists resented the taxes and resisted the quartering (为……提供食宿) of soldiers. Insisting that they could be taxed only by their own colonial assemblies, they rallied behind the slogan "no taxation without representation".

II. The War of Independence

On April 19, 1775, some British soldiers were sent to Concord (康科德) to search for weapons and "rebellious" colonists. When the troops reached Lexington (列克星顿) at dawn, they encountered militiamen (民兵). Fighting broke out and the first shots in the American War of Independence were fired.

In May 1775, the Second Continental Congress was held in Philadelphia and acted as a provisional government of the 13 colony-states. It established the Continental Army and Navy under the command of George Washington. Thomas Jefferson (1743-1826) drafted the Declaration of Independence, which the Congress adopted on July 4, 1776. The Declaration presented a public defense of the American War of Independence, and most importantly, it explained the philosophy behind the war, that men have a natural right to "Life, Liberty and the pursuit of Happiness", that governments can rule only with "the consent of the governed", that any government may be dissolved when it fails to protect the rights of the people. This theory of politics is central to the Western political tradition.

独立战争

托马斯·杰斐逊   乔治·华盛顿

At first, the war went badly for the Americans. After endless hard fighting, in October 1777, the Americans won a great victory at Saratoga (萨拉托加). This was the turning point of the war, resulting in an alliance between the U.S. and France. Finally, in 1781, the Americans won a decisive victory at Yorktown. On October 19, 1781, the British soldiers were forced to surrender. In 1783 the British and the Americans signed the Treaty of Paris (《巴黎条约》), and the United States of America won its independence.

III. The Civil War

奴隶买卖交易

American slavery existed after the first immigrants from Europe founded their settlements. In the South, the land was abundant and suitable for farming, and the planters had to manage their plantations using black African slaves, who were regarded as the property of the planters. They could be bought, sold and were often treated cruelly. However, in the North, there was a growing demand for labor to work in factories. Some Northerners wanted to get slaves from the South, so they supported the abolition (废除) of slavery.

What's more, the Northerners demanded a law to protect tariffs and asked the government to finance the building of railways and roads. However, the Southerners were against it and advocated free trade so that they could purchase cheaper goods from foreign countries. The conflicts between the North and the South were growing.

When Abraham Lincoln (1809-1865) was inaugurated as President in 1861, some of the southern states had seceded (脱离) from the Union. Lincoln's first priority was to keep the United States as one country; freedom for black people was a secondary objective. However, Lincoln realized that by making the war a battle against slavery, he could win support for the Union at home and abroad. Accordingly, on January 1, 1863, he issued the Emancipation Proclamation (《解放宣言》), which granted freedom to all slaves.

In July 1863, the turning point of the war came at Gettysburg (葛底斯堡)—the Union army defeated the Confederate army led by General Robert. E. Lee. On April 2, 1865, Lee was forced to abandon Richmond (里士满), the Confederate capital. A week later, he surrendered to General Grant of the Union army, and all other Confederate forces soon surrendered.

林肯

The war resolved two fundamental issues. Slavery was completely abolished and America became a single, indivisible nation.

IV. America in the 20th Century

At the start of World War I, President Wilson (1856-1924) issued his proclamation of neutrality on behalf of the people of the United States. Nevertheless, the U.S. later entered the war in 1917 for several reasons. First, the Germans announced that submarines were to be used to sink ships going to England, which would greatly injure American trade. Second, Germany promised the Mexicans a chance to regain its lost territory by going to war against the U.S. Third, after more than two years of fighting, both sides grew weary. This was a good chance for the U.S. to successfully influence the result of the war.

American troops played an important role in turning the tide of the war. In the face of combined attacks, the German government appealed to Wilson for a negotiated peace settlement.

In January 1918, President Wilson proposed his Fourteen Points as the basis for peace negotiation. In his Fourteen Points, he defined a new world order of justice, peace and property, promoting freedom of seas, removal of trade barriers, among others. However, his attempt to secure the world was in essence an effort to establish the U.S. domination in the world. This met with strong opposition from Britain and France. The Versailles Treaty was signed on June 28, 1919, but the U.S. Congress refused to ratify the treaty as almost all the points Wilson had proposed were rejected.

After World War I, America saw a short-term development in the 1920s, but unexpectedly, the Great Depression broke out. In October 1929 the stock market crashed. By 1933, industrial production had fallen to just 56% of its 1929 level, and at least 13 million people were unemployed.

Franklin D. Roosevelt (1882-1945) was elected President in 1933. In order to deal with the economic depression, he introduced the "New Deal"[1], which to some extent helped the country get out of the depression.

In the early days of World War II, the U.S. government adopted a sit-on-the-fence (持观望态度的) policy. The American capitalists wanted to continue their profitable trade with the warring countries, including the aggressors.

The American policy underwent great changes in 1940. In Europe, the British had been driven out of the continent and suffered repeated air raids by the German air force. In Asia, Japan had openly announced its "New Order"[2] in an attempt to extend its control to the Pacific. The American government began to fear that the Axis countries (轴心国) were winning the war and that their victory would threaten America's security and interests.

The Japanese air raid on Pearl Harbor was the direct cause for America's entrance into the war. On December 7, 1941, Japanese planes suddenly showered bombs on the American fleet and military installations at Pearl Harbor, Hawaii. About 3,400 Americans were killed or wounded, with the loss of more than 180 planes and eight battleships. A few minutes later, Japan declared war on America and the U.S. government responded by declaring war against Japan the following day.

In June 1944, American, British and Canadian forces landed on the beaches of Normandy (诺曼底), opening the long-delayed western front to attack the Germans. In May 1945, Germany surrendered. On August 6 and 9, American airplanes dropped two atomic bombs on Hiroshima (广岛) and Nagasaki (长崎). On August 14, Japan surrendered and World War II ended.

---

1 the New Deal: 新政，1933 年富兰克林·罗斯福任总统后颁布实行的一系列经济政策。
2 New Order: 大东亚新秩序，二战期间日本军国主义妄图建立大东亚殖民帝国、称霸亚太的战略构想和扩张计划。

In April 1945, a conference was called in San Francisco to organize the United Nations. Fifty-one countries altogether attended the conference and the United Nations was established.

During World War II, the development of the American economy reached a higher stage. As a result, America became the strongest power in the Western world. In the early post-war period, the Cold War was the most important political and diplomatic issue. It grew out of disagreements between the Soviet Union and the United States. The United States wanted to spread its sphere of influence and restrict the Soviet Union and communism. Thus began the conflicts between the two camps of the superpowers.

In the spring of 1947, President Truman (1884-1972) declared the "Truman Doctrine"* in order to establish the U.S. hegemony (霸权) in the post-war world. This marked the beginning of the Cold War. The Cold War exerted great influence in Europe and two Germanys were founded. In April 1949, the U.S. allied with other Western countries, forming the North Atlantic Treaty Organization. While seeking to prevent communist ideology from gaining further adherents (追随者) in Europe, the United States also responded to the challenges elsewhere. The Korean War started in June 1950 and ended in 1953 when the ceasefire agreement was signed.

---

* the Truman Doctrine: 杜鲁门主义，以遏制共产主义作为国家政治意识形态和对外政策的指导思想。

诺曼底登陆

The United States of America

越战纪念碑

The Vietnam War (1954-1975) was started under Eisenhower (1890-1969) and was continued by John F. Kennedy (1917-1963) and Lyndon B. Johnson (1908-1973). In 1960, Kennedy was elected President and his government policy was to contain communism in Vietnam. Johnson became President in 1963 after President Kennedy was assassinated. He promised not to send American soldiers to Vietnam, but failed to keep his word. More and more American people opposed the war. Critics rose throughout the country to demand American withdrawal.

In 1968, Richard M. Nixon (1913-1994) was elected President. In 1973, he signed an agreement to announce the U.S. military involvement in the Vietnam War ended. The total number of the killed or missing American soldiers during the war reached over 58,000. The war greatly weakened America and sharpened the country's internal contradictions.

In terms of diplomacy, Nixon achieved two diplomatic breakthroughs: reestablishing U.S. relations with China and negotiating the first Strategic Arms Limitation Treaty (《战略武器限制条约》) with the Soviet Union. In 1972, he easily won the reelection, but resigned from office in 1974 because of the Watergate Scandal*.

In the 1980 election, Ronald Reagan (1911-2004) was elected President. Soon after taking office, Reagan presented to Congress an economic program in which he called for reductions in income taxes and business taxes in order to encourage investment, and proposed deep cuts in federal spending in every area except defense. He requested that many government regulations be eliminated to reduce the federal government's

---

* Watergate Scandal: 水门事件，美国政治丑闻。共和党总统竞选连任委员会于 1972 年 6 月 17 日派人潜入水门大厦民主党总部安装窃听器，当场被捕。此事的暴露导致尼克松辞职。

Chapter 9 History

里根   布什

role in the day-to-day operation of business.

With his support of the tight money policy, inflation was finally brought under control and by 1983, a recovery was underway. Although many Americans were better off financially than they had been in 1980, Reagan's policies led to an increasing gap between rich and poor, and social welfare programs had been drastically curtailed (缩减). Despite this, Reagan overwhelmed the Democratic Party and won the 1984 election. At the end of his administration, the nation was enjoying its longest recorded period of peacetime prosperity without a recession or depression.

George H. W. Bush (1924-) was elected President in 1988. In his first two years in office, Bush followed Reagan's economic program and concentrated on solving social and economic problems. His greatest test came when the former Iraqi President Saddām Hussein invaded Kuwait in 1990, and threatened to move into Saudi Arabia. Vowing to free Kuwait, Bush sent 425,000 American troops. They were joined by troops from allied nations. After weeks of air and missile bombardment (轰炸), the allied military coalition drove Iraq's armies out of Kuwait.

Despite unprecedented popularity from this military and diplomatic triumph, Bush was unable to withstand discontent at home from a faltering (衰退的) economy, rising violence in inner cities and continued high deficit spending. In 1992, he lost his bid for reelection to Democrat Bill Clinton (1946-).

At age 46, Clinton became one of the youngest Presidents in American history. He acted on many important issues that affected the United States and other countries. Measures for economic recovery were taken and developments began to take shape during Clinton's first term. His second term saw a vigorous economic development.

One of the major foreign policy goals Clinton gained in his first administration was made in November 1993. Congress approved the North American Free Trade Agreement (NAFTA) (《北美自由贸易协定》). The agreement called for the elimination of most import taxes among the United States, Canada and Mexico. The agreement also called for ending restrictions on the flow of goods, services and investments among the three countries.

In 1998, American politics entered a period of turmoil (混乱) with the revelation that Clinton had an affair with a young intern (实习生). In the midst of the House impeachment (弹劾) debate, the President announced the largest budget surpluses (预算结余) in the country's history. Public opinion polls showed Clinton's approval rating remained high despite his impeachment.

签署《北美自由贸易协定》

Chapter 9　History

V. America in the 21st Century

9·11恐怖袭击事件

  In the presidential election of 2000, George W. Bush (1946-), son of the former President Bush, became the 43rd President of the United States. The theme of Bush's inaugural address was national unity. Bush listed a number of priorities for his administration, such as reforming education, cutting taxes, shoring up (加强) social security and medicare, and strengthening the country's defenses.

  The President quickly discovered that he had to deal with an economy that was beginning to slip from its peak of the late 1990s. This helped him to secure the passage of a tax cut in June 2001.

  On September 11, 2001, the United States suffered the most devastating foreign attack ever against its mainland. That morning, some terrorists hijacked (劫持) four airplanes and used two of them as suicide vehicles to destroy the twin towers of the World Trade Center. A third crashed into the Pentagon (五角大楼), the Defense Department's headquarters just outside of Washington, D.C. The fourth, probably meant for the U.S. Capitol (国会大厦), crashed in the Pennsylvania countryside as passengers fought the hijackers.

  The Bush administration's response to the September 11 event was swift, wide-ranging and decisive. They attributed responsibility for the attack to Osama bin Laden and the al-Qaeda (基地组织). The U.S. launched a military operation in October 2001 against the Taliban regime[1]. As a result, the Taliban regime was removed from power. In his 2002 State of the Union Address[2], Bush named an "axis of the evil" that he thought threatened the U.S. among which Iraq seemed to him and his advisors the most immediately troublesome.

On March 20, 2003, American and British troops, supported by small contingents (分遣队) from several other countries, began an invasion of Iraq. Baghdad fell on April 9. On May 1, Bush declared an end to major combat in Iraq.

Saddām Hussein was captured on October 13, 2003. On December 30, 2006, he was hanged for crimes against humanity. On May 2, 2011, the American army raided Osama bin Laden's house in Pakistan and killed him.

---

1 Taliban regime: 塔利班政权，阿富汗武装派别之一。
2 State of the Union Address: 国情咨文，每年由美国总统发表，总结一年来的国家发展情况和未来一年的工作计划。

Exercises

I. Read the following statements and decide whether they are true (T) or false (F).

_____ 1. America was named after Amerigo Vespucci, who arrived on the new continent after Columbus.

_____ 2. The Second Continental Congress was held in Philadelphia, and the Continental Army and Navy were established under the command of Thomas Jefferson.

_____ 3. The American Civil War not only put an end to slavery, but also made America a single, indivisible nation.

_____ 4. Most American people approved of the Vietnam War.

_____ 5. In 1990, American troops and the troops from allied nations took joint military action in order to drive Iraqi troops out of Kuwait.

_____ 6. According to the American government, Saddām Hussein and Osama bin Laden were responsible for the terrorist event on September 11, 2001.

_____ 7. The Bush administration regarded Iraq a nation among the "axis of the evil".

_____ 8. On March 20, 2003, American and United Nations' troops, supported by several other countries, began an invasion of Iraq.

II. **Choose the best answer to complete each of the following statements.**
   1. The first successful English colony in North America was founded at _____ in _____.
      A. Jamestown, Louisiana   B. Boston, Massachusetts
      C. Jamestown, Virginia   D. Plymouth, Georgia
   2. The Seven Years' War occurred between _____.
      A. the French and the American Indians   B. the French and the Spanish
      C. the French and the British   D. the British and the American Indians
   3. "No taxation without representation" was the rallying slogan of _____.
      A. the settlers of Virginia   B. the people of Pennsylvania
      C. the colonists in New England   D. the people of the 13 colonies
   4. In May 1775, _____ was held in Philadelphia and began to assume the functions of a provisional government.
      A. the First Continental Congress   B. the Second Continental Congress
      C. the Boston Tea Party   D. the Congress of Confederation
   5. Abraham Lincoln issued the _____ to grant freedom to all slaves.
      A. Declaration of Independence   B. Constitution
      C. Emancipation Proclamation   D. Bill of Rights
   6. The policy of the United States was _____ at the beginning of the two World Wars.
      A. neutrality   B. full involvement
      C. partial involvement   D. appeasement
   7. President _____ introduced the New Deal to deal with the problems of the Great Depression.
      A. Wilson   B. Truman   C. Roosevelt   D. Kennedy
   8. The Vietnam War was a long-time suffering for Americans, and it continued throughout the terms of Presidents _____.
      A. Johnson, Nixon and Ford   B. Truman, Eisenhower and Kennedy
      C. Kennedy, Johnson and Nixon   D. Eisenhower, Kennedy and Johnson

III. **Give brief answers to the following questions.**
   1. Why did America change its policy and enter World War II?

   2. What were Nixon's well-known contributions during his presidency?

3. What were the measures of Reagan's economic program?

   _____

   _____

IV. **State your understanding of the following questions.**

1. What was the cause of the American Civil War?
2. What made the United States a powerful country by the end of World War II?

○ Learn and Check

Discovery of America: by Christopher Columbus in 1492

English colonies in North America: 13 English colonies being established by 1733

The Declaration of Independence: drafted by Thomas Jefferson, adopted by the Congress on July 4, 1776

The War of Independence: 1775-1783

The Civil War: 1861-1865

The Cold War: started with the declaration of the "Truman Doctrine" in 1947

The Vietnam War: 1954-1975

Some U.S. Presidents: George Washington, Abraham Lincoln, Woodrow Wilson, Franklin D. Roosevelt, Harry S. Truman, Dwight D. Eisenhower, John F. Kennedy, Lyndon B. Johnson, Richard M. Nixon, Ronald Reagan, George H. W. Bush, Bill Clinton, George W. Bush

Chapter 10 Government

▼ **Think and Talk**
▶ What are the characteristics of the American Constitution?
▶ What is the Bill of Rights?
▶ What is "winner-takes-all" in American elections?

I. Constitution

The Constitution of the United States, which was drawn up in 1787 and came into effect in 1789, is the basic law of the land. For over two centuries, it has guided the development of government institutions and has supplied the basis for the nation's political stability, economic growth and social progress.

There are two obvious characteristics in the Constitution. One is "checks and balances"*. This goes back to the tradition that everybody in the United States was afraid that one person or group, including the majority, might become too powerful or seize control of the country and create a tyranny. To guard against this possibility, the delegates who drafted the Constitution set up a government consisting of three branches: the legislature, the executive and the judiciary. Each branch has powers that the others do not have and each branch has a way of counteracting and limiting any wrongful action by other branches. Another characteristic is that the Constitution specifies the respective powers of the federal government and of the state government. The states are allowed to run their own government as they wish.

The Constitution begins with the "Preamble" (导言) stating its purpose: "We the people of the United States, in order to form a more perfect union, establish Justice, insure

---

* checks and balances: 三权分立，其核心是立法权、行政权、司法权相互独立、互相制衡。

domestic Tranquility (平静), provide for the common defense, promote the general Welfare, and secure the Blessings of Liberty to ourselves and our posterity (子孙), do ordain (命令) and establish this Constitution for the United States of America."

When the Constitution was first drawn up in 1787, nothing was mentioned about the rights of individuals. Then, in 1791, the first 10 amendments were created. This is the well-known Bill of Rights (《人权法案》), which guarantees freedom of religion, speech and the press, the right of peaceful assembly and petition, the right to keep and bear arms, and freedom against unreasonable search and seizure, among others. Altogether, 27 amendments have been added to the Constitution since 1789.

The Constitution of the United States takes precedence over all state constitutions and laws, and over laws made by the U.S. Congress. The founders of the country left behind a Constitution, which is the first of its kind in the world and has inspired dozens of other countries seeking political reform.

II. Government

The form of government is based on three main principles: federalism, the separation of powers and respect for the Constitution and the rule of law. The federal government is the central government of the United States. It is divided into three equal and separate branches and they are checked and balanced by one another.

国会大厦

The Legislature

Congress is the legislative branch of the federal government. It is the law-making and the supreme legislative body of the nation. It consists of two houses: the Senate and the House of Representatives.

The Senate has 100 voting members, two from each of the 50 states. They may be reelected for an unlimited number of six-year terms. Senators are chosen directly by all the voters in their states. A Senator must be over 30 years old, a resident in the state which they represent, and must have been a U.S. citizen for at least nine years.

The House of Representatives has 435 voting members, divided among the 50 states in proportion to their total population. In addition, there are six non-voting representatives from Puerto Rico (波多黎各), the District of Columbia and four other territories of the U.S. The Representatives must be at least 25 years old and a U.S. citizen for at least seven years. A Representative serves for a term of two years.

The main function of Congress is to pass laws for the Union. However, the law-making process is very complicated.

Both houses have the power to introduce legislation on any subject except the revenue bills (税收法案) which must originate in the House of Representatives. A member of either house of Congress has the right to introduce a bill or legislative proposal. When bills are introduced, they are immediately sent to a proper committee. Committees are formed on special subjects such as education, agriculture and foreign affairs. The committee often sets up a sub-committee, and the sub-committee holds a series of sessions, at which people who wish to argue for or against a new policy offer their written statements. After the hearings (听证会), the committee votes on the bill to see if it should proceed further. If not favorably voted, the bill "dies".

If it is favorably voted, then after the hearings, recommendations regarding the bill are reported to the House of Representatives or the Senate by the committee. The committee's recommendations are very important because when the legislators vote on a bill, they usually follow the committee's report. If the two houses approve similar bills with different opinions, both bills are sent to a Conference Committee, which works out a compromise. If the committee does not reach an agreement, the bill is "lost".

If the bill is passed, it is called an "Act". Once a bill is passed by both houses, it goes to the President for approval. The President may either sign it into law or veto (否决) it. If it is vetoed, Congress can override the veto by a two-thirds majority.

The United States of America

白宫

The Executive

The executive branch consists of 15 departments and many independent agencies. The department heads form the Cabinet, which is the major source of advice and assistance to the President, who is the chief of the executive branch. The President's status makes him the most prominent figure as the first citizen of the United States, and his wife is called the First Lady.

The President has powers to manage national affairs and the working of the federal government. He can issue rules, regulations and instructions, which are called executive orders. He is Commander-in-Chief of the armed forces of the United States, so he has the power to raise, train, supervise and deploy (部署) American armed forces, provided Congress approves.

The President controls American foreign policy. He appoints the Secretary of State (国务卿) with the approval of the Senate. The Secretary of State is the official spokesperson for U.S. foreign policy and is the President's chief foreign affairs adviser.

The President also holds significant influence in law-making. The Constitution invests Congress with all legislative powers, but much of the American legislation is made by proposals of the President. If Congress passes any bills he does not like, he may veto them by refusing to sign them.

The President can also influence the decision of the federal courts. He has the power to nominate justices of the Supreme Court and the other federal courts.

There is a nucleus of leadership under the President in the administrative branch. It is called the Cabinet, which serves the President as a presidential council. The Cabinet is made up of the heads of the 15 executive departments, appointed by the President and confirmed by the Senate.

According to the Constitution, the President must be a natural-born American citizen, at least 35 years of age, and a resident of the United States for at least 14 years. He can only serve two successive four-year terms. Throughout American history, Franklin D. Roosevelt was the only President who served more than two successive terms.

The White House, the official presidential residence, is located in Washington, D.C. The President works and lives in this building and the offices for his senior staff are also located here.

The President has enormous powers, but his powers are not unlimited. He must ask Congress for every dollar his administration spends. His nomination of officials and his foreign treaties must be confirmed by the Senate. He has to report to Congress on his military action abroad for approval. Finally, if he abuses his power or commits a crime, he may be impeached by Congress.

The Judiciary

The judicial branch of the federal government consists of a series of courts: the Supreme Court, the courts of appeals and the district courts.

The Supreme Court is the highest court of the United States. It now has one Chief Justice and eight Associate Justices. Decisions are made by the majority. They are all appointed by the President with the Senate's approval. Only Congress can remove them from office through a difficult impeachment process.

最高法院

The major powers of the Supreme Court are as follows: a) to interpret laws; b) to hear appeals from any federal court cases; c) to hear appeals from state court cases that involve the Constitution or national laws; d) may declare a law unconstitutional; e) may declare a presidential act unconstitutional. The powers can be limited by the President who appoints judges and may grant parole (假释) and reprieves (死刑撤销令). The powers can also be limited by Congress. Congress may impeach and convict (宣判……有罪) any federal judges, and may propose an amendment to the Constitution if the Supreme Court declares a law unconstitutional. The Supreme Court opens on the first Monday of October till the late June of the next year. During the opening time, the Supreme Court holds public conventions from Monday to Friday each week.

The courts of appeals have been set up to share the burden of the Supreme Court, but they are under the Supreme Court. The whole country is divided into 12 appeal regions. Each region has a court of appeals made up of several judges. Then, the 50 states are divided into 94 federal judicial districts, each having a district court, which is the lowest unit of the federal judicial system. The court of appeals can review decisions of the district courts.

Besides the federal judicial system, each state has its own judicial system, courts of law, a police force and a prison system. All cases concerning ordinary crimes, such as theft, murder and disputes between residents of the same state, come under the jurisdiction of the state. State judges and police officers are responsible for upholding the state law, not the Supreme Court. All American courts use the jury system and common law. All the criminals not yet convicted are called suspects. After hearing the evidence, the judge explains the applicable law to the jury who then, in a separate room, reaches a verdict (裁决) in secret. The death penalty has not been abolished in every state of America, but usually only crimes such as treason and serious murder receive the death penalty.

III. Political Parties

As in Britain, a two-party system has been dominant in the United States. Today, the two major parties in America are the Democratic Party and the Republican Party. The symbol of the Democratic Party is a donkey and an elephant represents the Republican Party.

Chapter 10 Government

The Democratic Party is historically the party of labor, minorities and progressive reformers. In the 1790s, a group of Thomas Jefferson's supporters called themselves "Democratic Republicans" to demonstrate their belief in the principle of popular government and their opposition to monarchism. In the 1830s, the party adopted its present name.

The Republican Party came into being in 1854. It was a party of northern capitalists who opposed slavery. In February 1856, the party held its first national convention and ever since, the name "Republican" has been used. In 1860, the Republican candidate, Abraham Lincoln, was elected President and the Civil War broke out a few months afterward. From then on the Republicans held the presidency for most of the years until 1913. They returned to power from 1921 to 1933. Since World War II, the two parties have held the presidency in turn.

Generally speaking, the Democratic Party has a liberal ideology, while the Republican Party is more conservative. This affects their attitudes toward economic issues, social issues and foreign affairs, etc.

The Democrats want the government to play an important role in the economy and emphasize full employment as a matter of national concern. They favor civil rights laws, a strong social security system, less restrictive abortion (堕胎) laws, among others.

The Republicans favor an economic system which gives enterprises greater freedom and demand that the government control inflation. They stress the need for law and order and oppose complete government social programs and free choice of abortion. In addition, they favor a strong military posture (立场) and assertive stand in international relations.

There are no special requirements for membership of the two major parties. There are no membership cards, no dues (会费) and no initiation ceremonies. Members are not required to attend meetings. They do not have to vote for party candidates or to pay for party expenses, so party membership is nothing but an expression by the voters of which party they prefer.

IV. Election

By law, any natural-born American citizen over 35 years can run for the presidency. However, in reality, only the candidates nominated by the two major parties, the Republican and the Democratic, have the chance to win a presidential election.

Selecting the right candidate for the presidency is extremely important for both parties. To do this, each party holds its national convention every four years, in the summer before the general election. Several months before the convention, all the aspirants (有抱负者) for the nomination begin their personal campaigns within the party. Their purpose is to have their supporters chosen as delegates to the convention. The more supporters they have, the greater the chance for them to be nominated for the candidacy. This process is called the primary election. In some states, the primaries (初选) are "closed", in which a voter can only vote within his own party, but in other states, they are "open"—anyone can vote in any party's primary.

Chapter 10 Government

It is true that the convention has to work out the party's general policy, but its main job is to choose a presidential candidate. This cannot be easily done, and a lot of bargains, compromises and manipulation by party leaders are needed. The final choice is made when one candidate has received more than half of the votes. If nobody gets the absolute majority on the first ballot (第一轮投票), a second or a third ballot will be held. After the convention, the whole party will help its candidate run for election all over the country.

To win a presidential election, a candidate has to spend millions of dollars, which come from their fund-raising activities, their party and a grant from the government. The candidate has to travel all over the country, making countless speeches and shaking hands with countless voters. They have to face the rival in debates on television, and try their best to arouse public confidence in their platform (政纲).

The general election is technically divided into two stages. During the first stage, presidential electors for each state will be chosen. Each state is allowed to choose a number of presidential electors, which is equal to the total number of its Representatives and Senators in Congress. Since the number of the representatives from each state depends on the population, a state with a large population, such as California, may have 55 presidential electors, while a state with a small population like Alaska may have only three. The total number of electors in the nation is currently 538; they compose the United States Electoral College (总统选举团).

All candidates of presidential electors are party nominees. They make it clear to the public that they will vote their party candidate for the presidency. They are put on two lists, a Democratic list and a Republican one. As a result, a voter is actually choosing a President when he casts his vote for an elector. American elections adopt a "winner-takes-all"* practice.

In the second stage, the electors meet and vote into office a President. Since all the electors are already committed to voting a certain candidate, the second stage is actually only a formality. As soon as the first stage is over, everyone knows who will be the next President of the country.

---

* winner-takes-all: 胜者得全票规则，赢得一州的简单多数选民票的候选人即赢得了该州的全部选票。

V. Foreign Policy

Neutrality

On August 19, 1914, immediately after the outbreak of World War I, President Wilson issued the Declaration of Neutrality. He said, "The effect of the war upon the United States will depend upon what American citizens say and do. Every man who really loves America will act and speak in the true spirit of neutrality, which is the spirit of impartiality (公正) and fairness and friendliness to all concerned." However, on January 31, 1917, the German government resumed unrestricted submarine warfare. After several U.S. vessels were sunk, America entered the war. President Wilson submitted his Fourteen Points to the Senate in January, 1918 and called for the following: abandonment of secret international agreements; freedom of the seas; free trade between nations; reduction of armaments (军备); adjustment of colonial claims in the interests of the inhabitants affected; self-rule for subjugated European nationalities; and most importantly, the establishment of an association of nations to afford "mutual guarantees of political independence and territorial integrity to great and small states alike".

With the Nazi conquest of Poland in 1939 and the outbreak of World War II, isolationist sentiment increased, even though Americans clearly favored the victims of Hitler's aggression and supported the Allied countries.

The United States immediately announced that under no circumstances could any country involved in the conflict look to America for aid. Neutrality legislation, enacted piecemeal (逐步地) from 1935 to 1937, prohibited trade in arms with any warring nations, required cash for all other commodities and forbade American merchant ships from carrying those goods. The objective was to prevent, at almost any cost, the involvement in the war.

After the Japanese attack at Pearl Harbor on December 7, 1941, American opinion was unified overnight. America declared war on the Axis powers the following day. The nation rapidly readied itself for mobilization of its people and its entire industrial capacity. American wartime objectives were the total destruction of the Axis powers and the establishment of a world order after unconditional victory in accord with American ideals and interests.

Containment[1] and Intervention

The United States dominated global affairs in the years immediately after World War II. Victorious in that struggle, its homeland undamaged from the ravages of the war, the nation was confident of its mission at home and abroad. The U.S. leaders wanted to maintain the democratic structure they had defended at tremendous cost. For them, this was the "American Century". For years, most Americans remained sure of it. They accepted the need for a strong stance against the Soviet Union as the Cold War unfolded after 1945. Naturally, the American post-war policy was containment. President Truman affirmed the policy of containment, and his statements inspired a wave of hysterical anti-communism throughout the country.

President Dwight D. Eisenhower made vigorous efforts to wage the Cold War. He placed new emphasis on developing nuclear strength to prevent the outbreak of war. He also frequently authorized the Central Intelligence Agency (CIA)[2] to undertake secret interventions to overthrow unfriendly governments or protect reliable anti-communist leaders whose power was threatened. The CIA helped topple (推翻) the governments of Iran in 1953 and of Guatemala (危地马拉) in 1954, but suffered an embarrassing failure in 1958 when it intervened in Indonesia. After Cambodia (柬埔寨), Laos (老挝) and Vietnam became independent from France, Eisenhower used U.S. power and prestige to help create a non-communist government in South Vietnam, an action that had disastrous long-term consequences.

Although containment and intervention were the basic policies that the United States adhered to during the Cold War era, the Nixon administration took historic steps toward closer ties with major communist countries. The most dramatic move was a new relationship with China. In 1972, Nixon became the first U.S. President to visit Beijing. The Shanghai Communiqué (《上海公报》) established a new U.S. policy that there is one China, that Taiwan is a part of China.

The Berlin Wall fell in 1989, and the Soviet Union broke into several independent countries in 1991. Though great changes have taken place, the United States has remained one of the most powerful countries in the world.

---

1 containment: 遏制政策，第二次世界大战后美国推行的对外政策，旨在通过军事包围、经济封锁、政治颠覆、武装干涉和政治冷战等手段遏制社会主义国家的发展和影响。
2 Central Intelligence Agency (CIA): 美国中央情报局，负责在世界各地的情报收集和颠覆活动。

Exercises

I. Read the following statements and decide whether they are true (T) or false (F).

_____ 1. The Bill of Rights was written into the Constitution in 1787.

_____ 2. The form of the American government is based on three main principles: federalism, the separation of powers and respect for the Constitution and the rule of law.

_____ 3. The U.S. Congress consists of two houses: the House of Commons and the House of Lords.

_____ 4. The judicial branch of the U.S. federal government consists of a series of courts: the Supreme Court, the courts of appeals and the district courts.

_____ 5. The Democratic Party is conservative in terms of its ideology.

_____ 6. The American presidential campaigns adhere to the "winner-takes-all" practice.

_____ 7. The American foreign policy throughout World War II was neutrality.

_____ 8. The American foreign policy during the Cold War period was containment and intervention.

II. Choose the best answer to complete each of the following statements.

1. The U.S. Constitution came into effect in _____.
   A. 1787   B. 1789   C. 1791   D. 1793

2. The Constitution of the United States _____.
   A. gives the most power to Congress
   B. gives the most power to the President
   C. tries to give each branch enough power to balance the others
   D. gives the most power to the Supreme Court

3. The Bill of Rights _____.
   A. defines the rights of Congress and the rights of the President
   B. guarantees citizens of the United States specific individual rights and freedom
   C. is part of the Declaration of Independence
   D. has no relationship with the Constitution

4. The terms for a Senator and Representative are _____ and _____ years respectively.
   A. two, four   B. two, three   C. two, six   D. six, two

5. All the following can make legislative proposals EXCEPT _____.
   A. the Senator   B. the Representative
   C. the Secretary of State   D. the President

6. The following are all powers of the President EXCEPT _____.
   A. vetoing any bills passed by Congress
   B. appointing federal judges when vacancies occur
   C. making laws
   D. issuing executive orders

7. The Supreme Court is composed of _____ justices.
   A. six   B. seven   C. eight   D. nine

8. The President is directly voted into office by _____ .
   A. all citizens of America   B. the citizens over 18 years old
   C. electors elected by the voters   D. the Senators and the Representatives

III. Give brief answers to the following questions.

1. What are the two characteristics of the U.S. Constitution?

2. What are the qualifications for a Senator and a Representative respectively?

3. What are the major powers of the Supreme Court?

4. What are the differences between the Democrats and the Republicans in terms of political ideology?

IV. **State your understanding of the following questions.**
1. How is the American President voted into office? What are your ideas about the American election?
2. What was President Eisenhower's foreign policy and what were the consequences?

Learn and Check

Constitution: drawn up in 1787 and coming into effect in 1789

Government: the legislature, the executive, the judiciary

Major political parties: the Democratic Party, the Republican Party

Election: a winner-takes-all practice

Foreign policy: neutrality (during the two World Wars), containment and intervention (after World War II)

Chapter 11

Economy

▼ **Think and Talk**
- What is Hamilton's economic development strategy?
- What makes American agriculture a success?
- What do you know about American high-tech industry?

The United States is currently the largest industrial nation in the world. It is an economic and technological giant. It ranks first in such fields as computer technology, space technology, nuclear energy and electronics. Although its dominance is decreasing, it produces a major portion of the world's machinery, automobiles, oil, electrical energy and chemicals.

The American free enterprise system emphasizes private ownership. Businesses are directly or indirectly owned and operated by private individuals. In such a system, individual people and companies are free to make their own economic decisions. This emphasis on private ownership arises, in part, from the American beliefs about personal freedom. The federal government is involved in the system by regulating businesses in certain ways. For instance, it establishes anti-trust laws* to prevent one company from controlling an entire industry and creating a monopoly.

I. History of American Economy

The modern American economy traces its roots to the quest of European settlers for economic gain in the 16th, 17th and 18th centuries. The New World progressed from a colonial economy to a small, independent farming economy, and then to a highly complex, industrial economy.

---

* anti-trust laws: 反托拉斯法案，旨在防止企业垄断与自由贸易受限的联邦法规。

The Colonial Period

Early settlers came to the United States for various reasons. Some of them, like the Pilgrims of Massachusetts, wanted to escape religious persecution. They were pious, thrifty and had strong self-discipline. Others came to the New World for profits as well as religious and political freedom, as those in Virginia and Pennsylvania.

Chartered companies* contributed a lot to Britain's colonizing process of the would-be United States. They were groups of stockholders (usually merchants and wealthy landowners) who sought personal economic gain and perhaps also wanted to advance Britain's national goals. While the private sector financed the companies, the King or Queen provided each project with a charter or grant, conferring (授予) economic rights as well as political and judicial authority. Because the colonies generally did not show quick profits, the British investors often turned over their colonial charters to the colonists. The political implications, although not realized at the time, were enormous. The colonists were left to build their own lives, their own communities and their own economy, in effect, to start constructing their own new nation.

Secondary industries developed as the colonies grew. A variety of specialized sawmills (锯木厂) and gristmills (磨坊) appeared. Colonists established shipyards to build fishing fleets and trading vessels. They also built small iron forges (锻铁炉). By the 18th century, regional patterns of development had become clear: The New England colonies relied on shipbuilding and sailing to generate wealth; plantations in Maryland, Virginia and the Carolinas (南卡罗来纳州和北卡罗来纳州) grew tobacco, rice and indigo (靛蓝属植物); New York, Pennsylvania, New Jersey and Delaware (特拉华州) shipped crops and furs. Except for slaves, the standard of living in the colonies was generally higher, in fact, than in Britain. As the British investors withdrew their support, the field was open for entrepreneurs among the colonists to establish themselves.

By 1770, the North American colonies were ready, both economically and politically, for self-government. The Americans hoped for a modification (减轻) of British taxes and regulations that would satisfy their demand for more

---

* chartered company: 得到英王特许而从事殖民活动的商业公司。

self-government. Few thought the mounting quarrel with the British government would lead to war against the British and to independence for the colonies. Like the British turmoil of the 17th and 18th centuries, the American Revolution was both political and economic, bolstered (加强) by an emerging middle class with a rallying cry of "inalienable (不可剥夺的) rights to life, liberty and property"—a phrase borrowed from English philosopher, John Locke.

Since American Independence

The U.S. Constitution was in many ways a work of creative genius. As an economic charter, it established that the entire nation was a unified or "common" market. There were no tariffs or taxes on interstate commerce. The Constitution provided that the federal government could regulate commerce with foreign nations and among the states, establish uniform bankruptcy laws, create money and regulate its value, fix standards of weights and measures, establish post offices and roads, and fix rules governing patents (专利) and copyrights. The last-mentioned clause was an early recognition of the importance of "intellectual property", a matter that began assuming great importance in trade negotiations since the late 20th century.

Alexander Hamilton, one of the nation's founding fathers and its first Secretary of the Treasury (财政部长), advocated an economic development strategy in which the federal government would nurture infant industries by providing overt (公开的) subsidies and imposing protective tariffs on imports. He also urged the federal government to create a national bank and to assume the public debts that the colonies had incurred during the War of Independence. The new government wavered (犹豫) over some of Hamilton's proposals, but ultimately it did make tariffs an essential part of American foreign policy, a position that lasted until almost the middle of the 20th century.

亚历山大·汉密尔顿

The Industrial Revolution began in Europe in the 18th century and quickly spread to the United States. By 1860, when Abraham Lincoln was elected President, 16% of the U.S. population lived in urban areas and one-third of the nation's income came from manufacturing. Urbanized industry was limited primarily to the northeast; cotton cloth production was the leading industry, with the manufacture of shoes, woolen clothing and machinery also expanding.

Northern victory in the Civil War, however, ensured the destiny of the nation and its economic system. The slavery system was abolished, making the large southern cotton plantations much less profitable. Northern industries, which had expanded rapidly because of the demand of the war, surged ahead. Industrialists came to dominate many aspects of the nation's life, including social and political affairs. The planter aristocracy of the South disappeared.

The rapid economic development following the Civil War laid the groundwork for the modern U.S. industrial economy. An explosion of new discoveries and inventions took place, causing such profound changes that some termed as a "second industrial revolution". Oil was discovered in western Pennsylvania. The typewriter was developed. The telephone, phonograph (留声机) and electric light were invented. By the dawn of the 20th century, cars were replacing carriages and people were flying in airplanes.

The 20th Century

The American economy in the early 20th century experienced a period of prosperity and then suffered the worst depression in American history following the Wall Street Crash in October, 1929. President Roosevelt, in his attempt to tackle the economic depression, introduced his famous New Deal in 1933. Roosevelt's first act was to deal with the banking crisis. He ordered all banks to close and asked Congress to pass legislation which guaranteed that savers would not lose their money if there were another financial crisis. He also set up the New York State Emergency Relief Commission to help those in desperate need. While trying to reduce unemployment, Roosevelt also attempted to relieve the misery for those who were unable to work. The New Deal was extremely popular with the electorate (全体选民) and led Roosevelt to be reelected President in 1936. Obviously, the government has always played an active and important role in America's economic development. The intervention of the government has ensured that economic opportunities are fair and accessible to the people. It has prevented flagrant (公然的) abuses of the system, dampened (抑制) the effects of inflation and stimulated economic growth.

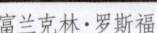
富兰克林·罗斯福

Chapter 11 Economy

After World War II, America recognized the urgent need to restructure international monetary arrangements. By ensuring an open, capitalist, international economy, American businesses entered a period of consolidation during the 1950s. The 1960s and the 1970s were a time of great change. President Johnson intended to build a "Great Society" by spreading the benefits of America's successful economy to more citizens. Various programs such as Medicare (health care for the elderly), Food Stamps (food assistance for the poor) and Education Initiatives (assistance to students as well as grants to schools and colleges) were launched by the government, which led to the drastic increase of the federal spending.

By the end of the 1970s, economic growth had decreased. Unemployment and inflation continued to rise. In the early 1980s, the Reagan administration adopted new monetary policies to fight inflation by increasing the supply of money.

Central to the Reagan administration's efforts to combat inflation was rigorous control over government spending deficit. In addition, taxes were cut to enhance economic development while interest rates were raised. These measures finally brought inflation and unemployment under control.

The economy saw a recession during the administration of President George H. W. Bush. Under President Clinton, the economy grew slowly at first. Then, measures taken during the Bush administration began to bear fruit and the economy recovered more quickly. Business earnings grew and new jobs were created. The economy had been growing continuously since the 1990s, the longest peacetime economic expansion in history.

When President Barack Obama took office in January 2009, the United States was in the midst of a deep recession, losing over 800,000 jobs per month. Since his first day in office, President Obama has focused on laying the foundation for an economy built to last. On February 17, 2009, Obama signed the American Recovery and Reinvestment Act of 2009, an economic stimulus package aimed at helping the economy recover from the deepening worldwide recession. The act includes increased federal spending for health care, infrastructure, education, various tax breaks and incentives, and direct assistance to individuals, which is being distributed over the course of several years.

II. Current American Economy

Agriculture

American agriculture assumes a richness and variety unmatched in most parts of the world. This is chiefly due to the vastness of the land and in part, due to the generosity of nature. Only in a relatively small area of the West are rainfall and snowfall so limited that deserts exist. Elsewhere, rainfall ranges from modest to abundant, and rivers and underground water allow for irrigation where necessary. Large areas of level or gently rolling land, especially in the Great Plains, provide ideal conditions for large-scale agriculture. Today the average American farm covers about 460 acres.

Large capital investments and increasing use of highly trained labor have also contributed to the success of American agriculture. Biotechnology has led to the development of seeds that are disease- and drought-resistant. Computers track farm operations, and even space technology is utilized to find the best place to plant crops. What's more, researchers periodically introduce new food products and new methods for raising them.

American agriculture has increasingly become an "agribusiness" (农业企业), a term created to reflect the big, corporate nature of many farm enterprises.

Agribusinesses include a variety of farm businesses and structures, from small, one-family corporations to huge conglomerates (联合企业) or multinational firms.

Both American and foreign consumers benefit from the American farm's low-cost output. American consumers pay far less for their food than people of many other industrial countries. Moreover, one-third of the crops are exported to Europe, Asia, Africa and Latin America. American agricultural exports are estimated to amount to $143 billion in 2013. Agricultural imports lag far behind, leaving a surplus in the agricultural balance of trade. Agriculture in America remains the foundation upon which American well-being and prosperity are based.

Manufacturing Industry

The United States has large manufacturing industries and nearly 12 million Americans (or 9% of the workforce) are employed directly in manufacturing. The four largest manufacturing industries are: computers and electronic products; chemicals; food, beverage and tobacco; and petroleum products. They account for about 51% of the U.S. manufacturing GDP. The American military industry is so highly developed that each year it makes a profit of billions of dollars by selling military products to foreign countries. The American auto-making companies reigned worldwide in 2012 as the biggest and most profitable. The Boeing Company is the foremost manufacturer of commercial jet transport aircraft in the world. It is also a leading producer of military aircraft, helicopters, space vehicles and missiles.

Service Industry

The service industry is significant to the American economy. A clear indication can be found in its effects on employment. Employment in manufacturing and agriculture has declined since the 1970s. By contrast, tremendous growth has occurred in the service sector.

The American service sector involves three categories: services for the affluent, welfare services and services provided by the poor. Services for the affluent include commercial banking, life insurance, real estate and law services. Welfare services include health care, education, government and social services. Services provided by the poor usually cover two major industries: services to buildings and dwellings, and retail services, both requiring little skill.

High-tech Industry

America has been undergoing profound economic change at the beginning of the 21st century. More emphasis has been laid on technological innovations in computing, telecommunications, biological sciences and space technology. Therefore, America's high-tech industry ranks first in the world and plays an important role in the country's economic growth. For example, in the fields of computers, engineering and information technology, American companies hold the dominant place in the world.

Foreign Trade

U.S. foreign trade has always been playing a significant role in the country's economic development. In the past two centuries, particularly since World War II, it has changed from a domestic-oriented trade pattern to a more internationally-oriented one. The U.S. government has made great efforts in reducing trade barriers and coordinating the world economic system because most U.S. leaders are well aware that open bilateral (双边的) trade will help advance American economic development, enhance its domestic stability as well as relationship with other nations.

The exports of U.S. goods and services reached an all-time record during 2012, totaling $2.2 trillion. The U.S. economy continues to make progress toward President

Obama's goal of doubling exports from their 2009 levels. The most important products for export are office machines, household appliances, transportation and communication equipment, chemicals, textile, metal manufactures, petroleum products, paper and other products made from wood and rubber. The United States ranks first in export of agricultural products. In addition, it is also the leading exporter of civil aircraft, services, technology and weapons.

America takes in the largest percentage of imports in the world. The major imported products are crude oil, engines, electronic equipment, vehicles, etc. Many U.S. industries are built around a continuous supply of essential raw materials.

In light of its tremendous influence on the world economy, the growth and decline of the U.S. foreign trade volume, to a large extent, affects the trend of the world economy.

Exercises

I. Read the following statements and decide whether they are true (T) or false (F).
    _____ 1. America is the world's largest industrial nation.
    _____ 2. In the U.S. Constitution, the recognition of the importance of "intellectual property" could be identified.
    _____ 3. Although slavery was abolished as a result of the Civil War, the owners of plantations in the South made more profits from selling their agricultural products.
    _____ 4. President Roosevelt's New Deal had little effect in dealing with the economic crisis in the early 1930s.
    _____ 5. The 1960s was a period of consolidation for the American businesses.
    _____ 6. American agricultural exports outweigh imports, leaving a surplus in the agricultural balance of trade.
    _____ 7. Auto production is one of the important sectors in American manufacturing industry.
    _____ 8. The growth and decline of the American foreign trade has little to do with the world economy.

II. Choose the best answer to complete each of the following statements.

1. America produces a major portion of the world's products in the following fields EXCEPT _____.

   A. machinery B. automobiles C. ore D. chemicals

2. The modern American economy progressed from _____ to _____, and then to _____.

   A. a colonial economy, a handcraft economy, an industrial economy

   B. a farming economy, a handcraft economy, an industrial economy

   C. a colonial economy, a farming economy, an industrial economy

   D. a handcraft economy, a farming economy, an industrial economy

3. Chartered companies were NOT granted the _____ by the British King or Queen.

   A. political authority   B. economic rights

   C. judicial authority   D. diplomatic authority

4. _____ urged the federal government to establish a national bank.

   A. George Washington   B. President Roosevelt

   C. Abraham Lincoln   D. Alexander Hamilton

5. The following inventions took place during the "second industrial revolution" EXCEPT _____.

   A. typewriter   B. telephone   C. electric light   D. refrigerator

6. President Johnson tried to build a "Great Society" by introducing various programs like the following EXCEPT _____.

   A. Medicare   B. Food Stamps

   C. Education Initiatives   D. Unemployment Pension

7. The following statements are all true EXCEPT _____.

   A. Agribusinesses reflect the big, corporate nature of many farm enterprises.

   B. Agribusinesses maintain a balanced trade pattern between agricultural imports and exports.

   C. Agribusinesses range from one-family corporations to multinational firms.

   D. Agribusinesses include a variety of farm businesses and structures.

8. Employment in the _____ sector has been increasing in the U.S. since the 1970s.

   A. service   B. agriculture   C. manufacturing   D. high-tech

Chapter 11 Economy

III. **Give brief answers to the following questions.**

1. What industrial developments took place during the colonial period in America?

   _____
   _____

2. How did the Civil War affect the American economy?

   _____
   _____

3. Why does America try to reduce trade barriers?

   _____
   _____

IV. **State your understanding of the following questions.**

1. How did the U.S. Constitution lay the groundwork for America's economic development?
2. Cite examples to illustrate the role of government intervention in America's economic development.

Learn and Check

Economic development: a colonial economy → a small, independent farming economy → a highly complex, industrial economy

Programs of benefits launched by the Johnson administration: Medicare (health care for the elderly), Food Stamps (food assistance for the poor), Education Initiatives (assistance to students and grants to schools and colleges)

Current economic sectors: agriculture, manufacturing industry, service industry, high-tech industry, foreign trade

Chapter 12: Education, Media and Holidays

> ### Think and Talk
> - What are the ideals of American education?
> - What do you know about the life of an undergraduate student in an American university?
> - What are the full names of CBS, NBS, ABS, CNN and VOA?
> - What do you know about Thanksgiving Day?

I. Education

Ideals of American Education

The first ideal of American education is that as many people as possible should have access to as much education as they want. This ideal is an outcome of the American assertions about equality among people.

The second ideal is producing a society that is totally literate and of local control. In the United States, education is governed by state and local governments, not by the Federal government. Each of the 50 states has its own laws regulating education. From state to state, some laws are similar; others are not. For example, all states require young people to attend school until the age of 16 or 18.

The third ideal is about the basic nature of knowledge and learning. The idea is that scholars and students should work to discover new information or conceive new ways to understand what is already known. Learning at all levels is considered not just a process of memorizing knowledge. Learning is an enterprise of exploration, experimentation, analysis and synthesis. American schools tend to put more emphasis on developing critical thinking than acquiring quantities of facts. The goal of American education is to teach children how to learn and help them reach their maximum potential.

Education in America is regarded as both an individual benefit and a social necessity. It is a general view that every American should have the right and obligation

Chapter 12 Education, Media and Holidays

to become educated. Americans believe that, through education, an individual acquires knowledge, skills, attitudes and abilities which will enable them to fit into society and improve their social status. They hold the view that the future of the nation depends largely on education.

Educational System

1) Elementary and Secondary Education

Formal education in the United States consists of elementary, secondary and higher education. Elementary and secondary education, the basis of public education, are compulsory and are divided into 12 grades. Generally, one academic year from September through June is required to complete each grade. The first academic institution that a child attends is called elementary school although many parents choose to enroll their children in kindergarten and even earlier, nursery school or daycare center. In some school systems, elementary schools include grades one through eight. The next four years are called high school. In other school systems, there are three divisions: elementary school (grades one through six), junior high school (grades seven through nine) and senior high school (grades 10 through 12).

Elementary schools teach reading, arithmetic and language arts such as creative writing, spelling and handwriting. Social studies, science, music, the arts and physical education are also part of the program. Class size is usually limited to between 20 and 30 students although schools generally try to have a smaller class size.

In high schools, subject matter becomes more specialized. English classes stress writing and literature. Social studies are split into separate courses in American history, American government or political science, European history, etc. Algebra and geometry are offered as well. High school students usually take a one-year general science course, and then more detailed courses in biology, chemistry and physics are provided. Most high school students study a foreign language, usually French or Spanish, with Chinese becoming more and more popular as a foreign language choice in some areas. Some high schools specialize in vocational education and train students for various technical careers.

In most high schools, students meet with a different teacher and a different group of students for each subject. The high school students' day may be divided into nine periods: five for academic subjects, one for physical education, a lunch period and two study periods. The study periods may be used to visit the library or participate in an extracurricular (课外的) activity such as the school orchestra, newspaper staff, or chess club.

Once a student has reached high school, they are very conscious of the need to obtain good marks on their schoolwork if they wish to go on to a competitive university. Some universities are very selective in their admission, while others admit any student provided they have passed all the high school courses and graduated. On the matter of admission, different colleges and universities have different requirements.

In America, there is no annual college entrance examination. College applicants are chosen on the basis of: a) their high school records; b) recommendations from their high school teachers; c) the impression they make during interviews at the university; d) their scores on the Scholastic Aptitude Test (SAT)[1]. Of all the high school graduates, more than 60% continue college after graduation.

2) Higher Education

Higher education in the United States began with the founding of Harvard College in 1636. In the past more than 300 years, it has developed into a large enterprise with a very complex system. The higher education comprises four categories of institutions: a) the university; b) the four-year undergraduate institution—the college; c) the technical training institution; and d) the two-year community college.

In America, the term "college" refers to an undergraduate institution that confers the degree of Bachelor of Arts (B.A.) or Bachelor of Science (B.S.) after four years of study or an associate degree[2] after two years of study. A university is generally a group of colleges, each serving a special purpose: college of business, college of arts and humanities, college of education, etc. The system of higher education in the United

---

[1] Scholastic Aptitude Test (SAT): 学习能力倾向测试，由美国大学入学考试委员会主持的高等学校入学前的预测性测试。
[2] associate degree: 准学士学位，某些美国高等专科学校授予的低于学士学位的一种学位。

Chapter 12 Education, Media and Holidays

States has three functions: teaching, research and public service. Each college or university has its own emphasis with regard to its functions. The majority of the higher education institutions are located in states that have a large population.

The American higher education institutions offer a wide variety of subjects, from the fine arts to practical and career-oriented fields such as engineering and marketing. The U.S. has a variety of higher education institutions, from large comprehensive universities to small traditional liberal arts colleges. Distinctions among these institutions are in size, level, educational quality, residential atmosphere and the time it takes to complete a degree. At the undergraduate level, students' personal preferences as to size, academic quality and location play a key role in their choice of college or university. At the graduate level, more attention is paid to the reputation of the faculty and department.

For a university student, an academic year is about nine months, usually from mid-September until early June or from late August until May. In most universities, it is divided into either two semesters or three semesters, excluding the summer session. The students usually enjoy a "break" of one week during each semester and a 30-day winter break.

Typically, an undergraduate student has to earn a certain number of "credits" (usually at least 120) in order to receive a degree at the end of four years of college. Credits are earned by attending lectures (or lab classes) and by successfully completing assignments and examinations. One credit usually equals one hour of class per week in a single course. A course may last 10 to 16 weeks, the length of a semester.

Living accommodations are usually not large enough to hold all university students, though large numbers of residence halls have been built. Many students live off campus and prepare their own meals.

It is common for students to work to earn their tuition and living expenses not only during vacations but also in their free time during the semester. Many colleges and universities offer work-study programs so that students can earn money while working at the school.

Sports have a significant place in American university life. Football (橄榄球) is the most popular university sport. Some universities award both football and basketball scholarships, and students admitted mainly as athletics or "jocks" (学生运动员) receive not only free tuition but also other financial assistance.

There are clubs and activities for almost every student's interests, such as art, music, drama, debate, foreign languages, photography, volunteer work, all aimed at helping students become successful in their later life while simultaneously pursuing their hobbies.

The United States of America

哈佛大学商学院

3) Famous Universities

Harvard University, the oldest institution of higher learning in the United States, is a comprehensive university. Harvard College was established in 1636 and was named for its first benefactor (捐助者), John Harvard[1]. The university has grown from nine students with a single master to an enrollment of more than 20,000 degree candidates, including undergraduates, graduates and professional students in 11 principal academic units.

Harvard University is known around the world for its outstanding academic achievements. The university has produced more than 40 Nobel laureates. Eight Presidents of the United States are graduates of Harvard.

Yale University was founded in 1701 as the Collegiate School (大学学院) in Killingworth, Connecticut. In 1716, it moved to its permanent location in New Haven (纽黑文). Elihu Yale, a wealthy British merchant, donated generously to the school, and it was renamed Yale College in 1718. In 1864, Yale College was renamed Yale University. The university is now comprised of three major academic components: Yale College (the undergraduate program), the Graduate School of Arts and Sciences and 10 professional schools. Yale encompasses a wide array of research organizations, libraries, museums and administrative support offices. Approximately 12,000 students attend Yale. And it embarks on a steady expansion. With strict teaching and enrollment, Yale University has a high academic standard and great prestige. Some of the world's most famous and powerful men today are graduates of Yale, including George W. Bush, John Kerry and William F. Buckley Jr.[2], etc.

---

1 John Harvard: 约翰•哈佛 (1607-1638)，英国牧师和慈善家。
2 William F. Buckley Jr.: 小威廉•巴克利 (1925-2008)，美国著名作家。

耶鲁大学

Chapter 12 Education, Media and Holidays

普林斯顿大学

Princeton University was known as the College of New Jersey from 1746 to 1896. It is well known for its History Department, Philosophy Department, English Department, Mathematics Department and Physics Department. The Woodrow Wilson School of Public and International Affairs has been continuously training government officials. President Wilson and over 80 Senators are graduates of Princeton University.

Massachusetts Institute of Technology (MIT) is an institute famous for its scientific and technological training and research. Established in 1861, the institute used to be a purely technical institution. It is comprised of five schools: the School of Architecture and Planning, the School of Engineering, the School of Humanities, Arts and Social Sciences, the MIT Slogan School of Management and the School of Science.

麻省理工学院

While attaching importance to teaching, the institute pays great attention to theory study and applied research. Both the undergraduates and the graduates participate in cooperative research work. MIT has achieved significant success in the fields of scientific research.

155

4) Multicultural Education

The schools in the United States have been greatly affected by the combination of population and increased immigration. For example, in California public schools one out of six students was born outside the U.S., and one in three speaks a language other than English at home.

Today, schools routinely teach the experiences and values of many ethnic cultures. Current textbooks incorporate a variety of ethnic individuals who have achieved success. Struggles for equality are vividly depicted, and past racism is bluntly acknowledged. Cultural pluralism is now generally recognized as the organizing principle of education. Concrete examples can be found at every grade level. Elementary school students learn not only about the traditional Thanksgiving celebration in the United States, but also about other harvest holidays around the world. High schools include literature from around the world, offering alternative perspectives on social problems and significant historical events. Ethnic studies departments can be found in high schools and colleges throughout the U.S.

II. Media

Technological advances in America have made mass communications inexpensive and immediately available to everyone. The media is perceived as more trustworthy than business, state and local governments, or the presidency.

Newspapers

No other country in the world has more daily newspapers than the U.S. The quality of some American papers is extremely high and their views are quoted all over the world. Many of the newspapers have columns by well-known journalists of different political and social views in order to present a balanced picture. To many readers, the most entertaining part of the paper is the "funnies" (滑稽漫画栏) or comics section. Almost everyone can find a comic strip that appeals to him, whether his taste is for slapstick (打闹剧) humor, violence, adventure or intellectual satire. Of all the newspapers, the following ones are the most influential in the U.S.

Chapter 12 Education, Media and Holidays

The New York Times was established in 1851, consistently ranking number one in the U.S. for editorial quality and news coverage. It is sold especially to the upper or upper-middle class and has a reputation for its serious attitude and great bulk.

The Washington Post, established in 1877, is the dominant newspaper in the U.S. capital and usually counted as one of the greatest newspapers in the U.S. Its main readers are government employees and it is closely linked to the American Congress. It was *The Washington Post* that first exposed the Watergate Scandal in 1972.

The Los Angeles Times, established in 1881, is one of the world's great newspapers. It is published by the Times Mirror Company* in Los Angeles. Being physically huge, it often covers 200 pages on Sunday. Furthermore, it makes a policy not to endorse (支持) candidates for high offices such as the the President and governors.

Television and Broadcast

In the United States, there is no government-owned television network. The major radio and TV networks are the Columbia Broadcasting System (CBS) (哥伦比亚广播公司), the National Broadcasting System (NBS) (国家广播公司) and the American Broadcasting System (ABS) (美国广播公司).

Nearly all TV is commercial and programs are frequently interrupted with advertisements. However, commercials (广告) do make it possible to show programs that are expensive to produce. There is one channel where there are no commercials. Programs on this channel are produced by the Public Broadcasting Service (PBS) (美国公共电视网) and can be seen all over the United States. Although PBS gets a grant from Congress, Congress does not interfere in any way regarding the content of its programs.

The Cable News Network (CNN) (美国有限电视新闻网) is a cable television network that was established in 1980 by Ted Turner. It is a division of the Turner Broadcasting System. CNN is widely credited for introducing the concept of 24-hour news coverage.

The Voice of America (VOA) is the most famous radio station in the United States for the dissemination of propaganda to foreign countries. Being supported and organized by the government, VOA was originally established to broadcast war information. Now its day-to-day operations are supported by the International Broadcasting Bureau. It sends news to the whole world in over 40 languages 24 hours a day.

---

* the Times Mirror Company: 时报－镜报公司，美国最重要的新闻媒体公司之一。

Chapter 12 Education, Media and Holidays

III. Holidays and Festivals

Thanksgiving

Thanksgiving is celebrated in the U.S. on the fourth Thursday in November. For many Americans it is the most important holiday apart from Christmas. Schools, offices and most businesses close for Thanksgiving, and many people make the whole weekend a vacation.

Thanksgiving is associated with the time when Europeans first came to North America. In 1620, when the Pilgrims first arrived, they had a very hard winter and could not find enough to eat, so many of them died. Native Americans showed them what crops were safe to eat and how to plant them, so next year they had a good harvest. They held a big celebration to thank God and the Native Americans for helping them survive the harsh winter and produce a bountiful harvest.

Thanksgiving Day became an official holiday in 1863. Today people celebrate Thanksgiving to remember the early days. The most important part of the celebration is a traditional dinner with foods that come from North America. The meal includes turkey, sweet potatoes and cranberry sauce (越橘沙司). Many families have their own special recipe.

On Thanksgiving, there are special television programs and sports events. In New York, there is Macy's Thanksgiving Day Parade*—a long line of people wearing fancy costumes march through the streets with large balloons in the shape of imaginary characters. Thanksgiving is considered the beginning of the Christmas season, and the next day many people go out to shop for Christmas presents.

Independence Day

The national day of the United States falls on the 4th of July and is America's most important patriotic holiday. It was on this day in 1776 when the Continental Congress representing the 13 colonies adopted the Declaration of Independence, which cut the ties with Britain and established the United States of America.

Independence Day is celebrated in all the states. The army marks the occasion by firing a 50-gun salute. Ceremonies may include parades, official speeches, visits to historic monuments, outdoor stage shows, dancing parties, boat races and fireworks displays. Each year on July 4th, Americans celebrate their freedom and independence with barbecues, picnics and family gatherings. Some people visit the birthplace of the nation, Philadelphia.

---

* Macy's Thanksgiving Day Parade: 梅西感恩节游行，是由美国梅西百货公司主办的一年一度的感恩节游行。这一传统始于 1924 年。

Exercises

I. Read the following statements and decide whether they are true (T) or false (F).

_____ 1. Education is governed by state and local governments instead of the national government in America.

_____ 2. All American children are offered 12 years of compulsory public education.

_____ 3. After 12 years of schooling, American students receive a bachelor's degree upon graduation.

_____ 4. When selecting a college or university, students have a great concern for its size, location and academic quality.

_____ 5. Usually, an undergraduate student has to earn at least 120 credits to receive a degree.

_____ 6. Outstanding graduates of Yale university include President Wilson and more than 80 Senators.

_____ 7. It is *The New York Times* that first uncovered the Watergate Scandal in 1972.

_____ 8. Thanksgiving Day falls on the fourth Tuesday in November.

II. Choose the best answer to complete each of the following statements.

1. Formal education in the United States consists of _____, secondary and higher education.
   A. kindergarten   B. public   C. elementary   D. private

2. Of the following subjects, _____ are NOT offered to elementary school students.
   A. mathematics and language arts   B. politics and business education
   C. science and social studies   D. music and physical education

3. Higher education in the United States began with the founding of _____.
   A. Yale University   B. Harvard College
   C. Princeton University   D. Massachusetts Institute of Technology

Chapter 12 Education, Media and Holidays

4. Of the following, _____ are NOT among the categories of American higher education.
   A. universities and colleges
   B. research institutions
   C. technical institutions
   D. community colleges

5. To get a bachelor's degree, all undergraduate students are required to do the following EXCEPT _____.
   A. attending lectures and completing assignments
   B. passing examinations
   C. working for communities
   D. earning a certain number of credits

6. _____ is sold especially to the upper or upper-middle class and has a reputation for its serious attitude and great bulk.
   A. *The Washington Post*
   B. *The New York Times*
   C. *The Los Angeles Times*
   D. *New York Daily News*

7. Of the following, _____ is NOT among the three major radio and TV networks in America.
   A. the National Broadcasting System (NBS)
   B. the Public Broadcasting Service (PBS)
   C. the Columbia Broadcasting System (CBS)
   D. the American Broadcasting System (ABS)

8. The National Day of the United States falls on _____ each year.
   A. June 4th   B. July 4th   C. June 14th   D. July 14th

III. Give brief answers to the following questions.

1. How does an American university choose its applicants?
   _____
   _____

2. What functions do American higher education institutions perform?
   _____
   _____

3. What similarities do the four famous universities share?

　　_____

　　_____

4. What are the origins of Thanksgiving Day?

　　_____

　　_____

IV. State your understanding of the following questions.

1. What are the ideals that guide the American educational system?
2. How does America carry out multicultural education?

Learn and Check

Educational system: elementary education, secondary education, higher education

Categories of higher education institutions: the university, the four-year undergraduate college, the technical training institution, the two-year community college

Famous universities: Harvard University, Yale University, Princeton University, Massachusetts Institute of Technology (MIT)

Major newspapers: *The New York Times, The Washington Post, The Los Angeles Times*

Major radio and TV networks: CBS, NBS, ABS, CNN

Important holidays and festivals: Thanksgiving (the fourth Thursday in November), Independence Day (the 4th of July)

Chapter 13 Literature

▼ **Think and Talk**
- What is Benjamin Franklin's *Autobiography* about?
- What do you know about Mark Twain and his famous works?
- What do you know about Ernest Hemingway and his major works?

The United States of America has a comparatively short history and accordingly, what we generally call American literature is confined to this short period. The rich native American writings before the colonial period are excluded and sometimes even the unrefined and indistinctive colonial writings could not count as American literature, but merely a branch of British literature. Though the nation won its War of Independence in 1783, its cultural independence did not arrive until the mid-19th century. Therefore, the history of American literature is also the story of the slow emergence of native elements and national characteristics.

I. The Colonial and Revolutionary Periods

The era from the founding of the first settlement at Jamestown (1607) to the outbreak of the American Revolution (1775) is often called the Colonial Period. Writings of this period are for the most part religious, practical or historical. The major topic deals with American Puritanism (清教主义), which stresses predestination (宿命论), original sin, total depravity (堕落), and limited atonement (有限的救赎) or the salvation of a selected few who would receive God's grace.

Jonathan Edwards (1703-1758) and Benjamin Franklin (1706-1790) are the epitome (典型) of this age. They respectively represent the dual nature of American Puritanism and American character: religious idealism and level-headed (头脑冷静的) common sense. With his powerful sermons, Jonathan Edwards ardently preached the Puritan ideas and condemned people's depravity. His best-known work is an intimidating sermon, "Sinners in the Hands of an Angry God" (1741). In order to revive Puritanism that had been weakened by ideas of the Enlightenment[1], he initiated the Great Awakening Movement[2].

On the other hand, Benjamin Franklin was a completely worldly man who also achieved great worldly success: His fame as a political leader, diplomat, scientist and inventor spread far and wide; his wealth accumulated in his printing and publishing enterprises.

本杰明·富兰克林

His *Poor Richard's Almanac* (1732-1757) was both a literary achievement and a profitable business. It was published continuously for a quarter of a century. "A penny saved is a penny earned" and "Early to bed and early to rise makes a man healthy, wealthy and wise"—these familiar sayings all come from his *Almanac*.

His most famous work is *Autobiography*. It records his rise from poverty and obscurity to wealth and fame. However, this worldly success is in line with Puritanism: Hard work is the right way to worship God and the material success of the believer is evidence of God's love. Thus, Franklin's *Autobiography* is also a record of spiritual growth in addition to self-examination and self-improvement.

The Revolutionary Period refers to the period between 1765 when the Stamp Act[3] was passed and 1790. The most representative work of this period is Thomas Jefferson's world-famous Declaration of Independence. Its rhetorical vigor, refined diction and polished style help express perfectly the nation's ardent longing for freedom.

---

1 the Enlightenment: 启蒙运动，17、18 世纪兴起于欧洲大陆的思想运动。它号召人们运用理性去除蒙昧、迷信和偏见，争取政治和信仰自由，反对封建制度。启蒙主义思想传到新大陆后掀起轩然大波，对当时的统治思想清教主义提出了挑战。
2 the Great Awakening Movement: 大觉醒运动，18 世纪北美殖民地的新教复兴运动。它提倡严格的道德和虔诚的生活，促进了更广泛的宗教自由和宗教生活的民主化，对后来的独立战争有一定的催化作用。
3 Stamp Act:《印花税法》，英国政府于 1765 年颁布的对北美殖民地人民征收直接税的法令，于 1766 年被废除。

II. The Romantic Period

The Romantic Period, one of the most important periods in the history of American literature, also called "the American Renaissance", stretches from the end of the 18th century to the mid-19th century.

During the period, most of the American writing place an increasing emphasis on the free expression of emotions and displayed an increasing attention to the psychic (精神的) state of the characters. The writing celebrated America's landscape with its virgin forests, meadows, endless prairies, streams and vast oceans. The strong tendency to exalt (赞美) the individual and the common man was almost a national religion in America. Although British influences were strong, American Romanticism exhibited from the very outset distinct features of its own.

Fiction

Regarded as the "father of American literature", Washington Irving (1783-1859) is the first American to achieve an international literary reputation. Irving provides the young nation with humorous, fictional accounts of the colonial past. His most famous stories are *Rip Van Winkle* (1819) and *The Legend of Sleepy Hollow* (1819), which help Irving earn great fame in the literary world.

James Fenimore Cooper (1789-1851) devotes two great figures to American mythology: the brave frontiersman and the bold Indian. James Fenimore Cooper is remembered today as the author of the "Leatherstocking Tales", a series of five novels that include *The Pioneers* (1823), *The Last of the Mohicans* (1826), *The Prairie* (1827), *The Pathfinder* (1840) and *The Deerslayer* (1841). The prominent figure throughout is a frontiersman hero, Natty Bumppo, who represents the ideal American.

Ralph Waldo Emerson (1803-1882) is acclaimed as the chief spokesman of New England Transcendentalism* (the summit of American Romanticism). Transcendentalism has been defined philosophically as the recognition in man of the capacity of knowing truth intuitively, or of attaining knowledge transcending the reach of the senses. Emerson's fame comes mainly from his ability as a speaker. His essays are usually derived from his lectures. Hence, his writing has a casual style. Emerson is generally known as an essayist. Among his best are *Nature* (1836) and *Essays* (1841, 1844).

Nathaniel Hawthorne (1804-1864) is an outstanding American Romanticist and a pioneer in psychological description. He tried to find out how men reacted in their mind when they found they had done something wrong. He exposed the evils of society by means of describing the psychological activities of human beings. His most famous novel is *The Scarlet Letter* (1850), in which he probes into the guilty conscience of two lovers, who commit adultery (通奸). *The Scarlet Letter* is not a praise of a sinning woman, but a hymn on the moral growth of her who had been sinned against. His other works include *The House of the Seven Gables* (1851), *The Blithedale Romance* (1852) and *The Marble Faun* (1860).

Edgar Allan Poe (1809-1849) is a lonely writer both in life and in literary history. His literary output is not small considering his short life: He wrote poetry, short stories and many reviews of literary works. Yet literary historians find it hard to categorize him. His strange theme and style makes him an outsider of the main current of American literature. In both his lifetime and many years after his death, his works were not well received by his own countrymen. Yet foreigners acclaimed him as a genius, especially the French poets of symbolism adored him as their precursor (先驱). His masterpieces include *The Raven* (1845), a long poem, and some excellent horror stories, like "The Fall of the House of Usher" (1839).

Herman Melville's (1819-1891) fame was established with *Moby Dick* (1851). It is now acknowledged to be one of the world's great masterpieces, but in the writer's lifetime, it suffered oblivion (遗忘) and misunderstanding. His theme may have been too far advanced for his contemporaries. When most people were extolling (赞美) the

---

* Transcendentalism: 超验主义，19世纪三四十年代在欧洲浪漫主义运动的影响下形成的文学和哲学思潮，宣称存在一种理想的精神实体，超越于经验和科学之外，可以通过直觉把握。

power of man and the progress of science and life, he presented a bleak view of the world, in which the universe is Godless and purposeless, and human life meaningless and futile.

Poetry

American poetry can be traced to two founts (源泉), Walt Whitman and Emily Dickinson. Being part of the Romantic Movement, their poetry explores and extols the emerging America and finds a poetic voice for its Americanness.

Walt Whitman (1819-1892) is remembered for his verse collection *Leaves of Grass* (1855), which is about man and nature. In his poetry, Whitman combines the ideal of the democratic common man and that of the rugged individual.

Whitman is one of the great innovators in American literature. The poetic style he devised is now called free verse, that is, poetry without a fixed beat or regular rhyme scheme. Whitman felt that the voice of democracy should not be limited by traditional forms of verse. He wanted his poetry to be for the common people, but ironically, it was ignored by the general public because of his unconventional style.

Emily Dickinson (1830-1886) is different from Whitman in many ways. Whereas Whitman turned to the outer world and embraced society, democracy and the nation, Dickinson cast her eyes inward to explore the inner feelings of the individual. Physically, the world she lived in was very small. For most of her life, she lived in her father's house in a New England village and seldom left it except for a short visit to Washington, D.C. Furthermore, due to her shy and sensitive nature, she generally avoided visitors and led a reclusive (隐居的) life. Her poems are short; the longest is but 50 lines. The real world, the great issues and events of her time, remain invisible in these concise lines, neither are there people. Nature with its marvelous creatures and phenomena dwells in her world, and metaphysical (形而上学的) thinking like death and immortality occupies her mind. Her most famous poems include "My Life Closed Twice Before Its Close", "Because I Could Not Stop for Death" and "A Narrow Fellow in the Grass". With a few plain and direct words, she constructs a wonderful world that is small, but intense, fresh, individual and original. That is where her charm lies.

惠特曼

III. The Realistic Period

American Realism came in the latter half of the 19th century as a reaction against Romanticism. It stresses truthful treatment of material. It expresses concern for the world of experience, for the commonplace, for the familiar and the low. The three dominant figures of the period are Mark Twain, Henry James and William Dean Howells.

Mark Twain (1835-1910) is the pen name of Samuel Langhorne Clemens. Early 19th-century American writers tended to be too flowery and sentimental, partially because they were still trying to prove that they could write as elegantly as the British could. However, Twain's style—based on vigorous, realistic, colloquial American speech—gave American writers a new appreciation for their national voice. Twain was the first major author to come from the interior of the country, and he well captured its distinctive, humorous slang and iconoclasm (对传统观念和习俗的反对).

马克·吐温

The Adventures of Huckleberry Finn (1884) is Twain's masterpiece, and Hemingway noted it as a book from which "all modern American literature comes". The story takes place along the Mississippi River. Huck, the son of an alcoholic bum (流浪汉), runs away from his abusive father. Another outcast (被遗弃者), the slave Jim, joins in his escape. Huck and Jim float on a raft down the majestic Mississippi. They go through many comical and dangerous adventures that show the variety, generosity and sometimes cruel irrationality of society. The book is concerned with Huck's inner struggle between his sense of guilt for helping Jim escape and his profound conviction that Jim is a human being. Through their escape down the river, he gets to know Jim better and finally accepts Jim not only as a human being, but also as a loyal friend.

Mark Twain's other famous novels are *The Adventures of Tom Sawyer* (1876), *The Prince and the Pauper* (1881), *Life on the Mississippi* (1883), *The Man That Corrupted Hadleyburg and Other Stories and Sketches* (1900), etc.

One of Mark Twain's great contributions is that he made colloquial speech an accepted, respectable literary medium in American literature. This style swept across the American literary world and its influence was far-reaching.

Henry James (1843-1916) is a writer who not only bridges the 19th and 20th centuries but also connects America and Europe. James' fame rests mainly upon his major fictional theme—the meeting of America and Europe. The Europeans in James' novels are more cultured, more concerned with art and more aware of the subtleties of social situations, while the Americans usually display a morality and innocence which the Europeans lack. For Americans, it is a process of progression from inexperience to experience, from innocence to knowledge and maturity. James seems to value both the sophistication of Europe and the idealism of America. His major works are *The American* (1877), *Daisy Miller* (1878), *The Portrait of a Lady* (1881), *The Wings of the Dove* (1902) and *The Golden Bowl* (1904).

William Dean Howells (1837-1920) is both an eminent critic and a prolific (多产的) writer. To him, realism is by no means mere photographic pictures of externals, but includes a central concern with "motives" and psychological conflicts. Howells wrote volumes of drama, poetry and novels in addition to criticism, travelogs (游记) and an autobiography. The greatest of all his works is *The Rise of Silas Lapham* (1885). Silas Lapham is a self-made man who starts his paint business from scratch and becomes a millionaire but ends up in ruin. Although he falls and suffers, he manages to keep a greater number of people from suffering. Falling, he achieves his moral and ethical "rise".

IV. The Naturalistic Period

In the 1890s, French Naturalism appealed to the imagination of the American younger generation of writers like Stephen Crane, Theodore Dreiser and Frank Norris. It applies the principles of scientific determinism to fiction and drama. It views human beings as animals in a natural world responding to environmental forces and internal stresses and drives, over which they have no control and none of which they can fully understand.

Stephen Crane (1871-1900) is an American novelist, poet and short-story writer. In his first novel *Maggie: A Girl of the Streets* (1893), he tells of a good woman's downfall and destruction in a slum environment. *The Red Badge of Courage* (1895) is Crane's finest book. Against the romantic view of war as a symbol of courage and heroism, Crane regards war as a slaughterhouse (屠宰场).

Theodore Dreiser (1871-1945) is one of the first important writers to come from the lower society. His novels deal with everyday life, often its sordid (卑鄙的) side. He finds that the American values are materialistic to the core. Living in such a society with such a value system, the human individual is obsessed with a never-ending, yet meaningless search for satisfaction of their desires. One of the desires is money, the other sex. He embraces social Darwinism and advocates the idea of "the survival of the fittest".

Dreiser is also famous for *Sister Carrie* (1900) and his *Trilogy* (三部曲) *of Desire*, which includes *The Financier* (1912), *The Titan* (1914) and *The Stoic* (1947). *An American Tragedy* (1925) is his masterpiece. It describes the life of a youth who becomes a corrupted murderer from a very innocent, naive boy. It exposes the evils of society that corrupt men, especially the young.

V. The Modern Period

The Lost Generation*

After World War I, many novelists produced a literature of disillusionment. F. Scott Fitzgerald and Ernest Hemingway are the spokesmen for the Lost Generation, which refers to the young American writers caught up in the war and cut off from the old values, yet unable to come to terms with the new era when civilization has gone mad.

F. Scott Fitzgerald's (1896-1940) major works are *Tales of the Jazz Age* (1922), *The Beautiful and Damned* (1922) and *Tender Is the Night* (1934). His *The Great Gatsby* (1925) is a masterpiece in American literature. The protagonist (主人公) of the novel, the mysterious Jay Gatsby, discovers the devastating cost of success in terms of personal fulfillment and love. Gatsby's life follows a clear pattern. There is, at first, a dream, then disenchantment (醒悟), and finally a sense of failure and despair. Gatsby's failure magnifies to a great extent the end of the American Dream.

---

* the Lost Generation: 迷惘的一代，第一次世界大战后美国的一个文学流派。其作品大多描写人们在"美国梦"破灭后的迷惘、彷徨和失落。

Chapter 13 Literature

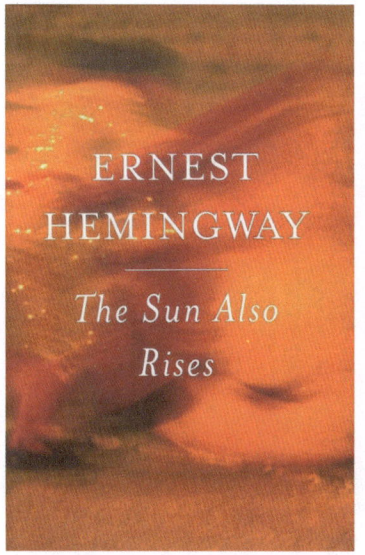

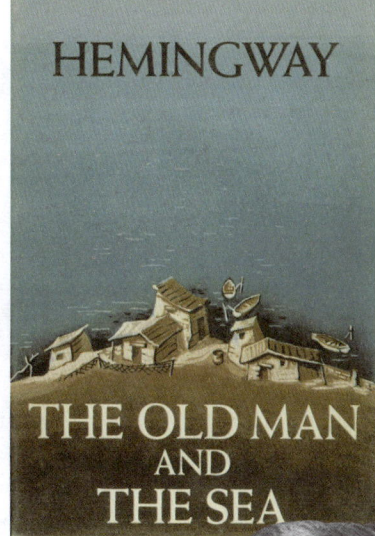

Ernest Hemingway (1899-1961), a Nobel Prize winner for literature, is one of the best-known American writers of the 20th century. His major works include *The Sun Also Rises* (1926), *A Farewell to Arms* (1929), *For Whom the Bell Tolls* (1940) and *The Old Man and the Sea* (1952).

Hemingway's world is essentially chaotic and meaningless, in which man fights a solitary struggle against a force he does not even understand. Being aware that it must end in defeat, no matter how hard he fights against it, the Hemingway hero still possesses a "despairing courage". It is this courage that enables a man to behave like a man, to assert their dignity in the face of adversity (逆境).

In terms of writing style, Hemingway follows Mark Twain's colloquialism. He chooses words concrete, specific, casual and conversational, and employs them in short, simple sentences, which are orderly and patterned, sometimes ungrammatical.

海明威

Modern Poetry

Ezra Pound (1885-1972) is one of the most influential American poets of the 20th century. He is a link between the United States and Britain, spearheading (充当先锋) the new school of poetry known as Imagism, which advocates a clear, highly visual presentation.

He argues for a modern-sounding, visual poetry that avoids clichés (陈词滥调) and set phrases. He defines "image" as something that "presents an intellectual and emotional complex in an instant of time".

171

Pound's interests and reading are universal. His translations introduce new literary possibilities from many cultures to modern writers. His life work is *The Cantos*, a collection of poems. They contain brilliant passages, but their allusions to works of literature and art from many eras and cultures make them difficult.

VI. The Contemporary Period

Black Writers

Since the 1930s black writers have got involved in the mainstream of American literature. Richard Wright's (1908-1960) *Native Son* (1940) and Ralph Ellison's (1914-1994) *Invisible Man* (1952) capture the wide attention of the white readers with truthful, open and shocking description of the life of black people. James Baldwin's (1924-1987) *Go Tell It on the Mountain* (1953) keeps the readers conscious of an oppressed race groaning and struggling for salvation.

Langston Hughes (1902-1967) is known as African Americans' poet laureate and one of the most important literary figures of the Harlem Renaissance* of the 1920s. He embraces African-American jazz rhythms and incorporates blues, spirituals (圣歌), colloquial speech and folkways (社会习俗) in his poetry.

He is not merely a poet, but a playwright, novelist, editor, translator and newspaper columnist as well. He received many awards and honors for his writings, which have been translated into over 25 languages. His most beloved poem is "the Negro Speaks of Rivers" (1921) which embraces his African and universal heritage. The poem suggests that, like the great rivers of the world, African culture will endure and deepen.

Jewish Writers

Jewish writers also assume great importance at this time. Saul Bellow (1915-2005) is one of the most outstanding representatives of Jewish literature and he won the

---

* Harlem Renaissance: 哈莱姆文艺复兴，美国最著名的、也是最重要的一次黑人文艺复兴运动。哈莱姆文艺复兴的主要内容是加强作品的艺术表现能力，反对种族歧视，批判并否定汤姆叔叔型驯顺的旧黑人形象，鼓励黑人作家在艺术创作中歌颂新黑人的精神，树立新黑人的形象。

Nobel Prize for Literature in 1976. His famous works include *Dangling Man* (1944), *The Victim* (1947), *The Adventures of Augie March* (1953), *Henderson the Rain King* (1959), *Herzog* (1964), *Mr. Sammler's Planet* (1970) and *Humboldt's Gift* (1975).

The Jewish writers not only focus upon Jewish characters and social questions, but also bring a distinctively Jewish sense of humor to their works. Their works often carry echoes of Yiddish, the language used by European Jews that has helped preserve Jewish culture isolated but intact (完好无损的) until the early 20th century.

The Beat Movement*

Led by Allen Ginsberg (1926-1997), the Beat Movement began in the 1950s. The word "beat" suggests a non-conformist, rebellious attitude toward conventional values concerning sex, religion and the American way of life, an attitude that results from the feeling of depression and exhaustion and the need to escape into an unconventional, communal mode of life. The central Beat writers include Allen Ginsberg, William Burroughs (1914-1997) and Jack Kerouac (1922-1969).

They reject the carefully written works of their contemporary writers. They want to express "raw" emotion, exactly as it is felt, rather than "cooked" emotion through memory and translation into art. Allen Ginsberg's *Howl* (1956), Jack Kerouac's *On the Road* (1957) and William Burroughs' *Naked Lunch* (1959) are representative works.

Literature of the Modern South

William Faulkner (1897-1962) is a giant in the realm of American literature. He is acclaimed throughout the world as one of the 20th century's greatest writers and was awarded the 1949 Noble Prize for Literature. His major works include *The Sound and the Fury* (1929), *As I Lay Dying* (1930), *Light in August* (1932), *Absalom, Absalom!* (1936) and *Go Down, Moses* (1942). Critics generally agree that he accomplished in a little over a decade more artistically than most writers could accomplish over a lifetime of writing. Although most of his stories are set in a small southern county, their exploration of basic human nature and basic patterns of human behavior makes them enduring works in the world literature.

---

* the Beat Movement: 垮掉的一代运动。垮掉的一代（the Beat Generation）是美国文学史上一个奇特的文学流派，是后现代主义的先驱、嬉皮运动的鼻祖，以离经叛道、惊世骇俗的生活方式与文学主张撼动了 20 世纪五六十年代美国的主流文化价值观与社会观，为青年人提供了一种新的生活选择，唤醒了美国民众的民主意识。

托尼·莫里森

Women's Voices

The feminist movement during the 1960s and the 1970s greatly affected women's relationship with the opposite sex as well as American culture. Many women writers exerted their influence on the world literature.

Toni Morrison (1931-) was awarded the Nobel Prize for Literature in 1993, and she was the first African-American writer to win a Nobel Prize. In her works, Morrison explores the experience of black women in a racist culture. Her famous novels are *The Bluest Eye* (1970) and *Beloved* (1987). The latter is about a slave who escapes with her children and when recaptured, attempts to kill her children rather than return them to a life of slavery.

Alice Walker (1944-) received the Pulitzer Prize[1] for *The Color Purple* (1982). She was active in the civil rights movement[2] of the 1960s and spoke for the women's movement and the anti-nuclear movement. Her works concern sexual and racial realities within black communities and unavoidable connections between family and society as well. Walker usually portrays men negatively. Her fiction weaves back and forth through time and individual perspectives, and her characters seek redemption (拯救), forgiveness and peace.

---

1 Pulitzer Prize: 普利策奖，于 1917 年设立。现设有新闻奖（14 项）和艺术奖（7 项）两大类奖项。
2 civil rights movement: 民权运动，第二次世界大战后美国黑人反对种族隔离与歧视、争取民主权利的运动。

Amy Tan (1952-) is a Chinese-American writer. Her books portray the lives of Chinese-American daughters and their Chinese immigrant mothers. Tan's first two novels, *The Joy Luck Club* (1989) and *The Kitchen God's Wife* (1991), focus on the relationship between mother and daughter. In her works, Tan deals with the characters' conflicting emotions, which are associated with being native-born Americans of Chinese ancestry.

Drama

The 20th century witnessed the rise of American drama. Drama began to turn up as an influential literary form in American literature. Eugene O'Neill, Tennessee Williams and Arthur Miller are three representative playwrights.

Eugene O'Neill (1888-1953) is undoubtedly America's greatest playwright. He won the 1936 Nobel Prize for Literature and the Pulitzer Prize four times. He is the first American playwright to regard drama as serious literature. O'Neill's plays are highly experimental in form and style, combining literary theories of symbolism, naturalism and expressionism. He has great influence on later American playwrights.

O'Neill's famous plays include *Beyond the Horizon* (1920), *Anna Christie* (1922), *The Hairy Ape* (1922), *Desire Under the Elms* (1924), *Strange Interlude* (1928), *The Iceman Cometh* (1946) and *Long Day's Journey into Night* (1956).

O'Neill is a sensitive artist. He feels "the discordant (不协调的), broken, faithless rhythm" of his time and tries to probe into the root of human desires and frustrations. The tragic sense of modern man being impotent (无能为力的) remains with O'Neill through his career. Most of his plays are very pessimistic, leaving the characters without illusion and hope.

Tennessee Williams (1911-1983) is also one of the great talents in American drama. Besides being a dramatist, he also wrote one novel, two volumes of poetry and six volumes of prose, including three collections of short stories. His representative works are *The Glass Menagerie* (1944), *A Streetcar Named Desire* (1947), *Cat on a Hot Tin Roof* (1955) and *Suddenly Last Summer* (1958). Williams was awarded the Pulitzer Prize for *A Streetcar Named Desire* and *Cat on a Hot Tin Roof*.

Williams portrays the isolated and lonely people in American society in his works. He is excellent at creating pathetic women, and Laura, heroine in *The Glass Menagerie*, is a typical one. As a fragile girl, Laura lives in her illusion, only to be smashed to pieces by a male intruder, who is the symbol of reality.

Arthur Miller (1915-2005) definitely deserves the title of "social dramatist" since all of his works concern the conflicts of the individual within society and present a social critique of the inhuman capitalist system.

戏剧《推销员之死》的海报

His masterpiece *Death of a Salesman* (1949) presents the miserable life and tragic death of the salesman Willy Loman. Willy is a hard-working and good-natured salesman who holds firm in his conviction about achieving the American Dream. His dream is indeed not very ambitious. He wants to establish his own business, pay off the mortgage on his house, have successful children and live happily and peacefully with his family. Unfortunately, reality is harsh and cruel. The company decides to dismiss him because he is getting old. His two sons turn out to be losers in society. Disillusioned, he desperately kills himself in order to get the life insurance money for his family.

Miller's other important plays include *All My Sons* (1947), *The Crucible* (1953) and *A View from the Bridge* (1955).

Exercises

I. **Read the following statements and decide whether they are true (T) or false (F).**

_____ 1. Walt Whitman introduced great innovations to American literature, and devised a poetic style, free verse.

_____ 2. Emily Dickinson's poems are usually long, exploring the inner life of the individual.

_____ 3. Stephen Crane is famous for his writings about the meeting of America and Europe.

_____ 4. Ezra Pound leads the School of Imagism, which advocates a clear, highly visual presentation.

_____ 5. Jack Kerouac's *On the Road* is a representative work of the Beat Writers.

_____ 6. Alice Walker was passionate about the civil rights movement and the women's movement of the 1960s, and *The Color Purple* is her masterpiece.

Chapter 13 Literature

_____ 7. America's most renowned playwright is Tennessee Williams, and his plays are highly experimental in form and style.

_____ 8. Arthur Miller is concerned with the conflicts of the individual within society, and *Death of a Salesman* is his masterpiece.

II. **Choose the best answer to complete each of the following statements.**

1. Of the following writers, _____ are from the Colonial and Revolutionary Periods.
    A. Benjamin Franklin and Edgar Allan Poe
    B. Edgar Allan Poe and Jonathan Edwards
    C. Benjamin Franklin and Jonathan Edwards
    D. Edgar Allan Poe and Washington Irving

2. _____ is regarded as the "father of American literature".
    A. James Fenimore Cooper   B. Ralph Waldo Emerson
    C. Thomas Jefferson   D. Washington Irving

3. Of the following, _____ is considered Herman Melville's masterpiece.
    A. *The Last of the Mohicans*   B. *The Legend of Sleepy Hollow*
    C. *Moby Dick*   D. *Daisy Miller*

4. Of the following, _____ is NOT characteristic of Mark Twain's works.
    A. colloquial speech   B. a sense of humor
    C. a realistic view   D. an idealistic view

5. Of the following writers, _____ is NOT included in the group of naturalists.
    A. Stephen Crane   B. Frank Norris
    C. Theodore Dreiser   D. Herman Melville

6. F. Scott Fitzgerald's finest novel is _____, and its theme is about _____.
    A. *The Great Gatsby*, the American Dream
    B. *Tender Is the Night*, love
    C. *Tales of the Jazz Age*, the loss of oneself
    D. *The Beautiful and Damned*, the evil of human nature

7. Of the following writers, _____ is NOT a Nobel Prize winner.
    A. Alice Walker   B. Ernest Hemingway
    C. William Faulkner   D. Eugene O'Neill

8. _____ is the first African-American winner of the Nobel Prize for Literature.
    A. Ralph Ellison   B. Toni Morrison
    C. Richard Wright   D. James Baldwin

III. Give brief answers to the following questions.

1. What is the essence of American Puritanism?

2. What is the Lost Generation?

3. What is the Beat Movement?

IV. State your understanding of the following questions.

1. What are the characteristics of the American writing during the Romantic Period?
2. Why is Eugene O'Neill regarded as the greatest American playwright?

Learn and Check

The Colonial and Revolutionary Periods: Jonathan Edwards, Benjamin Franklin, Thomas Jefferson

The Romantic Period: Washington Irving, James Fenimore Cooper, Ralph Waldo Emerson, Nathaniel Hawthorne, Edgar Allan Poe, Herman Melville, Walt Whitman, Emily Dickinson

The Realistic Period: Mark Twain, William Dean Howells, Henry James

The Naturalistic Period: Stephen Crane, Theodore Dreiser, Frank Norris

The Modern Period: F. Scott Fitzgerald, Ernest Hemingway, Ezra Pound

The Contemporary Period: Richard Wright, Ralph Ellison, James Baldwin, Langston Hughes, Saul Bellow, Allen Ginsberg, William Burroughs, Jack Kerouac, William Faulkner, Toni Morrison, Alice Walker, Amy Tan, Eugene O'Neill, Tennessee Williams, Arthur Miller

Chapter 14 Geography and History

> ### ▼ Think and Talk
> ▶ What do you know about the major cities of Canada—Ottawa, Toronto, Montréal, Québec city, Vancouver?
> ▶ How did Canada get its name?
> ▶ Who were the first Europeans to settle in Canada?

I. Geography

Location and Size

Canada has a landmass of nearly 10 million square kilometers, almost as big as the whole of Europe. The country's vast territory makes it the second largest country in the world in area after Russia. Its 10 provinces and three territories cover about two-fifths of the North American continent. From north to south, its territory sprawls (延伸) more than 4,600 kilometers. From east to west, the country stretches from the Atlantic Ocean to the Pacific Ocean, a distance that spans six time zones.

Geographical Regions

Canada's expansive area can be divided into five geographical regions, each with a distinct landscape and climate. These regions are the Atlantic Region, the Central Region, the Prairie Region, the Pacific Region and the Northern Region.

Canada has numerous lakes which cover about 7.6% of its landmass. Among them, the Great Lakes on the border between Canada and the U.S. are the largest group of freshwater lakes in the world. Canada shares with the U.S. Niagara Falls, one of the most spectacular natural wonders on the North American continent.

Canada is abundant in forest resources. In fact, about 45% of the country is

落基山脉

covered with forest. Westward, toward the Pacific Ocean, the area is covered by mountain ranges from north to south including the Rocky Mountains. The country's highest peak is Mount Logan (洛根山), about 5,959 meters.

Climate

Canada has a typical continental climate, characterized by cold winters, hot summers and sparse rainfall. The country's vast territory and unique topography (地形) result in a climate with wide regional variations. The Pacific Region has a relatively moderate climate. Mild summers and winters, high humidity and abundant rainfall are all characteristics of this region. In the central southern area of the interior plains, the climate is marked by cold winters, hot summers and sparse precipitation. Canadians enjoy four very distinct seasons. However, the average temperature is below freezing for seven months a year along the Arctic Circle.

Canada

Major Cities

渥太华圣母大教堂

Canada's capital and its major cities are situated in the south, near its border with the United States. Ottawa (渥太华) is the fourth largest city and the capital city of Canada. Unlike the capital cities of countries like the United States and Australia, there is no federal capital district in Canada. Ottawa is a municipality (自治市) within the province of Ontario (安大略省).

多伦多

Toronto (多伦多), the capital of Ontario, is the largest city in Canada, with an area of about 630 square kilometers. Toronto is one of the most multicultural cities in the world. About 2.5 million people from about 80 different ethnic backgrounds call Toronto their home. Toronto also has the distinction of being Canada's financial and commercial center.

蒙特利尔体育场

Montréal (蒙特利尔), in the province of Québec (魁北克省), is the second largest city in Canada and the largest city of the province. It held the 21st Olympic Games in 1976. It is often said to be the second largest French-speaking city in the world after Paris.

Chapter 14 Geography and History

魁北克

Located on the shores of the St. Lawrence River, Québec city is the capital of the province of Québec. To differentiate between Québec the city and Québec the province, the city is commonly referred to as Québec city while the province is referred to as Québec. Québec city is the second largest city in Québec and the second oldest existing European settlement in Canada. The majority of the population is Roman Catholic and French-speaking, along with a sizable Jewish and Protestant population.

Vancouver (温哥华) is a city in the province of British Columbia. It is the major urban center of western Canada and the third largest city in the country. As Canada's main connection to the Pacific Rim countries (环太平洋国家), Vancouver has become increasingly ethnically diverse as large numbers of Chinese, Japanese and other East Asians settled in the city. Chinese are by far the largest ethnic minority group in Vancouver. Vancouver has the second largest Chinatown in North America after San Francisco. Compared to other cities and regions, Vancouver has a very low rate of church attendance, and the majority of its population does not practice religion seriously. Vancouver is internationally renowned for its scenic setting and it regularly ranks among the top cities worldwide in annual quality-of-life surveys. It has one of North America's largest urban parks, Stanley Park (斯坦利公园).

温哥华

II. History

Discovery and Exploration

Canada is a relatively young country. Before the European discovery, Canada was populated by Indian and Inuit[1] tribes. The name "Canada" is said to have derived from the Huron[2] word "Kanata", meaning "a village or settlement".

In 1497 an Italian sea captain, John Cabot, sailed west from Bristol (布里斯托尔), Britain, searching for a new route to Asia. Instead, this voyage led to the discovery of the eastern shores of Canada, which Cabot claimed as Newfoundland. The French exploration of Canada began in 1534. Jacques Cartier, a French navigator, also in an attempt to find new routes to the Orient (东方国家), explored the Canadian coast and the St. Lawrence River (1534, 1535, 1541-1542), and visited what is today Québec city and Montréal.

When the European explorers returned home, they brought back the news that their Newfoundland was abundant in fish and other natural resources. Consequently, throughout the rest of the 16th century, European fishing fleets continued to make almost annual visits to the eastern shores of Canada. Thus, trading with the local Indians began to develop at the fishing site. At the same time, with the development of unorganized traffic in furs, the Canadian fur trade, later fur monopoly, gradually began to take shape.

---

1 Inuit: 指生活在西伯利亚北部、加拿大、阿拉斯加和格陵兰岛的伊努伊特人。
2 Huron: 休伦语，休伦族人的语言。

Chapter 14 Geography and History

European Settlement

In the early 1600s, both Britain and France founded permanent settlements in Canada. In 1608, France founded a colony at what is now Québec city, the root of French Canada. Through the 17th century, French colonies extended from the St. Lawrence River to the Great Lakes and from there to the Great Plains and the Mississippi Valley. Later, with the rapid growth of English colonies along the Atlantic seaboard, Britain and France soon became rivals in the gradual conquest of those parts of North America which had not been claimed by the Spanish. The decisive struggle took place during the 1750s when the famous Seven Years' War started. After the war, France lost all of its colonies, and the whole Canada came under the British control. The British named the French colony on the St. Lawrence River the province of Québec, but still allowed the French colonists to stay on.

British Canada

Britain faced immediate problems in the vast territory. In order to deal with the French population, in 1774, the British Parliament passed the Québec Act (《魁北克法案》), which granted the people of Québec linguistic and religious freedom, and guaranteed the use of French civil law and British criminal law. The Québec Act was the first important milestone in a long line of efforts to cope with the differences between the French and the British people.

After the American War of Independence, thousands of American refugees who called themselves Loyalists and claimed to remain loyal to Britain made their way north to settle in such areas as present-day southern Ontario and laid the base of English-speaking Canada. Due to the protest of these colonists, with the Constitutional Act (《宪法法案》) in 1791, Canada was split into Upper Canada (English-speaking Ontario) and Lower Canada (French-speaking Québec). Both colonies have limited self-government and political organization. Consequently, revolts broke out in 1837 because of economic and religious discontent between the British and French communities. After the rebellions were put down in 1841, Upper Canada and Lower Canada united as the British colony, the Province of Canada.

Canadian Nation

Canada's road to political self-government began with the British North America Act (《英属北美法案》), 1867, also known as the Constitution Act, which created the self-governing Dominion of Canada. After confederation, under the leadership of the nation's major political parties, Canada experienced rapid growth in the following decades. After World War I, Canada's economy and business advanced significantly so that the country became an important member among the nations in the world. With the passage of the Statute of Westminster[1] in 1931, Canada was recognized as an equal partner of Britain. Since then, Canada has been a member of the British Commonwealth of Nations. During World War II, Canada fought as an ally of Britain. Like the U.S., Canada's geographic location protected it from the wartime destruction. After the war, tremendous development took place in industry and agriculture, and Canada emerged as the world's fourth largest industrial nation.

The federal government's power increased in the 1950s to its historical height. With taxing and spending power gained from the provinces, the Liberal government led by Mackenzie King laid the foundations of the Canadian welfare state. Old age pensions were increased, unemployment insurance was expanded and federal-provincial welfare programs grew rapidly. In 1949, Newfoundland was incorporated into Canada as the 10th province.

Between 1946 and 1961, Canada's population increased from 12 million to 18 million due to the post-war baby boom and immigration, mostly from Europe. The face of urban Canada began to change. By 1961, the country had become one of the world's most urbanized nations, with more than 70% of all Canadians living in towns and cities. Television and other mass communications, mass merchandising and suburbanization accelerated social and cultural mobility. Women's roles were changing, too, with a significant increase in female participation in the workforce.

With its economic strength, Canada began to take an active role in international relations. Since the 1950s, Canada has involved itself in foreign aid programs for developing nations and peacekeeping missions to settle disputes in foreign countries. Canadian diplomat and politician Lester Pearson (1897-1972) won the Nobel Prize for Peace in 1957 for organizing a peacekeeping force to defuse (平息) the Suez Crisis[2].

莱斯特·皮尔森

---

1 Statute of Westminster:《威斯敏斯特法案》，它正式确立了英国和各自治领的关系，承认其自治领在内政、外交上独立，均为英联邦内自由和平等的国家。
2 Suez Crisis: 苏伊士运河危机。战争源于埃及将苏伊士运河收归国有，由于涉及石油运输等问题，英国、法国、以色列组成的联盟国家与之发生冲突。为避免局势进一步恶化，当时作为加拿大驻联合国常任代表的莱斯特·皮尔森出面调停，最终战争得以结束。

Chapter 14 Geography and History

In the 1960s, Québec wanted to separate from Canada and to establish a French-speaking nation. The Québec sovereignty movement led to referenda in 1980 and 1995, with its proposals for independence being rejected by the voters.

When the Organization of Petroleum Exporting Countries (OPEC)* cut back oil production in 1973, the world oil price rose dramatically. As an oil exporter, Canada profited from the oil-price increase. However, the Canadian economic stagnation persisted through the 1970s. Inflation continued to soar; chronic unemployment rose to double digits; though taxes continued to rise, the national budget deficit increased. While Canada struggled with its domestic problems, it played an increasingly important and more independent role in world affairs not only economically but also politically. During the 1970s, Canada strengthened its ties with China and the Soviet Union, and opposed the American war in Vietnam. Therefore, the relationship between Canada and the U.S. became strained.

Canada Since the 1980s

The Canada Act (《加拿大法案》) of 1982 made Canada a fully sovereign state. Around mid-1982, Canada was in its worst economic recession since the 1930s. Nearly 13% of the labor force was out of work. Meanwhile, as the Canadian dollar fell to a record low against the U.S. dollar, the annual rate of inflation rose to more than 11%. Partly because the government had not been able to reverse the economic trend, the Liberal Prime Minister Pierre Trudeau retired from his post as head of the government and party leader. Brian Mulroney, the leader of the Progressive Conservative Party, became Prime Minister in 1984. He made national unity a high priority and sought to amend the Constitution so that Québec could accept it. In 1987, the federal and provincial governments signed the Meech Lake Accord (《米其湖协议》) that was acceptable to the Premier of Québec. It gave all the provinces substantial new powers and recognized Québec as a "distinct society".

Many people saw the Meech Lake Accord as an attempt to weaken or even dismantle (取消) the power of the federal government, and regarded the special status of Québec as unfair and problematic. In 1990, the Accord was defeated. In 1992, the Mulroney government came up with another accord known as the Charlottetown Accord (《夏洛特敦协议》), which addressed greater autonomy for both Québec and

---

* the Organization of Petroleum Exporting Countries (OPEC): 石油输出国组织，简称"欧佩克"，成立于 1960 年 9 月，现有 12 个成员国。

the aboriginal population. It also failed in a national referendum.

The Mulroney government adopted a different economic agenda. It weakened government intervention in the national economy. Many state-owned enterprises such as the publicly-owned airline and oil companies were privatized. The government's investment in developing regions was greatly reduced. After Mulroney retired from the post as Prime Minister, Kim Campbell became Canada's first woman Prime Minister in June 1993. However, she and her Progressive Conservative Party were defeated by the Liberals in the national election that October.

The Liberal government, led by Jean Chrétien, continued with many of the Progressive Conservative Party's economic and social policies. It cut government spending and at the same time maintained the high tax rates. It strongly supported private rather than public enterprises as the key source of economic growth. Therefore, Chrétien's government gained popularity among the Canadian people in its early years. However, the Canadian unemployment rate still stayed very high. Particularly, his government's failure to fulfill the promise to remove Mulroney's goods and services tax created a severe impact on the government's credibility. Despite these, Chrétien was the first Canadian Prime Minister since 1945 to win three consecutive majorities, and by the end of his premiership, his government had succeeded in ending 20 years of federal budget deficit and lowering the persistently high unemployment rate.

In 2003, the new leader of the Liberal Party, Paul Martin took office as Prime Minister. Martin's Liberal government tried to improve Canadian-U.S. relations, which had noticeably cooled in the later years of the Chrétien era, and it also forged a closer relationship with China by announcing the strategic partnership initiated during the Chinese President Hu Jintao's state visit to Canada in September 2005. Martin's Liberal government proposed a bill to legalize same-sex marriage across Canada. In 2005, the Civil Marriage Act was passed, making Canada the fourth country in the world to allow same-sex marriage.

Canada entered the 21st century with considerable wealth and prosperity, and the country, which has become a magnet for immigrants from throughout the world, has established its own distinctive cultural, economic and political identity.

Chapter 14 Geography and History

Exercises

I. **Read the following statements and decide whether they are true (T) or false (F).**

　　_____ 1. Canada is the second largest country in the world in terms of territory.

　　_____ 2. The lakes in Canada cover about 7.6% of the Canadian landmass.

　　_____ 3. Canada has a typical oceanic climate influenced by both the Atlantic Ocean and the Pacific Ocean.

　　_____ 4. The Seven Years' War led to the British control of most of the territories in Canada.

　　_____ 5. Canada was split into Upper Canada and Lower Canada in 1791.

　　_____ 6. During World War II, neutral policy protected Canada from the wartime destruction.

　　_____ 7. Chrétien's Liberal government succeeded in lowering the persistently high unemployment rate.

　　_____ 8. Canada was the first country in the world to allow same-sex marriage.

II. **Choose the best answer to complete each of the following statements.**

1. Canada's fur trade, later fur monopoly, gradually began to take shape in the _____ century.
   A. 15th　　　B. 16th　　　C. 17th　　　D. 18th

2. The Liberal government led by Mackenzie King did the following to lay the foundations of the Canadian welfare state EXCEPT _____.
   A. increasing the old age pensions
   B. promoting federal-provincial welfare programs
   C. expanding unemployment benefits
   D. introducing health insurance

3. _____ won the Nobel Prize for Peace in 1957 for organizing a peacekeeping force to defuse the Suez Crisis.
   A. Pierre Trudeau　　　B. Lester Pearson
   C. Jean Chrétien　　　D. Brian Mulroney

4. In the _____, Canada was obsessed with economic recession.
   A. 1950s   B. 1960s   C. 1970s   D. 1990s
5. Pierre Trudeau retired from his post as head of the government and party leader partly because _____.
   A. he opposed the American war in Vietnam
   B. he agreed Québec to be an independent French-speaking nation
   C. he had not been able to reverse the declining economic trend
   D. he weakened government intervention in the national economy
6. _____ recognized Québec as a "distinct society".
   A. The Meech Lake Accord   B. The Québec Act
   C. The Constitutional Act   D. The British North America Act
7. _____ was Canada's first woman Prime Minister.
   A. Pierre Trudeau   B. Brian Mulroney
   C. Jean Chrétien   D. Kim Campbell
8. Martin's Liberal government tried to do the following EXCEPT _____.
   A. legalizing same-sex marriage in Canada
   B. giving the Québec city sovereignty
   C. improving Canadian-U.S. relations
   D. forging a closer relationship with China

III. Give brief answers to the following questions.

1. What was the original purpose of John Cabot and Jacques Cartier when they came to Canada?

2. Why did the Meech Lake Accord fail in 1990?

3. How did Jean Chrétien's government gain popularity among the Canadian people in its early years?

Chapter 14 Geography and History

IV. **State your understanding of the following questions.**
   1. What is the Québec Issue in Canada?
   2. What are the similarities between the major cities of Canada?

Learn and Check

Geographical regions: the Atlantic Region, the Central Region, the Prairie Region, the Pacific Region, the Northern Region

Climate: a typical continental climate with cold winters, hot summers and sparse rainfall

Major cities: Ottawa (capital city), Toronto, Montréal, Québec city, Vancouver

Discovery and exploration of Canada: John Cabot in 1497; Jacques Cartier in1534, 1535 and 1541-1542

Major acts: the Québec Act (1774), the Constitutional Act (1791), the British North America Act (1867), the Canada Act (1982)

Chapter 15

Government and Society

▼ Think and Talk
- Who is the official head of Canada?
- What is the role of the Governor General?
- What is the difference between a "melting pot" and a "cultural mosaic"?
- What are the requirements for students to enter the Canadian universities?

I. Government

Canada is a constitutional monarchy with a federal system of parliamentary government and strong democratic traditions. The Canadian government consists of three parts: the legislature, the executive and the judiciary. The political system under which modern Canada operates is known as the Westminster system*. Since Canada's political structure is modeled after that of Britain and the United States, it can be described as both a federation like the U.S. and a constitutional monarchy like Britain.

The Legislature

The Parliament of Canada consists of the House of Commons, whose 308 members are elected, and the Senate, whose 105 members are appointed by the Governor General on the advice of the Prime Minister. The Senate functions primarily to investigate, review government legislation and debate key national and regional issues. The Prime Minister is often the leader of the majority party in Parliament, and selects the ministers who make up the Cabinet. Together, they are responsible to the House of Commons.

---

* Westminster system: 威斯敏斯特体系。它是一种特殊的议会民主制，源于英国。在这种体系中，行政体系必须向立法体系负责，政府首脑以国家元首的名义行使职权。

Chapter 15 Government and Society

On average, members of the House of Commons are elected for a maximum of five-year term. If the House of Commons loses confidence in the government, the Prime Minister and his Cabinet are expected either to resign or to ask for Parliament to be dissolved so that a general election can be held.

The Executive

As a self-governing member of the Commonwealth, Canada recognizes the British monarch as the official head of state. While all government actions are carried out in the King's or Queen's name, it is in fact the people of Canada, through their elected representatives, who have the authority to exercise the power.

In the Canadian parliamentary system, the Governor General holds the highest position and is theoretically the source of executive power. It is the Governor General's responsibility to summon the House of Commons and the Senate, to give Royal Assent to all federal laws passed by the House, to open and end sessions of Parliament, and to dissolve Parliament before an election. In practice, however, the Governor General is only the symbolic executive who can act only on the advice of the Canadian Prime Minister and the Cabinet.

The Canadian government is divided into the federal government, provincial governments and territorial governments. The provincial governments share many

议会大厦

of the federal government's features except that none of the provinces has a second chamber equivalent to the Canadian Senate. A Lieutenant Governor represents the King or Queen in each province; their duties are similar to those of the Governor General. In addition, each province has a Premier who plays a public leadership similar to that of the State Governor in the United States. Canada's three territories also have their own governments, but with less power than those of the provinces.

The Judiciary

The courts in Canada are organized in a four-level structure. The Supreme Court serves as the final court of appeals in Canada. As the country's highest court, it hears both civil and criminal appeals from decisions of the courts of appeals in all the provinces and territories, as well as the federal court system headed by the Federal Court of Appeal. The Supreme Court also plays a special role as advisor to the federal government on questions concerning the Constitution and controversial or complicated areas of private and public laws.

The next level down from the Supreme Court consists of the Federal Court of Appeal and the various provincial courts of appeal.

Chapter 15 Government and Society

The next level down consists of the Federal Court, the Tax Court of Canada, and the provincial and territorial superior courts of general jurisdiction. These latter courts are the only courts in the system with inherent jurisdiction in addition to jurisdiction granted by federal and provincial statutes.

At the bottom of the hierarchy are the provincial courts. These courts are generally divided within each province into various divisions defined by the subject matter of their respective jurisdiction.

Political Parties

There are three main political parties in Canada, including the Liberal Party, the Conservative Party and the New Democratic Party.

The Liberal Party, founded in 1867, has been in office in Canada for most of Canadian history. The party combines a liberal social policy with a moderate economic policy.

The Conservative Party was formed by the merger of the Canadian Alliance (加拿大联盟党) and the Progressive Conservative Party (进步保守党) in 2003. The party formed a government in 2006. The party generally supports conservative social and economic policies, a strong federal system of government, and the use of Canada's armed forces in international peacekeeping missions.

The New Democratic Party, a democratic socialist party in Canada, was founded in 1961. It favors a mixed public-private economy, broadened social benefits and internationalist foreign policy.

Election

In Canada, each province has its own electoral system, and there is a national electoral system for the federal Parliament. Different systems share many similarities as well as significant differences. Canada's current electoral system is the result of increasing changes since the establishment of the Dominion of Canada in 1867. Nowadays, citizens aged 18 or older have the right to vote. In Canada, only two citizens cannot vote: the Chief Electoral Officer and the Deputy Chief Electoral Officer. The Chief Electoral Officer is responsible for administration of elections and referenda and other important aspects of Canada's electoral system. There is no fixed time for the elections in Canada. Constitutionally, elections must be held every five years, but by tradition, they are usually held at approximately four-year intervals, and can be called at any time especially when no single party has a majority in the House of Commons.

II. Society

Population

Canada is the second largest country in the world in terms of landmass, yet it ranks only 35th in terms of population with a population of about 35 million (2013). More than two-fifths of the people are Roman Catholics and nearly two-fifths are Protestants. Canada's population density is roughly four people per square kilometer, but this statistics is misleading because most parts of Canada are sparsely inhabited. Owing to the country's geographic and climate situation, the majority of the Canadian population is mainly concentrated along the southern border with the United States, an area that constitutes only about one-tenth of Canada's landmass.

Multicultural Society

1) Multilingualism

For historical reasons, the Canadian population is mainly characterized by its linguistic duality (双重性), with English and French being the two predominant languages. However, Canada is becoming a multilingual society. While most Canadians still speak either English or French at home, nearly one-fifth of the people are reported to have a mother tongue other than English or French. The most common mother tongues reported include Chinese, Italian, German and aboriginal languages, among which Chinese has become the third most common mother tongue in Canada.

2) Multiculturalism

Canada is also recognized as a multicultural nation in the wake of its diversified ethnic groups. Among the Canadian population, there are more than 30 ethnic groups, and many of these ethnic groups keep their own distinctive cultural characteristics.

Many factors have influenced the introduction of multicultural policy in Canada. The 1960s was marked by increasingly troubled British-French relations. A Royal Commission was set up to examine and recommend solutions to the outstanding problems. Organized ethnic communities demanded that their heritage also be

Chapter 15 Government and Society

acknowledged and argued that the old policy of assimilation was both unjust and a failure. In addition, the commissioners found that one-third of Canadians were neither English nor French. In its final report, the Royal Commission recommended the Canadian government to acknowledge the value of cultural pluralism and to encourage Canadian institutions to reflect this pluralism in their policies and programs. This new model of citizen participation, unlike the model of the United States which encourages citizens to be absorbed into the so-called "melting pot", promotes a "cultural mosaic"[1] in which people of diverse origins and communities are free to preserve and enhance their own cultural heritage while participating as equal partners in Canadian society.

In 1971, the government of Canada implemented a multicultural policy to recognize that pluralism was a fact of Canadian life. In 1988, the Canadian Multiculturalism Act (《加拿大多元文化法》) was passed. Canada became the first country in the world to pass a national multiculturalism law. As a result, the diversity of ethnicity, coupled with the government's multiculturalism policy, led to the emergence of multicultural Canada.

With globalization and the ever-increasing movement of people from one country to another, Canada's future depends on all its citizens committing to a unified Canadian identity while still taking pride in the uniqueness of their individual heritage. The multilingualism and multiculturalism together constitute a distinctly identifiable Canadian culture.

Immigration into Canada

Canada is an immigrant country, and immigration has played and continues to play a key role in shaping the character of Canadian society. However, before World War II, Canada used to have a racist immigration policy which actively discriminated against racial and religious minorities. It was after World War II that the Canadian government began to adopt a new policy, the "point system"[2], to eliminate prejudice. Since then, Canada has opened its door to immigrants of all races and religions from any countries.

---

1 cultural mosaic: 文化马赛克，指一种由多种文化元素结合而成的文化形式。在这种文化形式中，各种文化元素都保存着其自身的特点和传统。
2 point system: 点数制度，加拿大移民评估方式。

197

People migrate to Canada for different purposes. Some come to Canada as skilled workers and wish to get a Canadian work permit. Others may be interested in migration to Canada as investors or entrepreneurs. Whatever the purpose, applicants are required to pass the point system that Citizenship and Immigration Canada (加拿大公民及移民部) sets. Take skilled worker applicants for example, they need to earn at least 67 points out of 100 and have the funds required for settlement. The government of Canada would describe desirable skills it wanted in immigrants and different point levels assigned to potential immigrants according to how closely they could meet the criteria (the criteria often change depending on what type of immigrants are needed). Applicants get points for educational level, age, work experience, language ability, relatives living in Canada and personal adaptability, among other things. If you meet the basic requirements for immigration to Canada, you need to take a medical exam and pay an application fee, which is non-refundable even if you are not accepted. You also have to pay a landing fee, which is refundable if you are not accepted.

At the end of the 20th century, a kind of anti-immigrant sentiment spread throughout Canada because the native-born people believed immigrants were competing with them for job opportunities and creating serious social problems. The federal government thus announced changes in the immigration policy that decreased the number of immigrants allowed into Canada. Nowadays, this change in attitudes toward immigration and the subsequent changes in immigration rules have made it more difficult for people to move to Canada.

III. Economy

Canada is one of the world's wealthiest nations and the majority of its citizens enjoy a high quality of life by world standards.

Canada is renowned for the wealth of its natural resources: vast forests, fresh water, oil and gas, etc. Canada also has the world's richest mineral deposits. The service sector in Canada is the largest industry, employing some three quarters of Canadians. Manufacturing and fishing are also important economic activities in Canada.

Chapter 15 Government and Society

温哥华港

Canada is a free market economy and is highly integrated into the global economy. Due to its small population and limited domestic market, Canada is dependent on international trade, especially trade with the United States. Canada is one of the leading trading nations in the world, with the U.S., China, Britain and Japan being its largest trading partners. In the early colonial period, the leading Canadian export commodities were fish and furs. During the 19th century, timber became the staple export item. In the early 20th century, with the improvement of railway lines, wheat became the chief export item. Now, the exploration of minerals enables the manufacturing industries to produce more than half of Canada's exports.

After the recession of the early 1990s, the Canadian economy has grown more rapidly than that of most other developed countries, resulting from its low inflation, low interest rates and a low Canadian dollar (with respect to other major currencies), all of which helped exports grow. Today, with its abundant natural resources, skilled labor force and modern capital plant, Canada enjoys solid economic prospects.

IV. Education

Education in Canada is compulsory, that is, children from ages 6 to 16 are required by law to attend school. Public education is free to all citizens and permanent residents up to the end of secondary school. For parents seeking a better education for their children, they can send their children to a private school instead of a public school. Overall, being comprehensive, diversified and available to everyone, coupled with considerable financial commitment toward education, the Canadian educational system reflects the government's deep belief in the importance of education.

In Canada, the 10 provinces and three territories are responsible for elementary, secondary and university education, which means there are significant differences between the educational systems of different provinces and territories. As a result, Canada has no national or federal department of education. Each provincial system, while similar to others, bears some characteristics with respect to particular history and culture. However, standards across the country are uniformly high.

Elementary and Secondary Education

By law, children must attend school until the age of 15 or 16, depending on where they live. Children begin their education in elementary school at the age of 6 or 7. Elementary school usually starts with kindergarten for little children, but it may vary from school to school, or from province to province. For example, some provinces do not offer kindergarten in their educational system. Elementary school runs through to grade 6 or 8, and is followed by secondary school or high school. In some provinces, high school is divided into junior high and senior high. Students must complete high school to be admitted to college or university.

Higher Education

Canada has a large selection of universities and colleges located in both urban and rural settings in every region of the country. These universities are internationally known for the quality of teaching and research. Degrees from Canadian universities are considered equivalent to those from American and other Commonwealth

Chapter 15 Government and Society

universities. Students do not have to pass a university entrance exam, but they do need to achieve a minimum level in their final exams at secondary school in order to enter the university. To qualify for a degree program at most English-speaking universities, students for whom English is not their first language must pass an English examination test. The TOEFL and CAEL Assessment* are commonly accepted, but Canadian universities often have their own tests for students or may accept other English tests such as IELTS.

Major Universities

Laval University (拉瓦尔大学), originally founded in 1663, is the oldest French-speaking university in Canada, with its main campus located in Québec city.

The University of Toronto (多伦多大学), established in 1827, is now the largest university in Canada. Four Prime Ministers, two Governor Generals and numerous internationally recognized academic and business leaders graduated from this institution. It also boasts most Nobel Prize winning graduates among Canadian universities.

---

* CAEL Assessment: 全称为 Canadian Academic English Language Assessment，加拿大学术英文水平考试。它测试非英语国家的中学生申请在英语国家高等院校学习所应达到的英文水平。

多伦多大学

Exercises

I. Read the following statements and decide whether they are true (T) or false (F).

_____ 1. Canada's political structure has nothing to do with that of Britain and the United States.

_____ 2. The Canadian government is responsible to the King or Queen of Britain.

_____ 3. The Canadian court system is divided into four levels.

_____ 4. All Canadian citizens aged over 18 have the right to vote.

_____ 5. Multilingualism and multiculturalism are characteristic of the Canadian culture.

_____ 6. In Canada, different provinces and territories share the same educational system.

_____ 7. In Canada, children have to pass a university entrance exam in order to enter the university.

_____ 8. Laval University is the largest higher education institution in Canada, while the University of Toronto is the oldest one.

II. Choose the best answer to complete each of the following statements.

1. On average, members of the House of Commons are elected for a maximum of _____ years.
   A. three   B. four   C. five   D. six

2. _____ holds the highest position in the Canadian parliamentary system.
   A. The British Crown   B. The Governor General
   C. The President   D. The Prime Minister

3. In each province, _____ represents the British Crown.
   A. a Lieutenant Governor   B. a Governor General
   C. a Premier   D. a Governor

4. _____ of Canada serve(s) as the final court of appeals in Canada.
   A. The provincial courts   B. The Federal Court
   C. The Supreme Court   D. The Federal Court of Appeal

Chapter 15 Government and Society

5. In Canada, the largest religious denomination is _____.
   A. the Protestant church   B. the Roman Catholic church
   C. the Puritan church   D. the Anglican church
6. If applicants meet the basic requirements for immigration to Canada, they need to do the following EXCEPT _____.
   A. applying for citizenship   B. taking a medical exam
   C. paying an application fee   D. paying a landing fee
7. In the 19th century, _____ was the principal export item of Canada.
   A. fish   B. fur   C. timber   D. wheat
8. Canada's major trading partners include the following EXCEPT _____.
   A. Britain   B. America   C. Mexico   D. China

III. Give brief answers to the following questions.

1. What are the Governor General's responsibilities?

   _____
   _____

2. What are the characteristics of population distribution in Canada?

   _____
   _____

3. What does "cultural mosaic" mean in Canada?

   _____
   _____

IV. State your understanding of the following questions.

1. What are multilingualism and multiculturalism in Canada?
2. What is the immigration policy in Canada?

203

Learn and Check

The legislature: the House of Commons (308 elected members) and the Senate (105 appointed members)

The executive: the federal government, provincial governments, territorial governments

The judiciary: a four-level structure—the Supreme Court; the Federal Court of Appeal and provincial courts of appeal; the Federal Court, the Tax Court of Canada and the provincial and territorial superior courts of general jurisdiction; the provincial courts

Major political parties: the Liberal Party, the Conservative Party, the New Democratic Party

Population: about 35 million (2013)

Immigration: the "point system"

Major trading partners: the United States, China, Britain and Japan

Major universities: Laval University, the University of Toronto

Australia

Chapter 16

Geography and History

▼ Think and Talk
- What are the major cities of Australia?
- What were the effects of the gold rush in the 1850s?
- What is "White Australia Policy"?
- How was Australia influenced by the two World Wars?

I. Geography

Location and Size

Australia lies in the Southern Hemisphere, between the Indian Ocean and the Pacific Ocean. The country is surrounded by sea on all sides: the Pacific Ocean on the east, the Indian Ocean on the west, the Arafura Sea (阿拉弗拉海) on the north and the Southern Indian Ocean on the south. The Commonwealth of Australia, established in 1901, consists of mainland Australia, the island of Tasmania (塔斯马尼亚岛) and some other smaller islands. It is the only nation to govern an entire continent and its outlying islands. With a total area of nearly 7.7 million square kilometers, Australia is the sixth largest country in the world, after Russia, Canada, China, the U.S. and Brazil.

Geographical Regions

Australia is one of the oldest continents and the flattest landmass on earth. Even so, Australia possesses many different types of landscapes. Broadly speaking, Australia can be divided into three geographical regions: the Eastern Highlands, the Central Lowlands and the Western Plateau.

Stretching along the eastern coast of Australia, the Eastern Highlands are a series of mountain ranges and plateaus bordered by sandy beaches and rocky cliffs. The highest

Chapter 16 Geography and History

point of elevation in Australia, Mount Kosciuszko (科修斯科山), which rises to some 2,228 meters above sea level, is located here.

There is more rainfall on the eastern coastal plain than anywhere else in Australia. Rivers provide the water supply for both the forests on the eastern slope and the crops cultivated on the fertile western slope.

The Central Lowlands, lying to the southwest of the Eastern Highlands, include the area between the Gulf of Carpentaria (卡奔塔利亚湾) and the Great Artesian Basin (自流大盆地). They are the flattest and lowest part of Australia, with an average elevation of only 152 meters. At Lake Eyre (埃尔湖), the lowest point in the country, the elevation drops to some 15 meters below sea level. The Great Artesian Basin, which runs beneath the Central Lowlands, is the world's largest example of this type of geographical formation and accounts for approximately 20% of the continental landmass. This region boasts the second longest river in Australia, the Murray River (about 2,530 kilometers). Indeed, many rivers flow through the lowlands after heavy rains, but principally in the south of the Central Lowlands. Riverbeds far inland are often too dry or too hot for farming. Accordingly, the area has a small population.

The Western Plateau is an extensive region in western Australia. The average elevation of this area is around 300 to 450 meters above sea level, higher than elsewhere. However, the terrain (地貌) is predominantly flat and expansive.

Rainfall is heavy in northern and southwestern Australia, but the central region is covered with desert. The largest deserts, such as the Great Sandy Desert (大沙沙漠), the Gibson Desert (吉布森沙漠) and the Great Victoria Desert (维多利亚大沙漠), can be found inland.

Climate

Australia is located in the Southern Hemisphere, which means that its seasons are the reverse of those in the Northern Hemisphere. January and February are the hottest summer months, while June and July are the coldest winter months.

The climate of Australia varies greatly from region to region. In the tropical area of the north, which occupies around 40% of the country's total landmass, it is warm to extremely hot all year round and there is no winter. By contrast, the temperate regions of the south enjoy a moderate climate, with hot summers and mild winters. The coldest areas are the highlands and plateaus of Tasmania and the southeastern portion of the mainland.

Australia is widely known as "the Dry Continent" due to its low rainfall. The aridity (干旱) of Australia stems from its proximity to the equator. The deserts of the central and western region have an annual rainfall of less than 250 millimeters. Lake Eyre in South Australia has the country's lowest annual rainfall, around 100 millimeters, while the northern Queensland area, with an annual rainfall of around 4,050 millimeters, enjoys the wettest climate.

Major Cities

Over two-thirds of the Australian population live in big cities. The major urban centers of Australia include Canberra (堪培拉), Sydney, Melbourne (墨尔本), Brisbane (布里斯班), Perth (珀斯), Adelaide (阿德莱德) and Darwin (达尔文).

Canberra is the capital city of Australia and is located in the Australian Capital Territory. The name "Canberra" originally means "meeting place" in the Aboriginal language. Canberra houses many breathtaking landmarks and heritage buildings, such as Parliament House, the High Court of Australia and the National Museum of Australia.

Sydney is the capital city of New South Wales (新南威尔士州) and is Australia's largest and oldest city. Sydney has a population of over 4.4 million, and most of them live in the suburbs. Greater Sydney includes a very diverse ethnic mix, resulting in some great dining and cultural variations. It is also home to a great deal of Australia's historic sites, wildlife parks, great beaches, waterways and national parks.

堪培拉

Chapter 16 Geography and History

墨尔本

    Melbourne is the capital city of Victoria and is Australia's second largest city. The city is notable for its distinct blend of Victorian and contemporary architecture, extensive tram network, expansive parks and gardens and multicultural society. Since 2002, Melbourne has been consistently ranked among the World's Most Livable Cities by *The Economist*.

    The capital of Queensland is Brisbane, situated in the southeast of the province. It has a population of around 2.2 million and is the third largest city in Australia. The city is about one hour's drive from the Gold Coast, a famous tourist attraction in Australia.

    Perth is the capital of Western Australia. With a population of around 1.7 million, Perth is the fourth largest city in the country and the largest city in Western Australia.

    Adelaide is the capital of South Australia. The city has well established itself as a center for festivals as well as German cultural influences.

    Darwin is the only large city in northern Australia and is the capital of the Northern Territory (北领地). It is a prosperous, cosmopolitan city, a booming tourist destination and an important military base. It serves both as the front door to Australia's northern region and as Australia's gateway to Asia.

II. History

Early History

Contemporary historians agree that the history of Australia begins with the arrival of the Aborigines. The Aborigines were the first inhabitants of Australia. Most anthropologists believe they migrated from Asia between 50,000 and 60,000 years ago, when low sea levels permitted the simplest forms of land and water travel. They explored and settled on this vast continent, surviving on what the land provided. Instead of remaining permanently in one place, the Aboriginal people lived a nomadic (游牧的) or semi-nomadic life, seeking fresh supplies of animals and plants across the continent and moving on when food in each temporary settlement became scarce.

The Aborigines have a unique relationship with the environment. Not only are the means of their livelihood provided by the land, their religious beliefs are firmly linked to the land and those living things associated with it. To the Aborigines, not only does the land contain the ancestral spirits, it is also the source of life for the continuation of the people or the clans. Special ceremonies are held at these sites at particular times of the year to revere the totem (图腾) and to enable sacred myths to be transmitted to the younger generation. Plants and animals are also sacred to them. These living things are thought to contain the reincarnated (转世的) spirits of the dead.

澳洲土著

Discovery and Exploration

The first documented and undisputed European sighting and landing of Australia was in 1606 by the Dutch navigator Willem Janszoon, who sighted the coast of Cape York Peninsula (约克角半岛). During the 17th century, the Dutch chartered the whole of the western and northern coastlines of what they named New Holland. The most successful Dutch expedition was that of Abel Tasman, who in 1642 sailed into the waters of southern Australia, discovering and naming the island Tasmania after himself.

Despite the increasing knowledge of the continent, no further detailed explorations were made until 1770, when the English captain, James Cook, sailed along the fertile eastern coast of Australia. James Cook named the coast New South Wales and formally claimed it for Britain.

European Settlement

Britain underwent significant changes in the late 18th and early 19th centuries. The Industrial Revolution transformed the country from a largely rural society almost entirely dependent on agriculture to a town-centered one engaged increasingly in commercial manufacturing. However, the rapid population growth in London and other areas brought about various social problems, such as unemployment, overcrowding, homelessness and poverty. The rising crime rate compelled Britain to find somewhere to house the population of its overcrowded prisons. As the United States had gained independence, the British government had to look around for another destination to send convicts. It was Joseph Banks, who had accompanied Cook on his 1770 voyage, that recommended Botany Bay as a suitable site.

In May, 1787, the First Fleet of 11 ships under the command of Captain Arthur Phillip sailed from Portsmouth, Britain, for Australia. The ships carried about 1,500 people—half of them convicts. They arrived in Sydney on January 26, 1788, a date now celebrated as Australia Day. Here, Phillip established Britain's first permanent colony. In the following decades, more convicts were transported to the continent and new colonies were established, including Hobart (霍巴特) in Tasmania, Brisbane at Moreton Bay (莫顿湾) and Albany (奥尔巴尼) in Western Australia.

Life was extremely harsh for the new arrivals. Their lack of farming or trading experience and lack of understanding regarding Australia's seasons led to initial failures in farming. The heavy dependence on ships from Britain for food and supplies made starvation the biggest threat for the colonies. It was at this time that Captain John Macarthur began breeding fine merino sheep (美利奴绵羊) for their wool. The wool trade flourished and later became Australia's most important industry. John Macarthur is considered one of the founders of the Australian wool industry.

Colonization

From the 1820s to the 1880s, Australia underwent major processes that laid the foundation for its present society. Among these were the establishment of new colonies along the eastern coast, the expansion of sheep and cattle raising in the interior and the discovery of gold and other minerals in the eastern colonies.

Apart from New South Wales and Tasmania, settlements were also established in Western Australia (1829), South Australia (1836), Victoria (1851) and Queensland (1859). The six colonies were later unified to constitute the Commonwealth of Australia.

The mid-19th century saw the rapid growth of population in the colonies. Although the transportation of convicts had ended in 1868, the discovery of gold in the 1850s greatly increased Australia's population. New settlers from Britain, Ireland and large numbers of continental Europeans, North Americans and Chinese immigrated to the colonies. As a result, in 1861, the Australian population reached almost 1.2 million. Most of these free immigrants were skilled and semi-skilled tradesmen, so

露天金矿

both farming and mining industries underwent rapid development. In addition, the improvement of free trade gained the colonies more authority. Large-scale grazing also developed in the 1830s and the 1840s.

The three decades following the gold rush in the 1850s became a period of great economic expansion in Australia. The population also expanded rapidly. The rapid increase of Australia's population contributed, in turn, to the growth of its six capital cities. Meanwhile, the development of the gold mining industry gave impetus to the development of the entire mining industry. Advances in railroad, telecommunications and ship transportation not only established a link between Australia and the international market, but also transformed the national economy.

The Road Toward Federation

The federation of the six colonies was achieved after several national conventions and a series of compromises and referenda. The idea of federation was proposed by Earl Grey, Britain's colonial secretary, as early as in 1847. During the 1880s, various concerns served to keep the idea of unification alive. By the end of the 19th century, Australia was suffering a great depression, the most severe the state had ever experienced. The six colonies were aware that the separation of governments and markets had restricted their development. They also realized the need to pursue uniform immigration rules in order to keep the unwanted immigrants out. The colonial governments feared that the nations of mainland Europe would attempt to invade or colonize Australia.

Those in favor of federation argued that uniform policies on matters such as tariffs, immigration and defense would be advantageous. In 1885, the Federal Council of Australasia was formed. The National Australasian Convention took place in 1891, and a draft constitution was put forth. Later, two federal referenda were introduced. The first was in June, 1898. Victoria, South Australia and Tasmania voted "Yes" for federation, but the "Yes" majority needed in New South Wales was not accomplished. The draft constitution was then amended and a second referendum was held in 1899, when New South Wales and Queensland also voted in favor of federation. Western Australia agreed to join the federation in 1900.

Australia Since the 20th Century

In 1901, the six colonies of Australia adopted a federal Constitution and became a self-governing dominion of the British Empire, thus the Commonwealth of Australia was established.

One of the first acts of the new Parliament was the Immigration Restriction Act in 1901, with the purpose of restricting non-European immigrants. The formal implementation of a "White Australia Policy"* was welcomed by a majority of the Australian population. People who applied for immigration were required to pass a "Dictation Test" in a European language.

The non-indigenous population at the time of establishment of the Federation was 3.8 million. Half of them lived in capital cities, three quarters were born in Australia, and the majority was of English, Scottish or Irish descent. The Immigration Restriction Act was dismantled after World War II. Today Australia has a global, non-discriminatory policy and is home to people from more than 200 countries.

Although World War I was fought in Europe, as a member of the British Empire, Australia automatically followed Britain into the war in August, 1914, and pledged to defend the "motherland" Britain to "our last man and our last shilling". This was surely a tremendous display of patriotism.

During the war, the Australian troops, joined by the New Zealand forces, were called the Australian and New Zealand Army Corps (ANZACs) (澳新军团). The ANZACs took part in some of the bloodiest battles, including the battle with the Turks at Gallipoli (加利波利). Though the Gallipoli Campaign ended in defeat for the Allies, it is still remembered as one of the glorious chapters in Australian history. The Australians were particularly proud of their great bravery and indomitable (不屈不挠的) spirit. Now, ANZAC Day (April 25) is one of Australia's most important national holidays to honor all those Australians who died in military conflicts.

Australia was far from the battlefield and did not suffer the economic or social distress of Europe. Indeed, the war brought benefits to the Australian economy. During the war, Britain bought Australia's wool, wheat, mutton and beef at inflated prices. Moreover, Britain took all the zinc (锌) that Australia could produce. All in all, the Australian agriculture and mining industries were booming.

---

* White Australia Policy: 白澳政策，是澳大利亚反对亚洲移民的种族主义政策的通称。1901 年被确认为基本国策，1973 年被取消。

澳新军团日纪念活动

As the war drew to a close in 1918 and the troops returned home, the Australians were determined to forget the bitterness of the war. Australia had grown up during the war and was able to take a place among the great nations. It experienced rapid industrial growth in the years following the war.

In February 1923, Stanley Bruce of the Nationalist Party was sworn in as Prime Minister, forming a coalition with the Australian Country Party leader Earle Page as Deputy Prime Minister. He laid out his economic development plan for Australia in the 1920s through "men, money and markets". "Men" referred to immigrants, to increase Australia's population; "money" referred to capital, mostly to be borrowed from the British government; and "markets" referred to imperial preference (帝国特惠制), that is, mutual preference for trade between Britain and the dominions. It was a prosperous time for most Australians and the boom reached an all-time high in 1928.

The Great Depression struck a devastating blow to the whole world. Australia was also severely affected. The main causes of the Australian depression were external—the collapse of wool and wheat prices and the cessation (停止) of overseas loans. Internal factors, including an existing recession and drought, exacerbated (使恶化) the situation. National income fell markedly between 1929 and 1932; unemployment rate rose to around 30% in 1932; more citizens were only able to obtain part-time work.

During the Great Depression, the Australian Labor Party split. Joseph Lyons and his supporters departed and helped to form the United Australia Party. Lyons advocated a deflationary (通货紧缩的) policy to deal with the Great Depression. He won the 1931 federal election and subsequently became Prime Minister. He first led a United Australia Party government until 1934, and then one in coalition with the Australian Country Party until 1939.

As in World War I, Australia automatically followed Britain into World War II in September, 1939. World War II struck Australia much closer to home than World War I. On February 19, 1942, the Japanese launched air raids on Darwin. In May and June, the Japanese attacked Sydney Harbor and Newcastle, causing some casualties and property damage.

With the beginning of the Pacific War[1], Australia developed a foreign policy independent of Britain for the first time. Australia thought that their primary line of defense in the Pacific was Singapore. However, Singapore fell in February, 1942. Australia had to look elsewhere for assistance to secure its safety. It was the United States that helped protect Australia from the Japanese in the Battle of the Coral Sea[2]. This event marked the beginning of a profound shift in Australia's allegiance away from Britain toward the U.S.

Australian servicemen made significant contributions to the Allied victory in Europe and the Asia-Pacific region. Some 30,000 people lost their lives. A further 65,000 were wounded. Such efforts were considerable for a nation of only 7 million people with a large and sparsely populated country to defend.

With the end of World War II, Australia entered a boom period. The number of Australians in employment grew steadily. In the 1950s, the economy was fortified by the opening up of mining resources and major national building projects like the Snowy Mountains Scheme, a complex project for the development of hydroelectric (水力发电的) power. Other developments included the expansion of social security nets and advances in communications. In sports, Melbourne's hosting of the Olympic Games in 1956 put an international spotlight on Australia.

---

1 Pacific War: 太平洋战争，第二次世界大战的一部分，是日本等轴心国和美国等同盟国之间的主战场之一，始于日本1941年12月7日偷袭珍珠港，结束于1945年8月14日日本投降。
2 Battle of the Coral Sea: 珊瑚海战役，第二次世界大战中在珊瑚海海域进行的一次大规模海战。美军通过这次战役挫败了日本南下控制珊瑚海和澳大利亚海上通道的战略计划。

Chapter 16 Geography and History

Post-war prosperity made Australians regard Australia as "the lucky country"—a land of economic opportunity and bountiful natural resources. Australia launched a massive immigration program, believing that with such a small population inhabiting such a vast landmass, Australia was under-protected and vulnerable to external threats. In keeping with the slogan—"populate or perish", millions of refugees and other immigrants, including large numbers of Jews, settled in Australia for the first time.

The 1960s was a period of change for Australia. The post-war generation—the so-called "baby boomers"—emerged as an active force, seeking changes in political, economic and social relationships.

The ethnic diversity produced by post-war immigration caused Australians to rethink their attitude toward racial issues. The movement to gain recognition of Aboriginal rights began, and a campaign against the White Australia Policy was also launched. In 1967, a referendum was held, the result of which gave the federal government the power to pass legislation on behalf of the indigenous people and to include the indigenous people in future censuses. It was widely seen as a strong affirmation that the government was to take direct action to improve the living conditions of the Aborigines. In 1973, the White Australia policy officially ended. Since then, the Australians live in harmony with people from the Asian countries.

With the decline of Britain as a world power, Australia could no longer depend on Britain for protection. In September 1951, Australia signed the ANZUS Treaty (《澳新美安全条约》) with America and New Zealand, pledging to keep mutual defense and support in case of war.

The long post-war domination of national politics by the coalition of the Liberal Party and the Country Party ended in 1972, when the Australian Labor Party under the leadership of Gough Whitlam was elected to power. The next three years witnessed major changes in Australia's social and economic policy agenda and legislative reforms in health, education, foreign affairs, social security and industrial relations. The Whitlam government established formal diplomatic relations with China, abolished the death penalty for federal crimes, reduced the voting age to 18 years of age, abolished the last vestiges (残余) of the White Australia Policy, introduced language programs for non-English speaking Australians, and also tried to pursue a more independent foreign policy, especially in its relations with America.

The years between 1983 and 1996 constituted the longest period of Australian Labor Party's rule in the federal parliamentary history. During this period, the

Labor government under Bob Hawke and Paul Keating brought about unprecedented economic reforms. The Australian financial market was deregulated, tariffs were greatly reduced, the labor market was deregulated, and state-owned enterprises were privatized. The goal of these economic reforms was to allow market forces to play a greater role in shaping a healthy national economy, in which the Australian industries would improve their efficiency and competitiveness. At the same time, salaries and supply and demand were well regulated.

Since 1996, the Howard government attempted to reduce Australia's government deficit. Beginning with the government-owned telecommunications corporation Telstra, Australia accelerated the pace of privatization. The Howard government continued to pursue some of the foreign policies of its predecessors, based on foreign relations with four key countries: the United States, Japan, China and Indonesia. In international affairs, the Howard government showed strong support for the U.S.

In November 1999, a public referendum was held in which Australians voted to decide whether the form of the Australian government should be changed into a republic with a President elected by Parliament as head of the state, or whether it would retain the existing system. The majority of the Australians voted not to change the constitution. The reason for this, it was argued, was not that the Australians wished to keep the British monarch or the Governor General as head of the state, but that they disapproved of the proposed political system which preferred that the President be publicly and directly elected.

In sports, Australia performed admirably in the Sydney 2000 Olympic Games and Paralympic Games (残奥会). Achieving the fourth place overall in the Olympic

competition, the Australians won 58 medals, including 16 gold, 25 silver and 17 bronze. Australia came in first at the Paralympics, with a total of 149 medals.

After the terrorist attacks on September 11, 2001, Australia invoked (实施) the ANZUS Treaty for the first time since the treaty was ratified in 1952. The Howard government committed Australia to fully supporting, politically and militarily, the war on terrorism.

Today, with its highly developed economy and diverse culture, Australia has become one of the most cosmopolitan and dynamic societies in the world. The nation has a thriving ethnic media, an international business reputation, an innovative artistic community, a manifold (多样的) religious and cultural heritage and a tremendous variety of foods, fashion and architecture.

Exercises

I. **Read the following statements and decide whether they are true (T) or false (F).**

　　_____ 1. In terms of landmass, Australia is the sixth largest country in the world.

　　_____ 2. The name "Sydney" means "meeting place" in the Aboriginal language.

　　_____ 3. The first documented European expedition to Australia was made by Abel Tasman.

　　_____ 4. Australia Day is on January 26, which originates from the establishment of the first British colony on this day in 1788.

　　_____ 5. There was a period of great economic expansion in Australia following the gold rush in the 1850s.

　　_____ 6. The purpose of the Immigration Restriction Act in 1901 was to restrict European immigrant numbers.

　　_____ 7. The economy in Australia developed rapidly by means of the policy of "men, money and markets" in the 1920s.

　　_____ 8. It was Britain that helped protect Australia from the Japanese in the Battle of the Coral Sea during World War II.

II. Choose the best answer to complete each of the following statements.
1. _____ is the lowest point in Australia.
   A. Lake Eyre   B. The Great Artesian Basin
   C. Mount Kosciuszko   D. The Great Victoria Desert
2. _____ is Australia's capital.
   A. Sydney   B. Melbourne   C. Brisbane   D. Canberra
3. Britain's first permanent colony was founded in _____.
   A. 1606   B. 1770   C. 1787   D. 1788
4. The Commonwealth of Australia was established in _____.
   A. 1847   B. 1885   C. 1900   D. 1901
5. The movement to gain recognition of Aboriginal rights was started in the _____.
   A. 1950s   B. 1960s   C. 1970s   D. 1980s
6. Australia completely abolished the White Australia Policy during the government of _____.
   A. Earle Page   B. Gough Whitlam
   C. Joseph Lyons   D. Stanley Bruce
7. The following were all aspects of the economic reforms which took place between 1983 and 1996 EXCEPT _____.
   A. enlarging the scale of the mining industry
   B. deregulating the financial market
   C. reducing tariffs
   D. privatizing the state-owned enterprises
8. The Howard government's foreign policies were based on relations with four key countries, namely, _____.
   A. the U.S., Japan, Britain, China   B. the U.S., Japan, China, Indonesia
   C. the U.S., Japan, Britain, Indonesia D. the U.S., Britain, China, Indonesia

III. Give brief answers to the following questions.
1. Why did the six colonies want the country unified at the end of the 19th century?

Chapter 16 Geography and History

2. What is "ANZAC Day"?

   _____
   _____

3. What was the aim of the economic reforms which took place between 1983 and 1996?

   _____
   _____

IV. **State your understanding of the following questions.**
   1. What were the effects of the two World Wars on Australia?
   2. What efforts did the Australian government make to deal with the racial issues in the 1960s and the 1970s?

Learn and Check

Size: nearly 7.7 million square kilometers

Geographical regions: the Eastern Highlands, the Central Lowlands, the Western Plateau

Climate: with great regional variations and low rainfall

Major cities: Canberra (the capital city), Sydney, Melbourne, Brisbane, Perth, Adelaide, Darwin

First inhabitants: the Aborigines, between 50,000 and 60,000 years ago

First British colony: in Sydney, on January 26, 1788 (Australia Day)

The Commonwealth of Australia: established in 1901

ANZAC Day: April 25, an important national holiday to honor those Australians who died in military conflicts

ANZUS Treaty: a collective defense treaty with America and New Zealand, signed in 1951

Chapter 17 Government and Society

▼ **Think and Talk**
- Why did the Australian government adopt a policy of multiculturalism?
- What do you know about immigration to Australia?
- What do you know about the Australian universities?

I. Government

The Commonwealth of Australia, formed in 1901, is comprised of six states and two mainland territories. These six states are New South Wales, Victoria, Queensland, South Australia, Western Australia and Tasmania. The two territories are the Northern Territory and the Australian Capital Territory. The Commonwealth of Australia is a constitutional monarchy, a federation and a parliamentary democracy. The King or Queen of Britain is the head of Australia, normally represented by the Governor General.

Australia's system of government reflects both the British and North American models of liberal democracy, but with some unique Australian features. In terms of its governmental system, Australia follows the federation model of the United States. The federal government has a three-tier system (三级体制): the federal government at the national level, governments at the state and territory level and local governments at the city, town, municipal and shire (郡) level. The federal government is based on a popularly elected Parliament with two chambers, the House of Representatives and the Senate. The party or group of parties with a majority in the House of Representatives forms the government, with ministers appointed from both chambers to serve in the Cabinet. The government is responsible to the Parliament.

Chapter 17 Government and Society

The Australian Constitution deals with the composition of the Australian federal government, the powers of the government and the relationship between the federal government and state governments. The Australian Constitution can be changed only by referendum. Formal changes to the Constitution must be approved by a majority of voters in at least four out of the six states and an overall national majority of voters.

The division of powers between the federal government and state governments is defined in the Constitution. The powers exercised by the federal Parliament and government include the responsibilities for foreign relations and trade, defense and immigration, while the governments of states and territories are responsible for all matters not assigned to the Commonwealth.

The government is divided into three branches: the legislature, the executive and the judiciary, which can act as checks and balances on each other.

The Legislature

The Parliament of the Commonwealth is the federal legislature of Australia. The Australian Parliament consists of the Queen and two Houses—the Senate (the Upper House) and the House of Representatives (the Lower House). On the principle of "separation of powers", the Parliament makes laws and provides a legislative framework for the operations of the other two arms of government.

国会大厦

参议院

众议院

The Senate consists of 76 Senators, 12 from each of the six states and two from each of the mainland territories. The Senators are elected by the proportional representation system[1] for a term of six years. The Senate has virtually equal power to make laws with the House of Representatives.

The Senate has a highly developed committee system, which enables Senators to inquire into policy issues in depth and to scrutinize the way laws and policies are administered by ministers and civil servants. The Senate is thus called the house of review and it constitutes a powerful check on the government.

The House of Representatives has 150 members, each representing an electoral division. Members are elected for a term of up to three years, by the preferential voting system[2], under which voters rank candidates in order of preference.

The central function of the House of Representatives is the consideration and passing of new laws and amendments or changes to existing laws. Another function is to determine the government, therefore, it is also called the house of government. After an election, the political party or party group with majority support in the House of

---

1 proportional representation system: 比例代表制。在这种选举制度下，竞选政党所获得的议席的比例和他们所得选票占全部选票的比例相符。
2 preferential voting system: 名次投票制。投票者可选择多名候选人，但需列出名次。

Representatives forms the governing party, with its leader becoming Prime Minister. The House of Representatives is also involved in such responsibilities as publicizing and scrutinizing the government administration, representing the people and controlling government expenditure.

The Executive

In Australia, executive authority is vested (赋予权利) in the Governor General, who is appointed by the British monarch on the advice of the Prime Minister. The King or Queen of Britain is recognized as the royal head of state, but has no real power in the government and plays a merely symbolic role. The Governor General is His or Her Majesty's representative in the Commonwealth. Six State Governors perform similar roles in their states.

Under the Constitution, the Governor General has many important constitutional, official and ceremonial duties to perform. In accordance with the long-established constitutional practice, however, the Governor General can only act on the advice of the Federal Executive Council or the Cabinet comprised of senior ministers and the Prime Minister. Federal policy, in practice, is determined by the Cabinet, which is chaired by the Prime Minister. The ministers are responsible for the individual departments of the federal government.

The Judiciary

The judiciary is the government branch concerned with the administration of justice. It is absolutely separate from the executive branch and the legislature so as to check the concentration of government power. The independence of the judiciary is crucial for a democratic community because when judges are presiding over a case, there must be no interference and intimidation from external forces.

The Australian judiciary includes the High Court, the Federal Court, the Family Court, the Federal Magistrates Court and state and territory courts. The High Court is the superior court in Australia. Its functions include interpreting and applying the law of Australia, deciding cases of special federal significance and hearing appeals from the federal, state and territory courts.

Political Parties

There are three major political parties in Australia: the Australian Labor Party, the Liberal Party and the Nationals. Australia has a two-party system. There are two dominant political parties or coalitions, and it is difficult for independents or other minor parties to gain seats.

The Australian Labor Party, nominally (名义上地) representing the trade unions, is Australia's oldest political party, formed in the 1890s and represented in the first Federal Parliament elected in 1901. It's the only party to have been in continuous operation since 1901. In the past more than 100 years, the Australian Labor Party had governed at the federal level for only 33 years. In the 20th century, the party experienced three traumatic (痛苦的) splits (1917, 1931 and 1955) and was kept out of office for many years.

The Liberal Party nominally represents urban business-related groups. It is a relatively young party, formally formed in 1944 by Sir Robert Menzies, out of the remains of the United Australia Party. Since then, it has remained one of Australia's major parties and has enjoyed a long period of success.

The Nationals is the second oldest political party in Australia. It was founded in 1920 as the Australian Country Party, but its name changed to the National Party of Australia in 1982 and then the Nationals in 2006. It has remained a solid bulwark (保障) of conservative support in rural areas.

Election

Australia is one of the few countries that have compulsory voting. At election time, it is compulsory for all citizens over the age of 18 to enroll and vote at a polling station.

Australian citizens have been called on to give their decisions in elections and referenda at a rate higher than that of most Western nations. With the three-tier government, Australian electoral laws, practices and systems vary greatly. Thus, Australian citizens have been faced with not only high frequency, but also complexity and diversity of the electoral systems. Both voters and political parties have been forced to accommodate themselves to the complexity of various systems.

Chapter 17 Government and Society

The majority of voters depend upon "how-to-vote" cards to guide them. Political parties hope that the voters will follow the cards, cast a valid first preference vote and mark their preferences as the party desires.

Of all the elections, the general election is the most important, the result of which determines which party leader will rule the country as the Prime Minister. In Australia, a general election can be called before the Parliament has served its full term. The final decision in such cases rests with the Prime Minister. It is possible to call an election at the moment most favorable to the government and a good result will add to the Prime Minister's stature (声望) and consolidate their control of the party.

There are three electoral systems which are important in Australia, namely the simple majority system*, the preferential voting system and the proportional representation system. The simple majority system is a straightforward form of voting whereby the option with a simple majority of votes wins. Under the preferential voting system, voters number the candidates on the ballot paper in the order of their preference. Proportional representation is an electoral system delivering a close match between the percentage of votes that groups of candidates obtain in the election and the percentage of seats they receive.

---

* simple majority system: 简单多数制，是一种直接投票的办法，即候选人以简单多数票获胜。

II. People

Population

Most Australians are of British and Irish ancestry and the majority live in urban areas. The population has more than doubled since World War II, spurred by an ambitious post-war immigration program. The population of Australia is about 22.9 million (2013). The indigenous population, the Australian Aborigines, estimated 300,000 at the time of the European arrival, numbered 517,000 in 2006. Though still more rural than the general population, the Aboriginal population has become more urbanized, with one-third of them living in major cities.

Australia is the most sparsely populated of the inhabited continents. In terms of landmass, Australia is the sixth largest nation in the world. However, it ranks 53rd in terms of population, with an overall population density of about 3 people per square kilometer.

Multicultural Society

Home to people from more than 200 countries, Australia has an enviable international reputation for diversity and tolerance. Australia accepts and respects the right of all Australians to express and share their individual cultural heritage so long as they have an overriding (首要的) commitment to Australia's democratic foundations and to English as the national language. Cultural diversity has become a touchstone of its national identity.

Multiculturalism as a policy was adopted in Australia in the 1970s. While recognizing the importance of social cohesion (凝聚力) and the common rights and obligations of all citizens, multiculturalism advocates a multicultural society based on the diversity of ethnic groups and cultural identities, and also favors the equality of all in the labor market and social life.

1) Diversity of Population

Australia, like Canada and the United States, is considered a traditional country of immigration. Migrants from culturally and linguistically different backgrounds constitute a diverse Australian population.

Three major contributors to Australia's diverse population are the indigenous peoples, the British colonial past and extensive immigration from different countries and cultures.

Chapter 17 Government and Society

Despite the fact that the indigenous Australians have inhabited Australia for at least 50,000 years, they make up only about 2.5% of the total population of Australia. The overwhelming majority are immigrants and their descendants. Over half of these immigrants are from Europe, predominantly Britain. In recent years, there has been a new trend of immigration from New Zealand, China, India and Vietnam.

2) Diversity of Language

While English is the dominant language in Australia, many people speak a language other than English within their families and communities. Collectively, Australians speak over 200 languages. The most common languages other than English are Italian, Greek, Chinese and Arabic. In addition, there are about 50 indigenous languages and Australian creoles (克里奥耳语，一种欧洲语言和其他语言的混合语) spoken by the Australians.

3) Diversity of Religion

The major religion in Australia is Christianity and Christians represent 69% of the population. The non-Christian religions include Judaism (犹太教), Hinduism (印度教), Buddhism (佛教) and Islam (伊斯兰教). Buddhism is the largest non-Christian religion and is practiced by 1.9% of the total population. Islam, the second largest non-Christian religion in Australia today, is practiced by 1.5% of the total population.

墨尔本圣保罗教堂

Immigration into Australia

Immigrants contributed a lot to Australian society, culture and prosperity, and played an important role in shaping the nation. Since 1945, more than 7.2 million people have come to Australia as new settlers. After World War II, immigration to Australia mushroomed as a result of a terrible labor shortage and a growing belief that substantial population growth was essential for the country's future. Recently, more than 100,000 people immigrate to Australia every year. Today, nearly one-fourth of Australians were born overseas.

The current Australian immigration program is global and does not discriminate on racial or ethnic grounds. Its emphasis is on attracting new immigrants who have education or work skills that will contribute to Australia's economic growth. People from any country can be considered for immigration to Australia. The success of their application depends on their ability to satisfy rigorous selection criteria that include being in good health and having a good character. Australia also accepts immigration on other criteria, such as family reunion and humanitarian grounds.

III. Economy

Australia has a prosperous Western-style capitalist economy. The nation's high economic performance stems from effective economic management and ongoing structural reform.

Australia is self-sufficient in food; the raising of sheep and cattle and the production of grain have long been the country's major occupations. Meanwhile, Australia is also a highly industrialized country. Australia's economy depends largely on foreign trade. Its chief export commodities are metals, minerals, wool, beef, mutton, cereals and manufactured products. The leading imports are machinery, transportation and telecommunications equipment, computers and office machines, chemicals and petroleum products.

Australia is renowned for its unique plant and animal species. It is estimated that there are around 27,700 different plants native to Australia. Australia is also a leading supplier of mineral resources to international markets. Almost all the ore production is exported, mainly to Japan and other important markets, including China, Germany and the Republic of Korea.

Despite its limited arable (适于耕种的) area, Australia is one of the world's leading exporters of agricultural products. Until the late 1950s, agriculture still accounted for up to 80% of the value of all Australia's exports. Today, however, as the Australian economy becomes increasingly diverse, the proportion has declined despite an increasing agricultural output.

Manufacturing in Australia was developed in the late 19th century. At that time, it was characterized by the decentralized (分散的) domestic market, backward technology and fierce international competition. In 1908, the Australian government began to take measures to promote the development of manufacturing, mainly through tariffs. By the end of World War II, manufacturing contributed more than one-fourth of GDP, peaking at about one-third from 1959 to 1960. Declining sharply from this high point, manufacturing now employs about 10% of the labor force and contributes about 9% of Australia's GDP.

Foreign trade has traditionally played an essential role in Australia's economic growth, largely dominated by the country's rich natural resources and comparatively small population. Today, trade continues to be the best-performing industry in Australia. Australia's largest trading partners are China, Japan, the United States, New Zealand, the Republic of Korea, Britain and Germany. Australia has always been a country of foreign investment, with its foreign capital coming mainly from Britain and the United States.

Tourism is one of Australia's largest and fastest-growing industries. The country's spectacular natural environment, multicultural communities, food and wine, the friendliness of its people, its weather and lifestyle, are all factors which contribute to its special appeal as one of the world's most popular tourist destinations.

Tourism employs 4.5% of the workforce and contributes about 2.6% of Australia's GDP. The main visitors to Australia are the British, Americans, New Zealanders, the Japanese and the Chinese. The strong growth in domestic tourism is ascribed to the expanding range of attractions in each state and territory, including amusement and theme parks, zoos, art galleries and museums, national parks, historic sites and wineries (葡萄酒厂). Among them, the main tourist attractions are the Great Barrier Reef (大堡礁), the Gold Coast, Uluru (艾尔斯巨石), the Sydney Opera House and the Sydney Harbor Bridge.

The Great Barrier Reef is the largest coral reef in the world and is one of the natural structures that can be seen from the moon. It stretches more than 2,000 kilometers along the northeast coast of Australia. The Great Barrier Reef possesses an abundance of various coral types, and is home to many thousands of species of plants and animals, the majority of which have not yet been properly named and identified.

The Gold Coast is located in the southeast corner of Queensland, to the south of Brisbane. With about 57 kilometers of coastline, it possesses some of the most famous beaches in Australia. It is regarded as a paradise by people from all over the world who holiday there.

大堡礁

Chapter 17 Government and Society

艾尔斯巨石

Uluru, also known as Ayers Rock, is located in Uluru-Kata Tjuta National Park (乌卢鲁-卡塔丘塔国家公园) in the south of the Northern Territory. Being the largest monolith (巨型独石) in the world, it measures 9.4 kilometers around its base and rises to 348 meters above the surrounding flat land. Uluru is notable for appearing to change colors as different light strikes it at different times of the day and year. It is also regarded as a sacred place by the Australian Aborigines. The Aborigines believe that it is hollow underground and contains a powerful energy source. They hold that it is inhabited by their ancestral "beings" who have given them laws, customs and the source of life for the continuation of their clans. Special ceremonies are still held nowadays at some of the sacred sites around Uluru.

The Sydney Opera House is situated on Sydney Harbor, New South Wales, and is regarded as an Australian icon. Designed by a Danish architect Jorn Utzon, it is one of the most recognizable images of the modern world and one of the most famous performing arts venues (举办地点) in the world. The Sydney Opera House has about 1,000 rooms, including five theaters, five rehearsal studios, two main halls, four restaurants, six bars and numerous souvenir shops. In 2007, the Sydney Opera House was designated a UNESCO World Heritage site.

悉尼歌剧院

233

悉尼港大桥

The Sydney Harbor Bridge was formally opened in 1932. Being the largest steel arch bridge in the world, it connects the Sydney central business district with the North Shore commercial and residential areas. Since its opening, the bridge has been the focal point of New Year and Australia Day celebrations, when fireworks are set off from its arch.

IV. Education

Australia has a well-developed educational system with a very high rate of participation and secondary completion. Education in Australia is primarily the responsibility of the individual states. The Australian educational system is divided broadly into five areas: preschool, primary school, secondary/high school, vocational training institutions, and university and other tertiary institutions. The system of teaching and school discipline is different from that of many other countries. Less importance is placed on outward discipline and memorizing. On the contrary, the emphasis is on self-discipline, learning by discovery and by questioning, and encouraging students' interest in and enthusiasm for learning. In many cases, the Australian models attract international attention and Australia is involved in the development of education programs in more and more countries.

Chapter 17 Government and Society

Elementary and Secondary Education

In Australia, when children are between 2 and 5 years old, they can go to kindergartens, day care centers and playgroups for schooling. Preschool attendance in Australia is usually part-time. Education is compulsory between the ages of 6 and 15 in all states except Tasmania, where the upper age threshold is 16. Most children start their primary school education at the age of 5 and finish at 12. They can either go to state schools for free, secular education or attend religious classes offered by the clergy of various denominations (宗教派别). About two-thirds of students obtain their education in state schools rather than private schools which are usually denominational and charge high tuition fees. The majority of private schools are Catholic.

Most boys and girls enter the secondary school at around 12. Secondary school usually lasts six years. During the first four years, students study a broad range of subjects. In the last two years, they are encouraged to specialize in the subjects they prefer. At the age of 17 or 18, they take state examinations for university entrance.

The Australian Broadcasting Corporation also provides a variety of primary and early education programs for children living in isolated areas. Classes are conducted with the help of radio, television, video cassette recorders and computers by schools of the air (空中学院) or correspondence schools (函授学校).

Higher Education

Higher education is provided through universities, vocational training institutions, and adult and community educational institutions. The standard, design and diversity of education offered by the Australian universities are among the most impressive in the world. There are 38 universities and a large number of public and private colleges offering advanced education in specific subject areas. In addition, the Commonwealth government maintains a number of specialized learning institutions, notably the Australian Film, Television and Radio School (澳洲广播电视电影学校), the Australian Maritime College (澳大利亚海事学院) and the National Institute of Dramatic Art (国立戏剧艺术学校).

Australia's universities have long enjoyed an international reputation for excellence in teaching and research. Academic staff in the Australian universities is recruited on an international basis. The Australian universities have strong international links across the entire range of their activities, from individual research collaborations to joint ventures with universities in other countries. In particular, Australia works to develop strong educational relationships with its neighbors in the Asia-Pacific region.

Apart from universities, vocational training institutions provide courses with a strong vocational focus such as travel, tourism, graphic design and many others. TAFE (Technical and Further Education) is the largest provider of vocational education and training in Australia. It is government-funded postsecondary education which not only meets the needs of various industries, but also gives people immediately usable skills which win them jobs. Adult and community education programs are of shorter duration and are therefore well-adapted to the needs of adult learners, whose domestic and work commitment frequently discourages them from entering long-term education programs.

Major Universities

The University of Sydney was established in 1850. It is a member of Australia's "Group of Eight"* and remains one of the country's largest and most prestigious educational institutions. It has an international reputation for outstanding research

---

* Group of Eight: 澳大利亚八校联盟，指在澳大利亚最负盛名的八所研究型综合性大学，正式组建于1999年，类似于美国的常春藤联盟。八所大学分别为：阿德莱德大学、澳大利亚国立大学、墨尔本大学、莫纳什大学、新南威尔士大学、昆士兰大学、悉尼大学和西澳大学。

Chapter 17 Government and Society

and teaching. The University of Sydney continues to rise in global rankings, confirming its place within the top 40 universities in the world.

The University of Melbourne, established in 1853 by Hugh Childers, is the second oldest university in Australia. It ranks among the top universities in Australia and is highly regarded in the fields of arts, humanities and biomedicine. The university aims to consolidate its three core activities—research, learning and teaching and engagement—in order to become one of the world's finest universities.

The University of Adelaide is a public university located in Adelaide. Established in 1874, the university is a member of the "Group of Eight". It has a reputation for academic excellence, having produced a large number of Nobel laureates. It is the first university in Australia to admit women to academic courses and to grant degrees in science.

悉尼大学

Exercises

I. Read the following statements and decide whether they are true (T) or false (F).

_____ 1. Australia's government system mainly reflects the British model of liberal democracy.

_____ 2. The party or group of parties with a majority in the House of Representatives forms the government in Australia.

_____ 3. The Australian Constitution can be changed either by the government's will or by referendum.

_____ 4. The Australian Senate has more power than the House of Representatives to make laws.

_____ 5. In Australia the King or Queen of Britain serves as the symbolic head of state.

_____ 6. For Australian citizens over the age of 16, it is compulsory to vote at election time.

_____ 7. Multiculturalism in Australia advocates a multicultural society based on European and Asian ethnic backgrounds.

_____ 8. Since Australia has a vast cultivable area, it has become the world's leading exporter of agricultural products.

II. Choose the best answer to complete each of the following statements.

1. Of the following, _____ is NOT among the three major Australian political parties.
   A. the Australian Labor Party   B. the Nationals
   C. the Liberal Party   D. the United Australia Party

2. Australia tries to attract immigrants from any country with _____.
   A. a good family background   B. education or work skills
   C. high social status   D. adequate work experience

3. Australia's high economic performance is due to its _____ and ongoing structural reform.
   A. open-up policy   B. effective economic management
   C. historical development   D. proper investment

Chapter 17 Government and Society

4. Australia is a leading supplier of _____ to international markets.
   A. hi-tech products
   B. agricultural products
   C. industrial products
   D. mineral resources

5. Australia's foreign capital mainly comes from _____.
   A. the United States and Japan
   B. Britain and Germany
   C. Japan and the Republic of Korea
   D. Britain and the United States

6. Among the following tourist attractions, _____ can be seen from the moon.
   A. the Gold Coast
   B. Uluru
   C. the Great Barrier Reef
   D. the Sydney Opera House

7. _____ is/are mainly responsible for education in Australia.
   A. The federal government
   B. The individual states
   C. The territory assemblies
   D. The municipal governments

8. The Australian system of teaching and school discipline puts emphasis on the following EXCEPT _____.
   A. learning by discovery and questioning
   B. self-discipline
   C. preparing for tests
   D. encouraging students' interest in learning

III. Give brief answers to the following questions.

1. What is the three-tier system of the Australian government?

2. What are the chief functions of the House of Representatives in Australia?

3. What's the status of tourism in the economy of Australia?

IV. State your understanding of the following questions.

1. Why can Australia attract people from over 200 countries worldwide to make their home there?
2. What are the main features of Australian higher education?

Learn and Check

States and mainland territories: New South Wales, Victoria, Queensland, South Australia, Western Australia, Tasmania, the Northern Territory, the Australian Capital Territory

The government: the legislature, the executive, the judiciary

Major political parties: the Australian Labor Party, the Liberal Party, the Nationals

Population: 22.9 million (2013)

Multicultural society: diversity of population, diversity of language, diversity of religion

Immigration: more than 100,000 immigrants to Australia every year in recent years

Major trading partners: China, Japan, the United States, New Zealand, the Republic of Korea, Britain, Germany

Main tourist attractions: the Great Barrier Reef, the Gold Coast, Uluru, the Sydney Opera House, the Sydney Harbor Bridge

Major universities: the University of Sydney, the University of Melbourne, the University of Adelaide

New Zealand

Chapter 18 Society and Culture

▼ Think and Talk
- What makes New Zealand a popular tourist attraction?
- Why do we call New Zealand the world's largest farm?
- What do you know about education in New Zealand?

I. Geography

Geographical Features

New Zealand is located in the Southern Hemisphere, in the southwest corner of the Pacific Ocean, nearly 1,600 kilometers southeast of Australia. With a total landmass of about 270,000 square kilometers, New Zealand is the largest in the islands of Polynesia (波利尼西亚), an island group in the central and southern Pacific Ocean.

New Zealand is comprised of two principal islands, the North Island and the South Island, and a number of smaller ones, of which the Stewart Island is the largest and is often referred to as "our third island". The North Island and the South Island are separated by Cook Strait (库克海峡).

New Zealand is a mountainous country. On the South Island, the largest of all the islands in New Zealand, the Southern Alps run almost the entire length of the island, forming a natural dividing range. To the west there is a narrow coastal plain and to the east a series of wide, flat, more extensive lowlands. The 30 highest mountains are all within the Southern Alps. Mount Cook (3,754 meters), which lies in the center of the Southern Alps, is the highest peak in New Zealand. Another distinctive feature of the South Island is its abundant glaciers. The North Island is less mountainous than the South Island, but is volcanically active. Most of the elevated regions of the North Island are the result of volcanic activity.

Chapter 18 Society and Culture

The dramatic and varied landscapes of New Zealand, such as lakes, rivers, geysers (间歇泉) and hot springs, make it a popular tourist attraction. Every year, visitors from all over the world come to New Zealand to enjoy the spectacular scenery.

Climate

Situated in the Southern Hemisphere, New Zealand's seasons are the opposite of those in the Northern Hemisphere. January and February are its warmest months and July is normally the coldest. Consequently, New Zealanders celebrate their Christmas in mid-summer, while most people in the world celebrate their Christmas in winter.

New Zealand's climate is dominated by two main geographical features—the sea and the mountains. Since the small landmass of New Zealand is surrounded by a large expanse of ocean, the climate of New Zealand is temperate oceanic, which means that the seasonal variations in New Zealand are much slighter than in continental countries. There are generally small variations between summer and winter temperatures; temperatures seldom fall below 0℃ or rise above 30℃. The country's mountain ranges, particularly those of the South Island, have influence on the average rainfall of the east and west coasts. On the North Island, the west coast receives slightly more rain than the east. The contrast in rainfall across the South Island is much greater. The west coast of the South Island is the wettest area of New Zealand, whereas the east coast is the driest.

Major Cities

Wellington (惠灵顿) is the capital of New Zealand. Located at the southern tip of the North Island, it is the world's most southern capital. In terms of population, it is New Zealand's second largest city. Wellington is the cultural, commercial and cosmopolitan center of the country. The city is home to the Royal New Zealand Ballet, the National Symphony Orchestra, four professional theaters and many national opera, drama, dance and music groups. New Zealand's best galleries, museums, restaurants, bars and cafés are also located in Wellington.

Auckland (奥克兰), located in the northern part of the North Island, is the largest city in New Zealand. It has about 1.5 million inhabitants, one-third of the country's entire population. In the Maori language (毛利语), Auckland means "the city of 100 lovers". It earned this name because it was a place desired by all and conquered by many.

Chapter 18 Society and Culture

II. History

Discovery of New Zealand

New Zealand is one of the last corners of the planet to be colonized. It is believed that the early settlers in New Zealand, the Maoris, arrived from Polynesia about 1,200 years ago. The first Europeans did not reach New Zealand until 1642, when Dutchman Abel Tasman sailed up the northwestern coast of the South Island. In the face of hostility from the Maoris, Tasman left New Zealand without setting foot ashore.

The first significant voyage of discovery was undertaken by James Cook, who began extensive exploration of the islands in 1769. It was Cook who proved that New Zealand consisted of two islands. Cook's voyage eventually led to the European colonization of it. An increasing number of settlers came to New Zealand either to trade or to buy land for farming.

New Zealand as a Colony

In 1840, the Treaty of Waitangi (《怀唐伊条约》) was signed by representatives of the British Crown and chiefs of the indigenous Maori people, making New Zealand a British colony.

According to the treaty, the chiefs of the Maoris gave the Queen of England complete governance of the islands. If owners wanted to sell land, only the Crown had the right to buy it. In exchange, the Queen of England guaranteed to protect all the Maori people and give them the same rights and duties of citizenship as British subjects. The treaty is considered New Zealand's founding document and it marks the beginning of modern New Zealand.

The Treaty of Waitangi has a major impact on all New Zealanders. Nowadays, the place where the treaty was signed has become a popular tourist attraction. In addition, the anniversary of the signing, February 6, is celebrated as New Zealand's National Day.

The Treaty of Waitangi did not provide an absolutely sound basis for British sovereignty. Ever since its ratification, there had been intermittent (断断续续的) fighting between the Maori tribes and the colonists over disputes about land and trading rights. Both the Maori people and the British colonists differed widely in their understanding of the treaty. The Maoris believed that the treaty might guarantee them the continued possession of their land and the preservation of their customs, while many of the British thought that it had opened up the country to mass immigration and settlement. In addition, the British did not always respect the spirit of the treaty. The New Zealand Company* was just a case in point. The company made hasty and dishonest deals for land with the Maoris. In addition, it aggressively brought settlers to New Zealand without the authorization of the British government. This situation led to hostility between the Maori people and the British authorities. Eventually, the Colonial Office was obliged to give in to the Maori people's resistance. In 1852, under the British Parliament's New Zealand Constitution Act, New Zealand was granted internal self-government. After the discovery of gold on the South Island in 1861, many more European settlers arrived to establish farms there. The South Island was seen as a place of hope, so the capital was officially moved from Auckland to the central city of Wellington.

New Zealand as a Dominion

In 1907, New Zealand changed from a British colony to a separate dominion, equal in status to Australia and Canada. New Zealand remained a member of the British Commonwealth and pledged an oath of allegiance to the British monarch.

In 1914 when World War I started, New Zealand enthusiastically backed Britain. It suffered large casualties in the war—about 18,000 New Zealanders died and 41,000 were wounded. Politicians and historians claim that the country earned full nationhood through its contribution of troops to the Allied forces.

The worldwide economic depression hit New Zealand in the late 1920s. Problems such as escalating (逐步升高的) unemployment and declining living standards were predominating. In 1935, the Labor Party came to power and began to launch a series of social reforms. A comprehensive social security system including welfare benefits and health care was introduced; the free education system was further expanded; some initiatives granting state support for arts and culture were taken; and state regulations in most areas of the economy and society were extended. Through these measures, New Zealand began to show signs of economic improvement.

---

* New Zealand Company: 新西兰公司，于 1839 年由首批英国移民建立。

In World War II, New Zealand sent nearly 200,000 people to serve overseas as soldiers, airmen, sailors and nurses. Once again it suffered extraordinary casualties —about 11,900 people died. New Zealand's involvement in World War II greatly stimulated its economy. After the war, there was full employment, and manufacturing and service industries expanded. In addition, during the war, New Zealand strengthened its relationship with the United States. In 1951, seeing the U.S. as its major ally and protector, New Zealand signed the ANZUS Treaty with the United States and Australia.

It was not until 1947, when the Statute of Westminster Adoption Act was issued that New Zealand was granted total independence from Britain. The monarch of Britain remained the monarch of New Zealand and New Zealand became an independent constitutional monarchy. In 1983, New Zealand became the "Realm of New Zealand".

New Zealand as a Realm

In the mid-1980s, New Zealand declared its anti-nuclear policy and became a nuclear-free zone. It strongly opposed French nuclear testing in the Pacific and banned all nuclear vessels, including American nuclear-powered ships from visiting its territorial waters. This policy led to America's suspension of the ANZUS security guarantees to New Zealand in 1986.

Between the mid-1980s and mid-1990s, New Zealand underwent radical economic reforms. A number of state-owned enterprises were privatized; subsidies, tariff barriers and corporate regulations were abolished; and many welfare systems were dismantled. With these radical economic reforms, New Zealand retained its economic stability.

In 1999, Helen Clark (1950-), the leader of the Labor Party, was elected as New Zealand's first female Prime Minister. She also won the following two elections in 2002 and 2005. John Key (1961-) of the National Party won the 2008 election and became Prime Minister. He was then reelected in 2011.

Nowadays, New Zealand is a unique blend of South Pacific and European cultures with a strong national identity of its own. Though it is still considerably influenced by its bonds with Britain, New Zealand has become far more independent in terms of foreign policy and played an increasingly active role in international affairs.

III. Government

As a member of the Commonwealth, New Zealand's political system is largely influenced by Britain. New Zealand is a constitutional monarchy. The Queen of Britain is the head of state. In practice, however, the British monarch plays no active role in the running of New Zealand. A Governor General, usually a New Zealander, represents the Queen by discharging various responsibilities. The Prime Minister of New Zealand is the head of government.

The government of New Zealand is derived from the British one. Accordingly, its fundamental tenet (原则) is the "separation of powers". In other words, government power is divided among three different branches: the legislature, the executive and the judiciary. The division of powers seeks to ensure that no branch can act unconstitutionally.

New Zealand is a unitary state rather than a federation, which means that regions are created on the authority of the central government. Local government representatives are elected by the citizens of each region or city district, yet local governments in New Zealand have fewer powers than those in federation countries. For example, the police force and education are administered by the central government in New Zealand rather than at the local level.

The Legislature

New Zealand's Parliament developed from the British parliamentary system known as the Westminster system of government, and is the law-making body of the New Zealand government. A bill is first examined and debated in Parliament and then passed as a law. However, New Zealand does not have a formal written constitution. New Zealand's constitutional arrangements are reflected in a number of important statutes, judicial decisions and customary rules known as constitutional conventions.

New Zealand's Parliament consists of the Sovereign and the House of Representatives, which usually has 120 elected Representatives. New Zealand citizens and residents, male or female, aged 18 years and over, are legally allowed to vote in the elections.

议会大厦

The Executive

The executive branch of the New Zealand government is made up of the Cabinet, the Prime Minister and the public sector. The Cabinet exercises executive authority. All Cabinet ministers are drawn from Parliament and are collectively responsible to Parliament. The Prime Minister, usually the head of the main political party or coalition of parties in the government, leads the Cabinet.

The Governor General is appointed by the Sovereign on the Prime Minister's recommendation for a term of five years. The Governor General exercises the British monarch's royal powers, which include summoning Parliament or appointing ministers, as well as carrying out ceremonial duties. A bill cannot be passed by Parliament and become law without the Royal Assent of the Governor General.

The Judiciary

The judiciary of New Zealand is independent of the policy makers. Judges make decisions by interpreting the laws passed by Parliament. Parliament passes laws that represent policy decisions which reflect the intentions or interests of the citizens collectively. Freedom from political interference is an essential feature of the judiciary's position.

New Zealand's general courts are structured like a pyramid. At the top is the Supreme Court. Below it, in a descending order, are the Court of Appeal, the High Court and the district courts.

Most court business takes place in the district courts, which form the base of the pyramid. Most criminal cases are heard in the district courts, as well as a large number of civil cases. The High Court has broad general jurisdiction. In practice, it tends to hear the more serious jury trials, the more complex civil cases, administrative law cases and appeals from the decisions of courts and tribunals (特别法庭) below it.

Appeals are to a higher court. A case that is decided in the district courts, for example, can be appealed to the High Court, or directly to the Court of Appeal where the law allows it. The Supreme Court is the final appellate court (上诉法院). Because the Supreme Court hears only a small proportion of cases, the Court of Appeal is in reality the last court for an appeal for most cases in the legal system.

Political Parties

Most historians regard the Liberal Party, which began its rule in 1891, as the first real party in New Zealand politics. During the long period of Liberal Party's control, the party's more conservative opponents founded the Reform Party. Gradually, Liberal and Reform found themselves working together more often. After the Labor Party eventually won office in 1935, Liberal and Reform came together to form the National Party. The Labor Party and the National Party currently are the two main parties of New Zealand. The parties which are currently in the New Zealand Parliament include Labor Party, National Party, New Zealand First (新西兰第一党), Green Party (绿党), Maori Party (毛利党), United Future (联合未来党), ACT New Zealand (新西兰行动党) and Mana Party (马纳党).

The Labor Party was established in 1916 and first entered Parliament in 1919. The Labor Party is a center-left, socially progressive party. It maintains a commitment to strengthening the economy, supporting families and funding the very best education and health systems possible.

The National Party is a center-right, socially conservative party. It has traditionally been Labor's main opponent. It supports free market economy, lower taxation and less legislative interference.

New Zealand First is a centrist and nationalist party. Its primary goals are limiting immigration, reducing Treaty of Waitangi payments, increasing sentences for crimes and buying back former state assets.

The Green Party is a left-wing environmentalist party. It denounces genetic engineering and heavily favors a carbon tax. It also promotes highly progressive social policies.

IV. People

New Zealand is a multicultural society, greatly affected by its diverse population. The culture of the Maoris, as well as the European and Asian cultures, has contributed to the formation of a unique and dynamic society.

New Zealand has a population of 4.4 million (2012). Among them, about 68% are of European descent, whose arrival succeeded that of Captain James Cook. The Maoris make up 14.6% of the population. Other ethnic groups, such as Pacific Island Polynesians, Chinese and Indians have also settled in New Zealand. A distinct feature of New Zealand's population is that most New Zealanders prefer to live in urban areas, despite the nation's focus on agriculture.

New Zealand is nominally Christian, but there is no official state religion.

New Zealand's indigenous Maori people have a unique and fascinating language and culture. The Maori way of life and their view of the world have a major and profound impact on all facets of New Zealand, including national cuisine, the arts and even the accent of its citizens. The vast majority of place names are of Maori origin.

毛利人

The Maori arts, including traditional and contemporary arts, are still kept alive and flourishing. Excellent examples of weaving and carving can be found in today's museums, shops and on marae* throughout the country. Craftsmanship of the Maoris is famous for its varied designs and rich forms. Nowadays, some Maori people, while replicating the techniques used hundreds of years ago, also adopt innovative techniques and forms to develop this ancient form of Maori arts.

---

* marae: 马拉埃，指聚会大厅及其周围土地，是毛利人村社生活的中心。

New Zealand

V. Economy

New Zealand is one of the most developed countries in the world. With a modern and highly developed economy, New Zealand provides its people with a high standard of living, ranking 5th in the Economist Intelligence Unit's* 2012 quality-of-life index.

The economy of New Zealand is strongly trade-oriented, with exports of goods and services accounting for around one-third of the total output. Its primary exports include agricultural, horticultural (园艺的), fishing, forestry and industrial products. In addition, New Zealand imports raw materials necessary for the functioning of the economy. Its major economic partners include Australia, China, the U.S. and Japan.

New Zealand has jokingly been called the world's largest farm because agriculture has traditionally been the major generator of wealth. Agricultural exports, including meat, dairy products, wood products, fruits, vegetables, fish and wool, make up more than half of New Zealand's total export earnings.

However, New Zealand's heavy reliance on international trade, especially on agricultural trade, has made its economic growth vulnerable to any change in worldwide prices of its export and import products. Therefore, since the 1980s, the

---

* the Economist Intelligence Unit: 经济学人信息社，是经济学人集团的一部分，一个研究和咨询公司。每年发布世界最佳居住城市和生活质量指数报告。

government of New Zealand has accomplished a succession of far-reaching economic restructuring reforms, moving the country from an agriculturally-based economy toward a more industrialized, free-market economy. This regulation has greatly diversified the country's economy. Other industries, such as the manufacturing and service sectors, have rapidly developed.

VI. Languages

Both English and Maori are official languages of New Zealand. In April 2006, New Zealand became the first country to declare sign language as an official language, alongside English and Maori. New Zealand Sign Language is the main language of the deaf community in the country.

Maori is only used in New Zealand and nowhere else in the world. Despite its official status, the language continues to struggle for life. It is only recently that the Maori language has gathered widespread support. Presently, the Maori language is commonly used in the media and at school.

VII. Education

New Zealand has a worldwide reputation as a country that provides quality education. It offers a professionally unique learning environment, ranging from early childhood education to polytechnic and university education.

New Zealand offers a wide range of early childhood agencies, namely kindergartens, play centers, preschools, etc. Most of these services are administered by voluntary agencies with government's assistance, and are monitored regularly by the Ministry of Education and the Education Review Office.

Schooling in New Zealand is compulsory for all children aged 6 to 16. The compulsory schooling is divided into primary, intermediate or middle, and secondary schooling. There is a wide choice of schools, ranging from state schools, state integrated schools, private schools, boarding schools to home-based schools. The school year, based on four terms, usually runs from late January to mid-December. Both single-sex and coeducational schooling options are available.

New Zealand

奥克兰大学钟楼

Most children start school at age 5. Primary education starts in Year 1 and continues until Year 8, with Years 7 and 8 mostly offered at either a primary school or a separate intermediate school. English, mathematics, science, social studies, the arts, physical education, health education and music are taught in primary schools.

New Zealand secondary education covers Years 9 to 13. Most secondary schools are government-established, but there are also a number of schools that have special philosophical or religious traditions. The entry requirements, courses and educational standard of all secondary schools are similar, and all secondary schools prepare students for the same national qualifications.

Tertiary education institutions in New Zealand include universities, institutes of technology and polytechnics, colleges, Maori tertiary educational institutions and various training establishments.

New Zealand has 8 government-funded universities offering degree programs in academic and professional studies. While all universities offer a broad range of subjects for degrees in commerce, science and the arts, each university has developed its own specialized courses. The quality of New Zealand university education is well recognized internationally.

There are currently 25 government-funded polytechnics and institutes of technology, which offer a wide variety of academic, vocational and professional programs.

New Zealand is internationally recognized as a provider of qualified teachers. Colleges of education, the schools of education at various universities, some polytechnics and other teacher training agencies provide teacher training courses at the primary, secondary and higher education levels. Apart from these teacher training providers, there are private training establishments which offer English-language training and various forms of continuing education.

Chapter 18 Society and Culture

Exercises

I. Read the following statements and decide whether they are true (T) or false (F).

_____ 1. New Zealand is mainly composed of two islands in the Pacific Ocean.

_____ 2. The highest peak in New Zealand is Mount Cook, which lies in the center of the Southern Alps.

_____ 3. In 1907, New Zealand changed from a British colony to a separate dominion like Australia and Canada.

_____ 4. Helen Clark served three terms as the Prime Minister of New Zealand.

_____ 5. Like many other countries, New Zealand has a formal written constitution.

_____ 6. There is only one chamber in New Zealand's Parliament—the House of Representatives.

_____ 7. Agriculture is important to New Zealand's economy, so most New Zealanders live in suburban areas.

_____ 8. The Maori language is one of the official languages in New Zealand.

II. Choose the best answer to complete each of the following statements.

1. _____ is often referred to as "our third island" of New Zealand.
   A. Polynesia				B. The North Island
   C. The South Island			D. The Stewart Island

2. The climate in New Zealand is _____.
   A. subtropical	B. arctic	C. temperate	D. tropical

3. The _____ were the first group of people who arrived on the islands of New Zealand.
   A. Maoris	B. Europeans	C. Australians	D. Chinese

4. New Zealand was granted internal self-government in _____.
   A. 1840	B. 1852	C. 1893	D. 1907

5. During World War II, New Zealand strengthened its relationship with _____.
   A. Britain	B. the United States	C. Australia	D. France

255

6. _____ is the head of the New Zealand government.
   A. The British monarch   B. The Governor General
   C. The Prime Minister   D. The President
7. The Cabinet is responsible to _____ in New Zealand.
   A. Parliament   B. the Prime Minister
   C. the British monarch   D. the Governor General
8. Schooling in New Zealand is compulsory for all children _____.
   A. from ages 6 to 12   B. from ages 6 to 14
   C. from ages 6 to 16   D. from ages 6 to 18

III. **Give brief answers to the following questions.**
   1. What did the Labor Party do to improve New Zealand's economy in the 1930s?
      _____
      _____
   2. Why did America suspend the ANZUS security guarantees to New Zealand in 1986?
      _____
      _____
   3. Since the 1980s, what did the New Zealand government do to change its heavy reliance on international trade? What are the results?
      _____
      _____

IV. **State your understanding of the following questions.**
   1. What is the Treaty of Waitangi?
   2. What is the significance of the following documents: the Treaty of Waitangi, the New Zealand Constitution Act and the Statute of Westminster Adoption Act?

Chapter 18 Society and Culture

Learn and Check

Composing parts: the North Island, the South Island and a number of smaller islands

Major cities: Wellington (the capital city), Auckland (the largest city)

Discovery of New Zealand: the Maoris about 1,200 years ago, Abel Tasman in 1642 and James Cook in 1769

New Zealand as a colony: the signing of the Treaty of Waitangi in 1840 making New Zealand a British colony

New Zealand as a dominion: New Zealand becoming a dominion in 1907

New Zealand as a realm: from 1983 onward

The Statute of Westminster Adoption Act: signed in 1947, granting New Zealand total independence from Britain

Government: the legislature, the executive, the judiciary

Major political parties: the Labor Party, the National Party, New Zealand First, the Green Party

Population: 4.4 million (2012)

Economy: a more industrialized, free-market economy

Official languages: English, Maori, New Zealand Sign Language

Education system: early childhood education, primary education, secondary education, tertiary education

Key to Exercises

The United Kingdom of Great Britain and Northern Ireland

Chapter 1 Geography, People and Language

I
1. F 2. T 3. F 4. F
5. F 6. T 7. T 8. F

II
1. A 2. B 3. D 4. C
5. D 6. A 7. C 8. C

III
1. Tourists from all over the world like to go to Scotland to enjoy the beautiful Scottish scenery, to drink Scotch whisky and to see Scotsmen wearing kilts and playing bagpipes.
2. The development of the English language can be divided into three periods: Old English, Middle English and Modern English.
3. The laboring and merchant classes grew in economic and social importance after the Black Death, and English thus grew in importance compared to French.

IV
1. The earliest known inhabitants of Britain were Celts who were the ancestors of the Welsh, Scottish and Irish people. Then came the Anglos, the Saxons and the Jutes who brought with them the English language. Many people from other countries came later. In modern times there are a lot of immigrants from many former colonies of the British Empire. Britain is thus a country of mixed cultures and the British people are of different ethnic and cultural backgrounds.
2. Standard English is based on the speech of the upper class of southeastern England. It is preferred by the educated and is widely used in the media and taught at schools. It has developed and has been promoted as a model for correct British English. It is also the norm carried overseas. Today, Standard English is codified to the extent that the grammar and vocabulary are much the same everywhere in the world where English is taught and used.

Key to Exercises

Chapter 2　History

I
1. T　　2. T　　3. F　　4. T
5. T　　6. F　　7. F　　8. T

II
1. D　　2. D　　3. C　　4. C
5. A　　6. B　　7. A　　8. C

III
1. Queen Victoria made tremendous achievements in almost every aspect. She promoted further industrialization, the building of railways and the growth of trade and commerce. During her reign, Britain developed into an empire including about a quarter of the global population and a quarter of the world's landmass.

2. In World War I the two camps were the Central Powers—mainly Germany, Austria-Hungary, Turkey and the Allies—mainly France, Great Britain, Russia, Italy and from 1917, the United States.

3. Britain cooperated closely with the United States after World War II since they were allied during World War II and shared the same concerns about the Soviet Union.

IV
1. The Industrial Revolution changed Britain in many ways. First, its industrial productivity increased dramatically. Britain became the most advanced industrial country in the world. Second, urbanization took place. Many new cities sprang up. Third, it caused great changes in the social class structure. The capitalist class became the most important force in the country and the proletariat class emerged.

2. Colonization of Newfoundland in 1583 marked the beginning of the British Empire. By 1837, Britain had been an empire which included the colonies in Canada, India and many small states in the West Indies. During the mid-19th century, the British government consolidated the existing colonies by bringing them under the direct control of the government. By the end of the 19th century, the British Empire included about a quarter of the global population and a quarter of the world's landmass. Before World War I, Britain was the largest colonial empire in the world. However, Britain suffered a great loss of its manpower in the two World Wars and exhausted its reserves of gold, dollars and overseas investment. Most of Britain's colonies gained independence as a result of World War II, which inevitably led to the fall of the British Empire.

Chapter 3 Government and the Commonwealth

I
1. T   2. F   3. F   4. F
5. F   6. T   7. F   8. T

II
1. C   2. D   3. B   4. A
5. B   6. B   7. D   8. C

III
1. The three functions of the House of Commons are: to draft laws, to scrutinize the activities of the government and to influence future government policy.
2. The Liberal Democrats is perceived as a "middle" party between the Conservative Party and the Labor Party. Many people see it as comparatively flexible and pragmatic in its balance of the individual and the social. It emphasizes the need for a change in Britain's constitutional arrangements to make the government more democratic and accountable.
3. Independent candidates are unlikely to win in the general election because even if they were elected, they would be powerless in Parliament against the larger parties. Therefore, voters usually do not vote for them.

IV
1. The electoral campaigns usually involve advertising in newspapers, door-to-door campaigning and leaflets. The main parties are given short periods of time on national television to present their policies to the public. Apart from the parties' own publicity, newspapers and TV programs spend a lot of time discussing the campaigns, interviewing politicians and predicting the results.
2. The Commonwealth of Nations is a voluntary association of independent sovereign states, all of which acknowledge the British monarch as the symbolic head of the association. The Commonwealth is not a political union, and its member states have full autonomy to manage their own internal and external affairs. It is primarily an organization in which countries with diverse economic backgrounds have an opportunity for close and equal interaction after gaining independence. Its primary purpose is to advocate democracy, human rights and to promote economic cooperation and growth within its members.

Key to Exercises

Chapter 4   Economy

I   1. T   2. T   3. F   4. F
       5. T   6. T   7. F   8. T

II 1. A   2. C   3. D   4. C
       5. D   6. B   7. A   8. C

III 1. The negative aspect of Thatcher's reform in the early 1980s was a rapid increase in unemployment. In 1982, the unemployment rate reached the level of the Great Depression years, with three million people out of work.

2. Britain's agriculture is characterized by a small proportion of the population engaged in agricultural activities with a high degree of mechanization. Although it employs only about 1.5% of the country's labor force, it meets around 60% of the national demand for food.

3. Britain's beef industry was hit badly by BSE in 1996, resulting in a ban on its beef exports until 2006.

IV 1. Britain's economy experienced a relative decline in the post-war period for several reasons. First, Britain suffered great losses in the two World Wars and had gone heavily into debt to finance the wars. Second, the era of the British Empire was over by the mid-20th century. India and other British colonies, which provided raw materials and large markets for British goods, gained independence. Third, Britain was forced to maintain an expensive military presence in many overseas locations until the end of the 1960s. What's more, Britain had to make substantial financial contributions to NATO and the U.N. Security Council. Finally, Britain failed to invest in industry after World War II, whereas its competitors like Germany and Japan caught up by investing in industry.

2. The service industry has played an increasingly important role in economy in the developed countries. On the one hand, it requires a large group of people working in it so that abundant employment opportunities are provided. On the other hand, the service industry causes little pollution.

Chapter 5 Education, Media and Holidays

I
| 1. F | 2. F | 3. F | 4. T |
| 5. T | 6. F | 7. F | 8. T |

II
| 1. D | 2. C | 3. B | 4. B |
| 5. C | 6. C | 7. D | 8. A |

III
1. Grammar schools were to train the most academically capable students and prepare them for university, whereas vocational schools were to help the less successful students to learn a trade.
2. British comprehensive schools provide a general education, offering both academic subjects like literature and science, and more practical subjects like cooking and carpentry.
3. British universities enjoy complete academic freedom because they can appoint their own staff, decide which students to admit, provide their own courses and award their own degrees.
4. The media plays an essential role in British leisure culture since it helps to shape the public's opinion, determine people's moral and political orientation and consolidate or undermine the rule of a government.

IV
1. Britain's independent schools require fees from students. Although the National Curriculum is optional in the independent system, most independent schools teach what the curriculum demands. Independent schools get their funding through the private sector as well as tuition fees, with minimal government assistance. Since they are generally better funded than most state schools, they are likely to recruit the best teachers and provide superior facilities. However, the high tuition fees have become an obstacle for many students to enroll although graduates of independent schools are more likely to be accepted by famous universities.
2. Among the 10 daily national newspapers in Britain, about half of them are regarded as the "quality press" since they carry in-depth articles of political and social importance, reviews and feature articles about "high culture", and they are generally read by well-educated people. *The Times*, *The Guardian* and *The Daily Telegraph* are good examples. The "tabloids", with color photos and striking headlines, usually cover scandals and gossip about celebrities. A typical example is *The Sun on Sunday*.

Key to Exercises

Chapter 6 Literature

I 1. F 2. T 3. T 4. F
    5. F 6. F 7. F 8. T

II 1. B 2. C 3. B 4. D
    5. C 6. A 7. B 8. A

III 1. Shakespeare's plays fall into three categories: comedy, tragedy and historical play. His representative comedies include *A Midsummer Night's Dream*, *The Merchant of Venice*, *As You Like It* and *Twelfth Night*. His great tragedies are represented by *Hamlet*, *Othello*, *King Lear*, *Macbeth* and *Romeo and Juliet*. His major historical plays include *Richard III*, *Henry V* and *Antony and Cleopatra*.

2. Critical Realism is a literary school which flourished in the 1840s and the early 1850s. The critical realists described the chief traits of society and criticized the capitalist system from a democratic viewpoint. The greatest English critical realist is Charles Dickens.

3. The new literary trends that prevailed at the end of the 19th century are Neo-Romanticism and Aestheticism. Those who advocated Neo-Romanticism put emphasis on the invention of exciting adventures and fascinating stories, and those of Aestheticism believed in "art for art's sake".

4. The stream of consciousness is a writing technique which puts the unorganized flow of thought onto page. Writers who adopt this technique give precedence to the depiction of the characters' mental and emotional reactions to external events, rather than the events themselves.

IV 1. Romanticism is a trend that appeared in English literature at the turn of the 19th century. It is a revolt against the prescribed rules of Classicism. Writers of Romantic literature are more concerned with imagination and feeling than with reason and intellect. Discontent with the development of capitalism, they seek literary refuge. William Wordsworth and Samuel Taylor Coleridge began the trend with their joint work *Lyrical Ballads*, whose preface is viewed as Romantic poetry's "Declaration of Independence". It was the second generation of Romantic poets such as Lord Byron, Percy Bysshe Shelley and John Keats who brought the Romantic Movement to its height.

2. English literature in the 20th century can be roughly divided into two periods: Modernism and Postmodernism. Modernism prevailed before World War II. It can be viewed as a deliberate departure from tradition and is characterized by the use of innovative forms of expressions. Modernist writing seems disorganized and hard to understand. It often portrays the action from the viewpoint of a single confused individual, rather than from the viewpoint of an all-knowing impersonal narrator. After World War II, Postmodernism began. Postmodernism differs in some ways from Modernism. Modernism, for example, tends to present a fragmented view of human subjectivity, but presents that fragmentation as something tragic and to be lamented as a loss. Postmodernism does not lament the idea of fragmentation, but rather celebrates it. Modernists look for buried meaning below the confusing surface, while postmodernists abandon that search.

The Republic of Ireland

Chapter 7 Society and Culture

I
1. F 2. F 3. F 4. T
5. F 6. F 7. F 8. T

II
1. B 2. C 3. C 4. D
5. B 6. C 7. A 8. B

III
1. Cork was given the nickname "the Rebel County" because people of Cork fought to overthrow the English rule as early as in 1491, and they are proud of their participation in the Irish War of Independence and the Irish Civil War.
2. The hunter-gathers came to Ireland from Britain around 6,000 BC. Then Celtic tribes came in the 6th century BC. The Gaels arrived in the 4th century BC. The Vikings came in the 8th century. In the 12th century, the Normans arrived.
3. Ireland remained neutral in World War II because the Irish had anti-British sentiment and they lacked military preparation to join World War II.

Key to Exercises

IV 1. The Act of Union made Ireland an integral part of the U.K. The Anglo-Irish Treaty made the 26 southern counties of Ireland become the Irish Free State, as a dominion within the British Commonwealth of Nations. The divergent attitudes toward it caused the Irish Civil War. The Anglo-Irish Agreement gave the Irish government a consultative role in the administration of Northern Ireland. The Belfast Agreement called for devolved government in Northern Ireland and improved the relations between the Republic of Ireland and Britain.

2. Fianna Fáil pursues complete political separation from Britain and supports peaceful reunification of the whole island. The key principles of Fine Gael are equality of opportunity, pro-enterprise policies, security, integrity and hope. It accepts the British partition of Ireland and has generally been less anti-British. The Labor Party advocates liberalization of laws on divorce and contraception, an active role for the state in managing the economy, and a moderate position on the eventual unification with Northern Ireland.

The United States of America

Chapter 8 Geography and People

I 1. F 2. T 3. T 4. T
5. F 6. T 7. T 8. T

II 1. B 2. C 3. A 4. B
5. C 6. D 7. A 8. D

III 1. The distribution of the American population is rather uneven. The most densely populated region is the northeastern part of the country. This region takes up about one quarter of the total land area, but about half of the population is living here. The Great Plains have a comparatively small population. The South has a population of over 100 million. The West is not densely populated, except for some metropolitan centers like Los Angeles and San Francisco.

2. The new immigrants in the United States, being poor and accustomed to poverty, were willing to work for very low wages. This made other workers

afraid that the immigrants would lower wage levels and take jobs away from them. This opposition led to the Immigration Act of 1924.

IV 1. The United States is not merely a nation, but a nation of nations. The immigrants came in waves, including the Europeans, the Africans and the Asians. Therefore, America is described as a "melting pot" where various racial and ethnic groups are assimilated into the American culture. Recently, America has been called a "salad bowl" in that people of different races and ethnic groups mix harmoniously, but at the same time keep their distinct culture and customs.

2. The best possible way to help assimilation in a multicultural society is to be open and tolerant toward different cultures. People from different racial and ethnic backgrounds should respect each other. Society should create opportunities to help immigrants become assimilated. At the same time the immigrants should keep their own language, customs and religion, contributing to the diversity of a multicultural society.

Chapter 9   History

I 1. T   2. F   3. T   4. F
   5. T   6. F   7. T   8. F

II 1. C   2. C   3. D   4. B
   5. C   6. A   7. C   8. D

III 1. The America's sit-on-the-fence policy changed in 1940. The American government feared that the Axis countries were winning the war, which might threaten America's security and interests. The Japanese air raid on Pearl Harbor became the direct cause for America's entrance into World War II.

2. Nixon made three well-known contributions during his presidency: 1) ending the U.S. military involvement in the Vietnam War; 2) reestablishing U.S. relations with China; 3) negotiating the first Strategic Arms Limitation Treaty with the Soviet Union.

3. Regan's economic program called for reductions in income taxes and business taxes in order to encourage investment, and proposed deep cuts

in federal spending in every area except defense. Regan also requested that many government regulations be eliminated so as to reduce the federal government's role in the day-to-day operation of business.

IV 1. The Southern planters of America needed a large number of black African slaves to manage their plantations and they regarded the slaves as their property. In the North, with the development of industry, there was a growing demand for free labor. What's more, the Northerners demanded a law to protect tariffs and asked the government to finance the building of railways and roads. But the Southerners were against it and advocated free trade so as to purchase cheaper goods from foreign countries. The accumulating conflicts led to the division of the North and the South and finally the American Civil War.
2. During the two World Wars, America remained neutral in the early stage. However, Americans continued their profitable trade with the warring countries. Therefore, they not only retained their military forces, but also accumulated great wealth. When America entered the wars, it was almost at the end of the wars. By sharing the fruit of victory with other allies, America greatly strengthened its power and became a powerful country by the end of World War II.

Chapter 10 Government

I 1. F   2. T   3. F   4. T
      5. F   6. T   7. F   8. T

II 1. B   2. C   3. B   4. D
      5. C   6. C   7. D   8. C

III 1. One characteristic of the U.S. Constitution is "checks and balances". The other is that the powers of the federal government and of the state government are specified in the Constitution.
2. A Senator must be over 30 years old, a U.S. citizen for at least nine years and a resident in the state which they represent. A Representative should be at least 25 years old and a U.S. citizen for no less than seven years.

3. The major powers of the Supreme Court are: a) to interpret laws; b) to hear appeals from any federal court cases; c) to hear appeals from state court cases that involve the Constitution or national laws; d) may declare a law unconstitutional; e) may declare a presidential act unconstitutional.
4. Generally speaking, the Democratic Party has a liberal ideology, while the Republican Party is more conservative. The Democrats want the government to play an important role in the economy and emphasize full employment as a matter of national concern. They favor civil rights laws, a strong social security system, less restrictive abortion laws, among others. The Republicans favor an economic system which gives enterprises greater freedom and demand that the government control inflation. They stress the need for law and order and oppose complete government social programs and free choice of abortion. They also favor a strong military posture and assertive stand in international relations.

IV 1. Each party holds its national convention every four years to choose a candidate for the presidency. To win a presidential election, a candidate has to spend millions of dollars, travel all over the country to make speeches and debate on television with the rival. The general election is technically divided into two stages. During the first stage, presidential electors for each state will be chosen. In the second stage the electors meet and vote a President. Since the second stage is only a kind of formality, everyone knows who will be the next President as soon as the first stage is over.

I think the candidates spend too much money on the electoral campaigns. And, the election cannot solve the social and economic problems of the U.S. as some candidates do not keep their word after they become President.

2. President Eisenhower made vigorous efforts to wage the Cold War. He placed new emphasis on developing nuclear strength to prevent the outbreak of war. He also frequently authorized the CIA to undertake secret interventions to overthrow unfriendly governments or protect reliable anti-communist leaders whose power was threatened. The CIA helped topple the governments of Iran and Guatemala, but it suffered an embarrassing failure in Indonesia. In addition, Eisenhower used U.S. power and prestige to help create a non-communist government in South Vietnam, which brought disastrous long-term consequences to the United States.

Key to Exercises

Chapter 11 Economy

I 1. T   2. T   3. F   4. F
     5. F   6. T   7. T   8. F

II 1. C   2. C   3. D   4. D
     5. D   6. D   7. B   8. A

III 1. During the colonial period of America, secondary industries developed as the colonies grew. A variety of specialized sawmills and gristmills appeared. Colonists established shipyards to build fishing fleets and trading vessels. They also built small iron forges. By the 18th century, regional patterns of development had become clear.

2. After the Civil War, the large southern cotton plantations became much less profitable. Northern industries, which had expanded rapidly because of the demand of the war, surged ahead.

3. America has made great efforts to reduce trade barriers because the federal government has realized that open bilateral trade will not only advance its own economic development, but also enhance its domestic stability and its relationship with other nations.

IV 1. The U.S. Constitution, as an economic charter, established that the entire nation was a unified or "common" market. There were no tariffs or taxes on interstate commerce. It provided that the federal government could regulate commerce with foreign nations and among the states, establish uniform bankruptcy laws, create money and regulate its value, fix standards of weights and measures, establish post offices and roads, and fix rules governing patents and copyrights. The last-mentioned clause was an early recognition of the importance of "intellectual property", a matter that began assuming great importance in trade negotiations since the late 20th century.

2. The government has always played an active and important role in America's economic development. In the early 1930s, the United States suffered the worst economic depression in American history. President Roosevelt introduced the New Deal to tackle the financial crisis. Besides, he set up the New York State Emergency Relief Commission to help those in desperate need and tried to relieve the serious problems of the jobless. At the end of 1970s, the American economy again suffered a recession. The Reagan administration combated inflation by controlling government spending

deficit, cutting taxes and raising interest rates. Both policies mentioned above helped to set the country's economic development on its right course. In all, the intervention of the government has ensured that economic opportunities are fair and accessible to the people. It has prevented flagrant abuses of the system, dampened the effects of inflation and stimulated economic growth.

Chapter 12 Education, Media and Holidays

I   1. T   2. T   3. F   4. T
    5. T   6. F   7. F   8. F

II 1. C   2. B   3. B   4. B
    5. C   6. B   7. B   8. B

III 1. American universities choose applicants on the basis of: a) their high school records; b) recommendations from their high school teachers; c) the impression they make during interviews at the university; d) their scores on the SAT.
    2. Higher education institutions in the United States have three functions: teaching, research and public service, with each college or university having its own emphasis with regard to its functions.
    3. The four universities all have a long history. They all have an excellent faculty, a large number of students and have made extensive academic achievements. Some of their graduates are very successful or influential in politics, arts, business, etc.
    4. Thanksgiving is associated with the time when Europeans first came to the New World. When Pilgrims first arrived in 1620, life was very hard and there was not enough food, so many of them died. The Native Americans helped them and then they had a bountiful harvest next year. So they held a big celebration to thank God and the Native Americans.

IV 1. The first ideal of the American educational system is that as many people as possible should receive as much education as possible. The second ideal is producing a society that is totally literate and of local control. The third ideal is that scholars and students should work to discover new information or conceive new ways to understand what is already known.

Key to Exercises

2. American schools routinely teach the experiences and values of many ethnic cultures. Current textbooks incorporate a variety of ethnic individuals who have achieved success. Struggles for equality are vividly depicted, and past racism is bluntly acknowledged. Cultural pluralism is now generally recognized as the organizing principle of education. Schools at all levels offer students opportunities to learn about different cultures.

Chapter 13 Literature

I
1. T 2. F 3. F 4. T
5. T 6. T 7. F 8. T

II
1. C 2. D 3. C 4. D
5. D 6. A 7. A 8. B

III
1. American Puritanism stresses predestination, original sin, total depravity, and limited atonement or the salvation of a selected few who would receive God's grace.
2. The Lost Generation refers to the young American writers caught up in World War I and cut off from the old values, yet unable to come to terms with the new era when civilization has gone mad. They produced works of disillusionment. Two representative writers are F. Scott Fitzgerald and Ernest Hemingway.
3. The Beat Movement began in the 1950s. The word "beat" suggests a non-conformist, rebellious attitude toward conventional values concerning sex, religion and the American way of life, an attitude which results from the feeling of depression and exhaustion and the need to escape into an unconventional, communal mode of life. The representatives are Allen Ginsberg, William Burroughs and Jack Kerouac.

IV
1. During the Romantic Period, most of the American writing placed an increasing emphasis on the free expression of emotion and displayed an increasing attention to the psychic state of the characters. They celebrated America's landscape with its virgin forests, meadows, endless prairies, streams and vast oceans. The Romantic writers of America had a strong tendency to exalt the individual and the common man.

2. Eugene O'Neill is the first American playwright to regard drama as serious literature. His plays are highly experimental in form and style, combining literary theories of symbolism, naturalism and expressionism. He has great influence on later American playwrights. Therefore, he is regarded as the greatest American playwright.

Canada

Chapter 14 Geography and History

I 1. T   2. T   3. F   4. F
    5. T   6. F   7. T   8. F

II 1. B   2. D   3. B   4. C
    5. C   6. A   7. D   8. B

III 1. Both John Cabot and Jacques Cartier originally wanted to find new routes to Asia. However, the voyage led them to Canada.
2. The Meech Lake Accord failed in 1990 because many people regarded the Meech Lake Accord as an attempt to weaken or even dismantle the power of the Canadian federal government, and also viewed the special status of Québec as unfair and problematic.
3. The Chrétien's government cut government spending while maintaining the high tax rates. It strongly supported private enterprises as the key source of economic growth. Therefore, it gained popularity among the Canadian people in its early years.

IV 1. In the early 1600s, both Britain and France founded permanent settlements in Canada. The French founded a colony in Québec city and extended from the St. Lawrence River to the Great Lakes and then from there to the Great Plains and the Mississippi Valley. The British settled along the Atlantic coast. Due to the competition for land, there were conflicts between Britain and France. The Seven Years' War brought the whole Canada under the British control. In 1774, the Québec Act granted the people of Québec linguistic

and religious freedom, and guaranteed the use of French civil law and British criminal law. According to the Constitutional Act of 1791, Canada was split into the English-speaking Ontario and the French-speaking Québec, both with limited self-government and political organization. In the 1960s, Québec wanted to separate from Canada and to establish a French-speaking nation. The Québec sovereignty movement led to referenda in 1980 and 1995, with its proposals for independence being rejected by the voters. Mulroney's government made national unity a high priority. In 1987, the Meech Lake Accord was passed, recognizing the distinctive state of Québec. However, the Accord was defeated in 1990. In 1992, the Charlottetown Accord which addressed greater autonomy for both Québec and the aboriginal population was also defeated in a national referendum. Hence, Québec still remains one of the provinces of Canada.
2. Canada's major cities include Ottawa, Toronto, Québec city, Montréal and Vancouver, all located near the Canadian-U.S. border. Each city has a large population with people from different racial and ethnic backgrounds. The climate in this area is comparatively moderate, with mild summers and winters, high humidity and abundant rainfall.

Chapter 15   Government and Society

I
1. F   2. F   3. T   4. F
5. T   6. F   7. F   8. F

II
1. C   2. B   3. A   4. C
5. B   6. A   7. C   8. C

III
1. The responsibilities of the Governor General include summoning the House of Commons and the Senate, giving Royal Assent to all federal laws passed by the House, opening and ending sessions of Parliament, and dissolving Parliament before an election.
2. The population distribution in Canada is rather uneven. The southern large cities are densely populated, while most other parts of Canada are sparsely inhabited.
3. "Cultural mosaic" indicates that people of diverse origins and communities are free to preserve and enhance their own cultural heritage while participating as equal partners in Canadian society.

IV 1. Canadians are composed of many different races and ethnic groups. They speak different languages at home apart from English and French. While participating as equal partners in Canadian society, they keep their own cultural heritage, constituting a "cultural mosaic". In 1971, Canada implemented a multicultural policy to admit pluralism as a fact of Canadian life. In 1988, the Canadian Multiculturalism Act was passed. Canada became the first country in the world to pass a national multiculturalism law. With globalization and increasing immigration, multilingualism and multiculturalism will remain a special feature of Canadian society.

2. Before World War II, Canada used to have a racist immigration policy which actively discriminated against racial and religious minorities. After World War II, the Canadian government began to adopt a new policy to eliminate prejudice. Since then, Canada has opened its door to immigrants of all races and religions from any countries. At the end of the 20th century, a kind of anti-immigrant sentiment spread in Canada, and the federal government made changes to its immigration policy that decreased the number of immigrants allowed into Canada. Now, it is more difficult for people to immigrate to Canada.

Australia

Chapter 16 Geography and History

I 1. T   2. F   3. F   4. T
    5. T   6. F   7. T   8. F

II 1. A   2. D   3. D   4. D
    5. B   6. B   7. A   8. B

III 1. At the end of the 19th century, the six colonies found that the separation of governments and markets had restricted their development. They also realized that they needed to pursue uniform immigration rules in order to keep the unwanted immigrants out. Moreover, they feared that the mainland

Key to Exercises

      European countries would invade or colonize Australia. So they all wanted to have the country unified.

2. During World War I, the Australian and New Zealand Army Corps (ANZACs) took part in some of the bloodiest battles, such as the Gallipoli Campaign, leaving one of the glorious chapters in Australian history. The Australians were very proud of their bravery and indomitable spirit. Now April 25 is celebrated as ANZAC Day to honor all those Australians who died in military conflicts.

3. The aim of the economic reforms between 1983 and 1996 was to make market forces play a greater role in shaping a healthy national economy so that the Australian industries would improve their efficiency and competitiveness.

IV 1. Australia joined both wars following Britain, and had heavy casualties in both wars. However, Australia also gained some benefits from the wars as it experienced industrial and social development and prosperity during or after the wars. Australia also got recognition for its role in the wars.

2. In the 1960s, the movement to gain recognition of Aboriginal rights began. According to the 1967 referendum, the Australian federal government was given the power to pass legislation on behalf of the indigenous people and to include the indigenous people in future censuses. There was also a campaign against the White Australia Policy. In 1973, the White Australia Policy officially ended. Since then the Australians live in harmony with people from the Asian countries.

Chapter 17 Government and Society

I   1. F   2. T   3. F   4. F
     5. T   6. F   7. F   8. F

II   1. D   2. B   3. B   4. D
     5. D   6. C   7. B   8. C

III 1. The three-tier system of the Australian government includes: the federal government at the national level, governments at the state and territory level and local governments at the city, town, municipal and shire level.

2. The central function of the House of Representatives in Australia is to consider and pass new laws and make amendments or changes to existing laws. It is also involved in determining the government, publicizing and scrutinizing government administration, representing the people and controlling government expenditure.
3. Tourism is one of Australia's largest and fastest-developing industries. It employs 4.5% of the workforce and contributes about 2.6% of Australia's GDP.

IV 1. There are two main factors that attract immigrants from over 200 countries to Australia. One is the Australian immigration policy and tradition. Australia has a great international reputation for its diversity and tolerance. It accepts and respects the right of all people to express and share their individual cultural heritage. It emphasizes the equality of all people in the labor market and social life. The other is Australia's good natural and living environment.
2. Higher education in Australia is provided through universities, vocational training institutions, and adult and community educational institutions. The standard, design and diversity of education offered by the Australian universities are among the most impressive in the world. The Australian universities have strong international links across the whole range of their activities. They especially develop strong educational relationships with its neighbors in the Asia-Pacific region.

New Zealand

Chapter 18   Society and Culture

I   1. T   2. T   3. T   4. T
    5. F   6. T   7. F   8. T

II 1. D   2. C   3. A   4. B
    5. B   6. C   7. A   8. C

Key to Exercises

III
1. In the 1930s, the Labor Party launched a series of social reforms. A comprehensive social security system including welfare benefits and health care was introduced; the free education system was further expanded; some initiatives granting state support for arts and culture were taken; and state regulations in most areas of the economy and society were extended. Through these measures, New Zealand began to show signs of economic improvement.
2. New Zealand declared its anti-nuclear policy and became a nuclear-free zone in the mid-1980s. It prohibited the American nuclear-powered ships from coming into its territorial waters. As a result, America suspended the ANZUS security guarantees to New Zealand in 1986.
3. Since the 1980s, the New Zealand government launched a series of far-reaching economic restructuring reforms, changing the country from an agriculturally-based economy toward a more industrialized, free-market economy. This regulation has greatly diversified the country's economy and helped develop other industries, such as the manufacturing and service sectors.

IV
1. The Treaty of Waitangi was signed in 1840 by representatives of the British Crown and chiefs of the indigenous Maori people, making New Zealand a British colony. According to the treaty, the chiefs of the Maori people gave the Queen of England complete governance over their land. In exchange, the Queen of England guaranteed to protect all the Maori people and give them the same rights and duties of citizenship as British subjects. The Treaty of Waitangi is also known as New Zealand's founding document and it marks the beginning of modern New Zealand.
2. The Treaty of Waitangi made New Zealand a British colony. The New Zealand Constitution Act granted New Zealand internal self-government. The Statute of Westminster Adoption Act granted New Zealand total independence from Britain.

Appendices

Appendix 1   Shires of the United Kingdom

Shire		County Town	
Bedfordshire	贝德福德郡	Bedford	贝德福德
Buckinghamshire	白金汉郡	Aylesbury	艾尔斯伯里
Cambridgeshire	剑桥郡	Cambridge	剑桥
Cheshire	柴郡	Chester	切斯特
Cornwall and Isles of Scilly	康沃尔和锡利群岛郡	Truro	特鲁罗
Cumbria	坎布里亚郡	Carlisle	卡莱尔
Derbyshire	德比郡	Matlock	马特洛克
Devon	德文郡	Exeter	埃克塞特
Dorset	多塞特郡	Dorchester	多切斯特
Durham	达勒姆郡	Durham	达勒姆
East Sussex	东萨塞克斯郡	Lewes	刘易斯
Essex	埃塞克斯郡	Chelmsford	切姆斯福德
Gloucestershire	格洛斯特郡	Gloucester	格洛斯特
Hampshire	汉普郡	Winchester	温切斯特
Hertfordshire	赫特福德郡	Hertford	赫特福德

Shire		County Town	
Kent	肯特郡	Maidstone	梅德斯通
Lancashire	兰开夏郡	Preston	普雷斯顿
Leicestershire	莱斯特郡	Leicester	莱斯特
Lincolnshire	林肯郡	Lincoln	林肯
Norfolk	诺福克郡	Norwich	诺里奇
North Yorkshire	北约克郡	Northallerton	诺萨勒顿
Northamptonshire	北安普顿郡	Northampton	北安普顿
Northumberland	诺森伯兰郡	Morpeth	莫珀斯
Nottinghamshire	诺丁汉郡	Nottingham	诺丁汉
Oxfordshire	牛津郡	Oxford	牛津
Shropshire	什罗普郡	Shrewsbury	什鲁斯伯里
Somerset	萨默塞特郡	Taunton	汤顿
Staffordshire	斯塔福德郡	Stafford	斯塔福德
Suffolk	萨福克郡	Ipswich	伊普斯威奇
Surrey	萨里郡	Kingston upon Thames	泰晤士河畔的金斯敦
Warwickshire	沃里克郡	Warwick	沃里克
West Sussex	西萨塞克斯郡	Chichester	奇切斯特
Wiltshire	威尔特郡	Trowbridge	特罗布里奇
Worcestershire	伍斯特郡	Worcester	伍斯特

Appendix 2 States of the United States

State		Capital		Postal Abbreviation	State Nickname
Alabama	亚拉巴马州	Montgomery	蒙哥马利	AL	Cotton State
Alaska	阿拉斯加州	Juneau	朱诺	AK	Last Frontier
Arizona	亚利桑那州	Phoenix	菲尼克斯	AZ	Grand Canyon State
Arkansas	阿肯色州	Little Rock	小石城	AR	Land of Opportunity
California	加利福尼亚州	Sacramento	萨克拉门托	CA	Golden State
Colorado	科罗拉多州	Denver	丹佛	CO	Centennial State
Connecticut	康涅狄格州	Hartford	哈特福德	CT	Constitution State
Delaware	特拉华州	Dover	多佛尔	DE	First State
Florida	佛罗里达州	Tallahassee	塔拉哈西	FL	Sunshine State
Georgia	佐治亚州	Atlanta	亚特兰大	GA	Empire State of the South
Hawaii	夏威夷州	Honolulu	檀香山	HI	Aloha State
Idaho	爱达荷州	Boise	博伊西	ID	Gem State
Illinois	伊利诺伊州	Springfield	斯普林菲尔德	IL	Land of Lincoln
Indiana	印第安纳州	Indianapolis	印第安纳波利斯	IN	Hoosier State
Iowa	衣阿华州	Des Moines	得梅因	IA	Hawkeye State
Kansas	堪萨斯州	Topeka	托皮卡	KS	Sunflower State
Kentucky	肯塔基州	Frankfort	法兰克福	KY	Bluegrass State
Louisiana	路易斯安那州	Baton Rouge	巴吞鲁日	LA	Pelican State
Maine	缅因州	Augusta	奥古斯塔	ME	Pine Tree State
Maryland	马里兰州	Annapolis	安纳波利斯	MD	Old Line State
Massachusetts	马萨诸塞州	Boston	波士顿	MA	Bay State
Michigan	密歇根州	Lansing	兰辛	MI	Wolverine State
Minnesota	明尼苏达州	Saint Paul	圣保罗	MN	Gopher State
Mississippi	密西西比州	Jackson	杰克逊	MS	Magnolia State
Missouri	密苏里州	Jefferson City	杰斐逊城	MO	Show Me State

State		Capital		Postal Abbreviation	State Nickname
Montana	蒙大拿州	Helena	赫勒纳	MT	Treasure State
Nebraska	内布拉斯加州	Lincoln	林肯	NE	Cornhusker State
Nevada	内华达州	Carson City	卡森城	NV	Silver State
New Hampshire	新罕布什尔州	Concord	康科德	NH	Granite State
New Jersey	新泽西州	Trenton	特伦顿	NJ	Garden State
New Mexico	新墨西哥州	Santa Fe	圣菲	NM	Land of Enchantment
New York	纽约州	Albany	奥尔巴尼	NY	Empire State
North Carolina	北卡罗来纳州	Raleigh	罗利	NC	Tar Heel State
North Dakota	北达科他州	Bismarck	俾斯麦	ND	Flickertail State
Ohio	俄亥俄州	Columbus	哥伦布	OH	Buckeye State
Oklahoma	俄克拉荷马州	Oklahoma City	俄克拉荷马城	OK	Sooner State
Oregon	俄勒冈州	Salem	萨勒姆	OR	Beaver State
Pennsylvania	宾夕法尼亚州	Harrisburg	哈里斯堡	PA	Keystone State
Rhode Island	罗得岛州	Providence	普罗维登斯	RI	Ocean State
South Carolina	南卡罗来纳州	Columbia	哥伦比亚	SC	Palmetto State
South Dakota	南达科他州	Pierre	皮尔	SD	Mount Rushmore State
Tennessee	田纳西州	Nashville	纳什维尔	TN	Volunteer State
Texas	得克萨斯州	Austin	奥斯汀	TX	Lone Star State
Utah	犹他州	Salt Lake City	盐湖城	UT	Beehive State
Vermont	佛蒙特州	Montpelier	蒙彼利埃	VT	Green Mountain State
Virginia	弗吉尼亚州	Richmond	里士满	VA	Old Dominion State
Washington	华盛顿州	Olympia	奥林匹亚	WA	Evergreen State
West Virginia	西弗吉尼亚州	Charleston	查尔斯顿	WV	Mountain State
Wisconsin	威斯康星州	Madison	麦迪逊	WI	Badger State
Wyoming	怀俄明州	Cheyenne	夏延	WY	Equality State

Appendix 3   Provinces and Territories of Canada

Province/Territory		Capital	
Alberta	阿尔伯达省	Edmonton	埃德蒙顿
British Columbia	不列颠哥伦比亚省	Victoria	维多利亚
Manitoba	马尼托巴省	Winnipeg	温尼伯
New Brunswick	新不伦瑞克省	Fredericton	弗雷德里克顿
Newfoundland and Labrador	纽芬兰与拉布拉多省	Saint John's	圣约翰斯
Nova Scotia	新斯科舍省	Halifax	哈利法克斯
Ontario	安大略省	Toronto	多伦多
Prince Edward Island	爱德华王子岛省	Charlottetown	夏洛特敦
Québec	魁北克省	Québec City	魁北克市
Saskatchewan	萨斯喀彻温省	Regina	里贾纳
Northwest Territories	西北地区	Yellowknife	耶洛奈夫
Nunavut	努纳武特地区	Iqaluit	伊卡卢伊特
Yukon	育空地区	Whitehorse	怀特霍斯

Appendix 4   States and Territories of Australia

State/Territory		Capital	
New South Wales	新南威尔士州	Sydney	悉尼
Victoria	维多利亚州	Melbourne	墨尔本
Queensland	昆士兰州	Brisbane	布里斯班
South Australia	南澳大利亚州	Adelaide	阿德莱德
Western Australia	西澳大利亚州	Perth	珀斯
Tasmania	塔斯马尼亚州	Hobart	霍巴特
Northern Territory	北领地	Darwin	达尔文
Australian Capital Territory	澳大利亚首都领地	Canberra	堪培拉

References

Paul, A. 1975. *A Guide to the English-Speaking World.* London: Longman Group Ltd.

Singh, B. 1997. *Canadian Society and Culture.* New Delhi: Vikas Publishing House.

Burner, D. 1985. *An American Portrait: A History of the United States.* New York: Scribner.

Kurian, G. T. 1990. *Facts on File National Profiles. Australia and New Zealand.* New York: Facts on File.

Mackay, H. 1993. *Reinventing Australia: The Mind and Mood of Australia in the 90s.* Sydney: Angus & Robertson.

Sinclair, K. 1980. *A History of New Zealand.* Auckland: Penguin Books.

Cathcart, M. 1993. *Manning Clark's History of Australia.* Victoria: Melbourne University Press.

Bromhead, P. 1977. *Life in Modern America.* London: Longman Group Ltd.

邓炎昌, 1988,《现代美国社会与文化》(I & II)。北京: 高等教育出版社。

黄源深, 1991,《当代澳大利亚社会》。上海: 华东师范大学出版社。

季任钧, 1978,《新西兰经济地理》。天津: 天津人民出版社。

阮西湖, 1986,《加拿大民族志》。北京: 中国社会科学出版社。

王彤福, 1990,《加拿大风情录》。北京: 知识出版社。

吴祯福, 1992,《澳大利亚历史: 1942-1988》。北京: 北京出版社。

肖惠云, 1996,《当代英国概况》。上海: 上海外语教育出版社。

余志远, 1996,《英语国家概况》。北京: 外语教学与研究出版社。

朱永涛, 1991,《英美文化基础教程》。北京: 外语教学与研究出版社。

图书在版编目（CIP）数据

英语国家概况 / 谢福之主编；白晓煌等编. -- 修订本. -- 北京：外语教学与研究出版社，2013.4（2025.6重印）
高等学校英语拓展系列教程. 语言文化类
ISBN 978-7-5135-2941-9

Ⅰ. ①英… Ⅱ. ①谢… ②白… Ⅲ. ①英语－阅读教学－高等学校－教材 Ⅳ. ①H319.4

中国版本图书馆 CIP 数据核字（2013）第 065347 号

出 版 人　王　芳
项目负责　赵春梅
责任编辑　高　颖
封面设计　孙敬沂
版式设计　涂　俐
出版发行　外语教学与研究出版社
社　　址　北京市西三环北路 19 号（100089）
网　　址　https://www.fltrp.com
印　　刷　河北泓景印刷有限公司
开　　本　787×1095　1/16
印　　张　18.5
版　　次　2013 年 4 月第 1 版　2025 年 6 月第 31 次印刷
书　　号　ISBN 978-7-5135-2941-9
定　　价　49.90 元

如有图书采购需求，图书内容或印刷装订等问题，侵权、盗版书籍等线索，请拨打以下电话或关注官方服务号：
客服电话：400 898 7008
官方服务号：微信搜索并关注公众号"外研社官方服务号"
外研社购书网址：https://fltrp.tmall.com

物料号：229410101